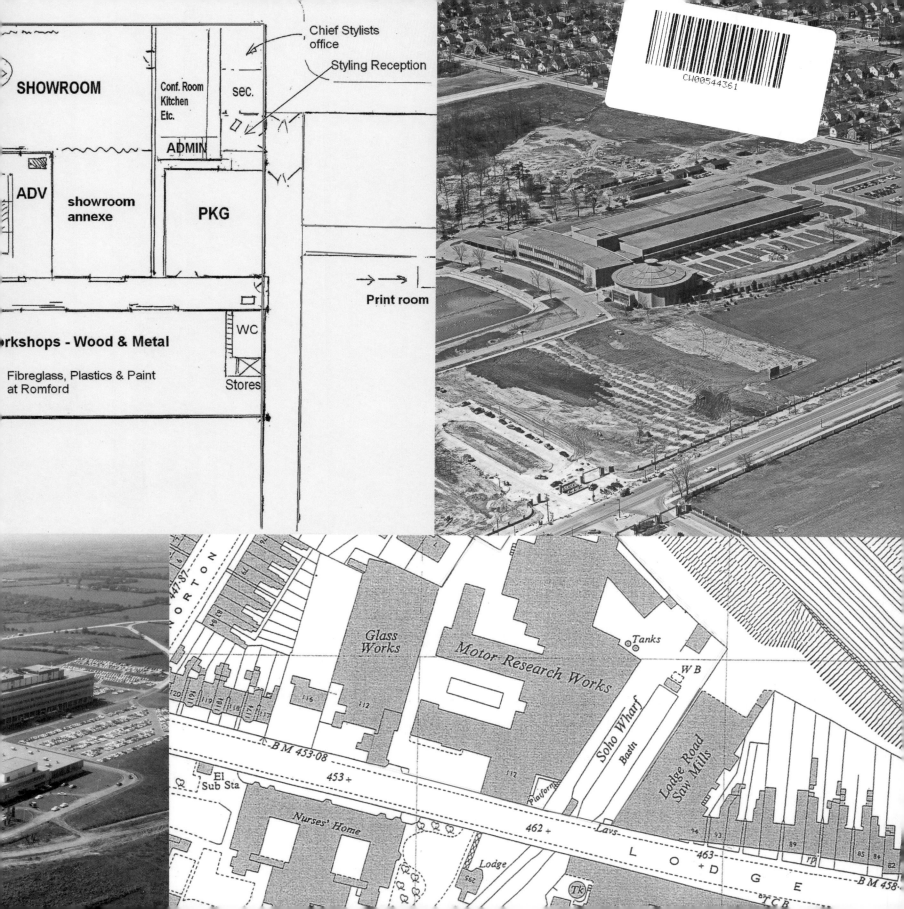

SHOWROOM

Chief Stylists office

Styling Reception

Conf. Room
Kitchen
Etc.

sec.

ADMIN

ADV

showroom annexe

PKG

Print room

WC

rkshops - Wood & Metal

Fibreglass, Plastics & Paint at Romford

Stores

NORTON

Glass Works

Motor Research Works

Tanks

W B

Soho Wharf

Bastn

Lodge Road Saw Mills

BM 453·08

453 +

El Sub Sta

112

112

462 +

Lavs

Lodge

463 +

L O D G E

BM 458·

Nurses' Home

TCB

Tk

447·87

64
62
68
69

120
119
118
117
117
116
112
94
93
89
85
84
82

Platform

rp

Ford
DESIGN
in the UK
70 years of success

NICK HULL

Contents

Foreword

Chris Svensson, Design Director – Americas

When I first heard that a dedicated book was going to be written on the topic of the Dunton Design facility, I was worried the truly special stories of the individuals that have inhabited the building over the years would be missed, the unsung heroes of design such as the modellers and designers that perhaps are not the well-known individuals of that world. But after meeting Nick Hull, talking to him about the book, and hearing his enthusiasm for the world of design, I realised he was as passionate about the people and their stories as he was the products that are created in the secretive studios, and he was the perfect author to bring the stories of Dunton Design to life.

The story of my time at Dunton starts as a student at the Royal College of Art. Gaining a summer internship with a major automotive manufacturer was a highly prized experience, and in the summer of 1991 I was extremely fortunate to be accepted by Ford to intern at Dunton, its UK design facility. Although this was not my first time in a design studio, the scale of Dunton was far beyond anything I had previously encountered, and the diversity of work was mind boggling! The students were given complete access to all programs within the facility, and were expected to contribute alongside the regular in-house designers.

The competition between designers to win sketch reviews, getting your ideas picked and going to 3D, was extremely tough, and I sketched cars all day, every day. I had never experienced anything that intense – even in the competitive world of being one of only nine students on the RCA Vehicle Design MA course – but the work ethic of the Ford Design team was inspiring. However, what I remember most from this time is the feeling of family and the warmth with which I was greeted. The help was unprecedented, and I learnt so much in such a short time.

After graduating in 1992, I took up a full-time role as an Exterior Designer in the Ford Cologne design studio, and have remained a Ford designer for the whole of my 25-year career, but it's that first experience with Ford and Dunton that would set the tone for my career with Ford: the family mentality, working hard and letting the rewards come, the tough but fair competitiveness. The extreme creativity, diversity of work, and the people have stayed with me to this day.

Introduction and acknowledgements

Despite the prevalence of books on Ford, there has never been one dedicated to the subject of Ford design and styling, particularly within the UK. With 2017 marking the 50th anniversary of Ford's Dunton design studio, and 70 years since the first UK studio was established, it seemed timely to produce such a book. A volume on all of Ford's design history in Europe and America would be an immense project, whereas starting with the UK seemed a more manageable task. Also, this is where Ford has had the longest and most continuous design presence outside of Detroit.

This book reflects the emphasis on the people, projects and process of design, and how this has changed over time. There is a fourth 'P' as well – places. Since arriving in Dagenham 70 years ago, Ford has had five design studios, and the history of the earlier ones is barely recorded. The identification and description of each of those studios and locations, where photos of various models were taken, is one aspect of this book that has never before been attempted in print, and it constitutes an important documentation of the company's history, particularly since most of those locations and buildings no longer exist.

As a profession, automotive design has changed hugely over the past 70 years, and it continues to evolve as new processes and methods are developed. In the early days there was little formal training available for new recruits, and designers came from a variety of backgrounds. Ford struggled to recruit good candidates with the right creative and drawing skills, which led to its involvement with the Royal College of Art in London and Coventry University. Today, the UK is a rich source of design talent in Europe.

Car design tended to be a male-dominated world, but Ford was unusual in being the first studio to employ a woman designer in the mid-1950s. It was also a forward-thinking company that recruited graduates when the rest of the UK car industry rather shunned them. Nowadays, young designers require a degree in Automotive Design (plus a stunning portfolio) as a basic requirement for entry into the profession, and women form a key part of any design team, too – and not just in the traditional area of colour and trim. Design studios today offer a full career structure, not just for the designers, but for clay and digital modellers and technicians, with migration of staff across companies and continents being commonplace.

Ford conducted exit interviews for senior design staff in the 1980s, and these proved invaluable as a record of older stories and anecdotes. Whilst researching this book, it also became obvious

that the preservation of design material for the archives was quite patchy. Each time the design department had moved, lots of material was cleared out, and potentially interesting sketches were inevitably lost. Not everything should be saved, of course, but it is important to document the key stages in any project in order for future generations of historians to make sense of it. Wherever possible, I have sought out rare photos of sketches, models and early prototypes, rather than simply using commonplace images of Ford production models.

Finally, a note on the use of terms. The book adopts the terms used within design and engineering, which are a mix of American and English terminology, chiefly due to the influence of Briggs Motor Bodies in the 1940s. Thus, 'fender' is the term used rather than 'wing,' and 'trunk' rather than 'boot,' because these are the descriptions used on all engineering drawings and in design discussions, not just at Ford but within most car companies globally. Some American spelling is also used for Ford terms, eg 'program', 'center' etc.

Acknowledgements

I would like to thank Joel Piaskowski, Chris Svensson, Paul Wraith, Simon Spearman-Oxx, Chris Bird, Martin Smith, Patrick le Quément, Jordan Bennett, Dave Hilton, Pierre Webster, Julie Francis, Alan Thorley, Maurice Ginn, Howard Mook, Harris Mann and John Stark for finding the time to be interviewed about their recollections and providing detailed information that allowed me to piece together the full story of the design studios.

The vast majority of images were supplied by Dave Hill at the Ford archives in Dunton, with a further tranche of new images supplied by Ford Design through the efforts of Paul Wraith and Simon Spearman-Oxx. During the writing of this book, the Ford image archives were relocated to Dearborn, Michigan, meaning that searching them in future will not be so easy.

Thanks also to Maurice and David Ginn, Dave Hilton, Tony Catignani and Steve Harper for providing images. Peter Lee from the Transit Van Club and Stephen Wickham from the Ford Classic and Capri Owners' club also gave valuable help with images and information.

Finally, I am indebted to Neil Birtley and Martin Burgess, who both provided a lot of detailed background information and support, and supplied a number of additional images from their own collections.

Nick Hull

Chapter

1

Early days of Ford in Britain

The early history of Ford Design in the UK is closely bound up with Ford Motor Company of America, as is that of Ford of Britain. Indeed, the UK operation was the first overseas venture undertaken by Henry Ford, who set up a franchise to sell Ford cars as early as November 1904, with the Central Motor Car Company in London, run by Aubrey Blakiston and Percival Perry. The first cars arrived in crates from the US, and were assembled and sold at a rate of just a few per month. The Ford Model B was offered from 1905, and proved successful, followed by the improved Model N in 1906, which sold for £120 – the cheapest four-cylinder car on the market. Central also offered two additional bodies for this model, a four-seater and a landaulette, to augment the standard two-seater offering.

The Model T arrived in October 1908, and was displayed by Perry at the Olympia Motor Show in London to much acclaim, with 400 being sold over the next couple of years. By this stage, Perry was running Central Motor Cars without Blakiston, and wanted to expand. He travelled to Detroit and met Henry Ford, who proposed that Perry set up a formal Ford organisation in the UK. Thus, in March 1911, Perry registered Ford Motor Company (England) Ltd as a company, operating from a showroom on Shaftesbury Avenue, central London.

Henry Ford had always planned for the Model T to be assembled overseas, and the UK was a prime candidate. With his Irish ancestry, Ford favoured a site in Cork, Ireland, for an initial assembly plant, chosen for its sea access and the fact that his father had emigrated from there in 1847. In addition, a plant in England was planned, and in the summer of 1911 a second 5½-acre site in Trafford Park, Manchester, was leased, with excellent rail sidings and good access to the sea via the Manchester Ship Canal. The first British-built Model T was assembled there on 23 October 1911 – the first Ford ever built overseas.

Chassis were produced in Cork and sent over to Manchester, but Joseph Sankey later supplied them from its factory near Birmingham. To avoid costly shipping charges on bulky bodywork, very early on Perry arranged to buy Trafford Park Woodworkers Ltd to manufacture bodies on site, and a variety of body styles were offered, including a 7cwt delivery van: one of the first available in Britain, and a popular choice for businesses looking to replace horse-drawn carts. Production had increased from 3000 in 1912 to over 8000 by 1914. Britain was now Ford's second biggest market after the US, and Perry's policy of producing parts locally, rather than importing everything from Detroit, proved very wise. With the outbreak of war, import duties and shipping losses in the Atlantic would have proved disastrous to the continuation of the company in the UK, without some local sourcing of components.

During the First World War, Trafford Park turned out over 30,000 vehicles based on the Model T, including staff cars, ambulances, and armoured vehicles for the army. Percival Perry became Deputy Controller of Mechanical Warfare for the British government, and ended the war with a CBE and a knighthood in 1918. In 1919 he departed from Ford following disagreements over policy, and soon afterwards retired to the Channel Islands as a very wealthy man.

With the establishment of the Irish Free State in 1922, it was becoming less economical to import parts from Cork, and further expansion at Trafford Park proved impossible. Hence, Cork plant manager Edward Grace was tasked with finding a new site on the British mainland. Perry had favoured a location on Southampton Water that had been purchased in 1919, but Grace selected a site alongside the Thames at Dagenham, east of London. Ford bought an initial 295 acre (119ha) site there in 1924, with the aim of setting up a completely integrated car factory, from blast furnaces to produce raw iron and steel to final assembly of finished cars. As such, the 'River Plant' at Dagenham was modelled on Ford's famed River Rouge plant in Detroit.

The original Ford Model T was rugged, lightweight, easy to repair, and well-suited to the poor roads of the day.

Model T and Henry Ford.

The early days of Model T production in Trafford Park, circa 1914. Over 8300 cars were produced that year. Rolling chassis are on the right, while finished cars are lined up on the left.

The establishment of the huge Dagenham plant took quite some time to plan and set up, and it wasn't until May 1929 that construction even commenced, with over 22,000 piles required to be driven into the marshy ground simply to allow buildings to be erected. Ford of America invested £5 million in the project – a huge sum for the time and a very bold move, given that the American economy was starting to falter. In October 1929 the stock market on Wall Street crashed, and this massive investment abroad was seen as risky, yet too late to cancel. In October 1930, Henry Ford visited the Dagenham construction site to inspect progress and to review the situation again with Sir Percival Perry. Two years previously, Ford had persuaded Perry to rejoin him in leading the newly-created Ford of Britain company, and needed a trusted chief to take the helm of these new expansion plans that were deemed critical to the success of Ford, not just in the UK, but as a beachhead for the whole of Europe. Ford Motor Company Ltd was capitalised with £7 million, with 40 per cent owned by UK shareholders. At this point Perry, as Managing Director of Ford Motor Company Ltd, set up other production plants in Europe, including Ford Automobiles in Asnières, France, and Ford Belgium in Antwerp, while Ford of America also set up assembly works, with Ford Werke AG in Cologne and Ford Spain in Barcelona.

Sir Percival Perry brought on board two senior managers to assist him: Patrick Hennessy and Rowland A Smith. Hennessy had worked at the Cork plant as a purchasing manager since 1920, and was well-known to Perry, while Smith had been involved with the Trafford Park factory before being appointed Works Manager at Standard Motor Company in 1928. Both men would become key names in the Ford of Britain story.

Meanwhile, the Trafford plant continued to turn out the Model T, with 250,000 produced by April 1925, but it was increasingly outdated as a design, and was being outsold by more modern models. The Austin Seven had been launched in 1922 and the Morris Minor in 1928, both proving much more popular to British motorists than the Model T.

Ford Model A and Model Y

Henry Ford remained wedded to the concept of the Model T for far too long during the 1920s and by early 1927 it was clear to many others within Ford that the company was on a path to doom without a newer design to sell to an increasingly sophisticated customer in America. The replacement Model A was hastily developed by a small team over a seven month period and was launched in November 1927 in New York, becoming an instant hit. Over 50,000 were ordered during the display at the Waldorf Hotel that month.

Interestingly, the Model A was introduced simultaneously in the UK from early 1928, with parts being supplied to Trafford Park and Cork immediately following the launch in America. However, the Model A demonstrated that Henry Ford's concept of a single model to appeal globally was deeply flawed, and when the Model

Early paint process

Up to the early 1920s, most British car makers used the traditional carriage making process of painting by hand brush, skillfully applying several coats with a 2½in badger-hair brush then topping off with a clear varnish coat. This whole laborious process could take several weeks, and was a major bottleneck to early mass production in car plants. Worse still, the paint job only lasted 2-3 seasons before requiring revarnishing.

Ford introduced gravity painting at Trafford Park, whereby paint could be flowed onto bodies through overhead nozzles in just three minutes, although curing each of the three coats required extensive drying in a gas oven and meant that hundreds of bodies in various stages of paint had to be stored to feed the production lines. Up to 1913, British Model Ts were all painted blue, then they were green with black fenders, and for 1914 all Fords were chocolate brown.

The fastest drying varnish was black, as it absorbs more heat, and that is the real reason behind Henry Ford's famous quote: "Any colour as long as it's black" rather than any effort to limit customer choice. From 1914 onwards Trafford Park followed Henry's edict.

Baked Japanese enamel was used on bicycles, but only came in black, due to the gilsonite pigment used that could withstand the 450 degrees needed to bake it. Thus, baked enamel could not be used for wooden framed bodies, but was used for parts without wood framing, such as fenders, hoods, front aprons, wheels, or radiator shells. This explains why these parts were black on so many early cars, including the Model T.

In 1924, GM and DuPont developed Duco nitrocellulose laquer, a solvent-based liquid celluloid film that dried extremely quickly and could be applied with a spray gun. It was also more flexible than the very brittle enamels, did not require expensive high-temperature gas ovens, and came in very bright colours. This revolutionised the car industry, and was in general use by 1926.

The term 'body in white' was originally used to mean an unpainted body with a white primer coat to prevent it from rusting. Later on, it came to mean any unpainted bodyshell.

1928 Model A.

Dagenham factory. The huge 'Ford' neon sign was added in 1936.

A was offered in the UK it struggled to sell, not least due to its large 3.3-litre 22hp engine that, while ideal for America, was heavily taxed in the UK. Thus, a smaller-engined version, the Model AF (for 'Foreign'), was rapidly introduced. The AF had a 2038cc engine with a smaller 3.05in (77.47mm) bore, but with the same stroke as the regular Model A, and was rated as a 14.9hp car. This meant it could find a ready market against other 10 and 12 horsepower models, with a price of £185 for the two-door saloon – a car that, although still large by British standards, was roomy, powerful, and reasonable value for money.

The Dagenham plant finally came on stream in October 1931, with the first vehicle off the line being a Ford AA 30cwt (1500kg) truck, driven by general manager Rowland Smith. Model A production was slow to get up to speed; only five being produced in the first three months in the changeover from Trafford Park production. This was followed by the introduction of the luxurious 30hp Ford V8 model and the Model AB: a larger version of the A using the 106in V8 chassis and more powerful variants of the Model A four-cylinder engines.

With a full-blown recession now in place, it was clear that the entire Dagenham venture would collapse without a successful volume model to sell, particularly an 8hp model to compete against market leaders in Britain. Therefore, in early 1931, Perry arranged for an Austin Seven and a Standard Nine to be shipped to Detroit for evaluation in a completely new project, known as Model 19 – later to become the Model Y. He also managed to include one of the first examples of the latest budget-priced £100 Morris Minor SV models, launched a few weeks previously. A small engineering team was then brought together in Dearborn to develop this new small car for Europe, as a matter of great urgency.

The layout for this new car would remain thoroughly conventional. A pressed steel channel-section chassis was used with transverse leaf springs and solid axles front and rear, together with a 3-speed transmission taking drive to the rear via a torque tube.

In December 1931, Rowland Smith went over to Ford headquarters in Dearborn, Michigan to view the finished prototype of the Model Y. The first 14 prototypes were subsequently shipped over to London and revealed to Ford's UK dealers in the Royal Albert Hall on 18 February 1932. Feedback from this presentation suggested that more cabin width would be required, and the production versions had

a 2in wider body, concealed radiator and fuel filler caps. A moulded coachline along the bodyside was added to make it appear sleeker, too. During testing it was also discovered that stronger side-valve engines with a 3-bearing crankshaft, rather than 2-bearing as on the prototypes, would be required. This new 'Model Y' was in production at Dagenham within a record six months, with body dies and jigs being supplied to Briggs Motor Bodies for a production start date of August 1932. Prices ranged from £120 for the two-door 'Tudor' to £135 for the four-door – or 'Fordor' in Ford-speak. The Model Y went on to become a very successful car, but it had been a disastrous first year for Dagenham – Ford of Britain reported a loss of £682,000 for 1932, although by 1933, once the Model Y was in full swing, this was turned around into a £388,000 profit

The price of the Model Y was reduced to just £100 in October 1935, providing low-cost motoring for many families.

Establishing Ford Design Department and Bob Gregorie

Styling for the new baby Model Y was entrusted to a new recruit to Ford, Eugene T (Bob) Gregorie. Gregorie had actually been recruited to lead the styling for Lincoln, and at this point we need to backtrack slightly to give the full picture.

The Lincoln Motor Co had been bought by Henry Ford in 1922 as a second car brand to be run by his son, Edsel Ford. Edsel had already been made President of Ford Motor Co on 30 December 1918 but the title carried little authority or real duties for the 25-year-old playboy, who, it was rumoured, had been presented with $1 million of gold by his father on reaching his 21st birthday. Lincoln, however was another matter. This was his 'plaything' and he had serious intentions to make Lincoln nothing less than one of most prestigious cars in America, right up there with established marques such as Pierce-Arrow, Packard, Peerless and Cadillac.

While Henry Ford paid scant attention to styling, Edsel was very different. He loved to draw cars and took a deep interest in the design of all Lincoln models throughout the 1920s. Whilst there was no in-house body design capability at Lincoln, Edsel personally made sure the company engaged the services of the best coachbuilders of the day, in particular Willoughby, LeBaron, Dietrich, Brunn and Judkins. Edsel would write long and detailed memos to the coachbuilders about their custom body proposals, including details of trim stitching and metal finishes, and over the next few years he gained a decent technical knowledge of body design. He also demanded his sign-off on any production runs of custom Lincoln bodies, usually produced in batches of 25 to 100.

For the 1928 Model A Ford, Edsel took a lead in directing the styling of the car, which was undertaken by Briggs with a wood and clay mock-up of the design. The Model A turned out as a nicely resolved design, quite delicate and feminine compared to the Model T, with neat detailing and handsome proportions, much like a baby Lincoln of the day.

Bob Gregorie grew up in a wealthy Long Island family with a privileged background of exotic cars and yachts, yet was determined to make his way as a car designer. Initially he worked in the boat-building industry, where he learned body drafting and lofting of full-size drafts. He briefly worked for Brewster and GM before being hired by Lincoln, arriving in January 1931, aged 23.

The immediate task was not creating a Lincoln, but rather styling the body for the British Ford Model 19 project. It seems he was the only person within Ford Motor Co at that time who could sketch and draw the exterior of a car, and he was immediately set to work on this urgent project. His sketches were sent to Edsel Ford, who approved the direction, and the subsequent Model Y was developed as a design very quickly during that spring of 1931.

Edsel found Gregorie easy to get on with and the pair could talk in an educated fashion for hours about architecture, art, yachts and car design – all topics close to Edsel's heart – and thus the two men soon developed a deep respect for each other. Gregorie wasn't afraid

Seen here is Ford's first Chief Designer, ET 'Bob' Gregorie, who set up Ford's first styling studio in Dearborn in 1937. Gregorie lost out to George Walker in 1947.

Edsel Ford.

of standing up and defending his position too, not least due to his outgoing personality and confidence gained through his privileged education, not a situation that most employees at Ford could claim at that time.

Not surprisingly, Edsel asked Gregorie to set up a body styling department that could serve both Lincoln and Ford and the group was set up in January 1935 as the Ford Design Department, based at Ford's engineering laboratory in Dearborn. By autumn 1937 the department had five designers covering all cars and Ford trucks, together with a clay modelling team largely recruited from Briggs or the Ford pattern shop. There was also a wood and metal fabrication shop and a plaster casting area. By 1939-'40 Gregorie had built up his staff to around 50 people and handled all the yearly styling changes and all body styles across the entire Ford and Lincoln range, including the new Mercury, Ford trucks, tractors, buses and accessories. Nevertheless, the Ford Design Department was a fraction of the size of GM's styling group under Harley Earl, which was already 450 strong at that point.

Expansion of the range

Back in the UK, the Ford range was expanded in 1934 by the addition of the Model C, a larger version of the Model Y with 1172cc 10hp engine and revised body styling that aped the larger V8 model. The Model C was designed in Dearborn as the Model 20 project, with body styling overseen (it is believed) by Gregorie. It competed with the Austin Ten, the Morris Ten and the new Hillman Minx, and the Model C became the market leader in this compact car category, much in the same way that the Escort would several decades later.

The luxurious 30hp Ford V8 received yearly updates to its style throughout the 1930s, but never sold in large numbers, due to the high annual road tax charge of £22 – almost 10 per cent of its list price. The initial models of the V8 were simply imported, but assembly in Dagenham started from 1935. Even so, production volumes rarely exceeded 4000 per year, and it is thought that body panels were never pressed by Briggs in Dagenham, but were assembled from crated parts brought over from North America.

At the other end of the range, the Model Y and Model C were replaced in summer 1937 with new models, the 7Y Eight and the 7W Ten respectively. These were effectively re-engineered versions of the previous cars, de-costed to suit the sometimes-superior manufacturing methods of UK suppliers, or introducing minor design changes rather than rigidly adhering to the Dearborn specifications.

The 7Y used the same 90in (2286mm) wheelbase from the older car, but the chassis was revised with steel panelling under the rear seat and longer rear springs to provide a better ride. The body, however, was all-new, and this time around was designed by Briggs Motor Bodies in Dagenham, rather than by Dearborn. The reason was simple: the design for the Model Y by Gregorie in 1931 had been charged to Ford of Britain to the tune of $535,360, although this was

Briggs Motor Bodies

Like many companies, Ford used Briggs Manufacturing Co styling staff to help it generate new models. In 1932, Briggs designer Ralph Roberts was dispatched to England to help set up the Briggs plant in Dagenham, and establish a British design team. He would return to the US several times a year, but in his absence the main Briggs design studio in Mack Avenue, Detroit was run by John Tjaarda. Tjaarda's son Tom would later work for Ghia in the 1970s.

The Briggs Motor Bodies plant in Dagenham produced bodies for the Model Y, Model C, 7Y Eight and the 7W Ten up to outbreak of the Second World War. By 1939 it employed around 3000 and started to supply body pressings and complete bodies to other manufacturers including Austin, Jowett, Rootes and Standard. During the war Briggs expanded massively, with plants in Southampton, Romford, Doncaster and Dundee with valuable aircraft contracts such as engine cowlings and parts for the Spitfire, with a peak workforce of 23,000.

Ford of Britain relied heavily on Briggs not only to develop and manufacture all their bodyshells but to act as the main styling studio, producing sketches and mock-ups for approval up until the 1950s. After the war Bob Bingman became Chief Stylist, building up a small styling team that became the nucleus of Ford of Britain's first styling studio in the mid-1950s.

Seen here are finished Prefect bodies at Briggs Motor Bodies, being readied for transfer to Dagenham's final assembly lines.

later reduced to $210,000 (£62,874) following protests from the UK company.

This time around Perry was determined to go his own way, although Edsel Ford was far from keen and took a lot of persuading to allow the project to go ahead. Patrick Hennessy was dispatched to go over to America with the prototypes, as this initiative was never authorised by Dearborn, and was something of a cheeky move on Perry's part. Surprisingly, Hennessy managed to strike up a good relationship with 'Old Henry' Ford, and managed to get his blessing for the two designs, at the same time striking up a good relationship with Edsel's teenage son, Henry Ford II, who always referred to Hennessy as 'Uncle Pat' right up to the 1960s when the two of them were senior executives within the organisation.

Briggs' Chief Designer in the UK, Ralph Roberts, would have had major input on those 1937 models, and it is presumed he had started to recruit a couple of assistants by the mid-1930s to work with him at the Chequers Lane site.

The resulting style was modern for the time and would come to define the small 'perpendicular' Ford in the UK for another 20 years, remaining in production in various revised forms until 1959. 'Easiclean' 17in artillery-style steel wheels were used rather than thin spoked wheels as on the older models. The price was £117.10s for the standard version, £10 more for the De Luxe.

The more powerful 7W Ten model had a larger bore engine of 1172cc giving 10hp – around 30bhp – and a chassis with a 4in longer wheelbase that could allow for a decent four-door body as an alternative to the standard two-door offering. The four-door gained an attractive six-light body style with an extra window in the C-pillar. Equipment was superior, too, including leathercloth upholstery, map pockets, a clock, interior light and chrome hubcaps, while a sliding roof and leather trim were available as options.

In October 1938, the Ten was renamed 'Prefect,' while in October 1939 the basic 7Y eight was renamed 'Anglia,' and gained a more upright squared-off grille.

Wartime and postwar struggles within Ford

Following the outbreak of war, Dagenham was rapidly turned over to production of military vehicles and equipment, including the 10cwt Fordson E83W van, which served as an ambulance and mobile canteen, amongst other duties. The E83W had a remarkably long life, with 188,577 produced up to the end of production in 1957. Dagenham also produced heavy trucks and Fordson tractors in considerable numbers, paving the way for the success of the Fordson tractor in the postwar years on British farms. Patrick Hennessy became a member of the Advisory Council to the Ministry of Aircraft Production for the British government, and, for his efforts in organising production of 34,000 Rolls-Royce Merlin engines, ended the war with a knighthood, as did Rowland Smith.

Production of the small 8hp Anglia and 10hp Prefect models resumed in June 1945 with minor improvements to the interior, while the large V8 model was redesigned and relaunched in 1947 with a 30hp 3.6-litre V8 engine, now known as the Ford Pilot.

Over in America, Ford was in deep trouble. In 1943 Edsel Ford had died of a rare stomach cancer, and, with the elder Henry Ford becoming too senile to run the company, Edsel's 25-year-old son, Henry Ford II, was rapidly discharged from the Navy to take over. This period now saw a series of bitter power struggles within the company, with product development in disarray. Gregorie's design department had been cut to just 25 staff and, with Edsel now gone, it came under the control of engineering. Gregorie protested but was fired.

However, that was not the end of the story. With the company losing $10 million per month and desperate to develop a new series of vehicles, six months later Henry Ford II phoned Gregorie, begging him to return. Gregorie agreed, although it turned out to

Henry Ford in later years. Henry Ford senior died in 1947, leading to disarray regarding control of the company in the immediate postwar years.

The three Ford brothers: Benson, William Clay, and Henry Ford II, seen here in 1949 with a scale model of the new Ford sedan.

1946 discussion for the proposed Engineering Research Center in Dearborn. Henry Ford II leans over the model. The Center featured two big lakes outside the styling studio. The Ford museum, with its distinctive spire, lies to the east of Oakwood Boulevard.

The eventual styling studio complex under construction in 1953, with two blocks of styling studios and an enclosed viewing yard. The circular presentation studio with the curved wing of styling executive offices overlooking the lake remains essentially unaltered today, although the entire site seen here is now covered with further design studios.

be a vicious struggle to retain his former influence within the fast-changing organisation. Realizing he could never save Ford alone, Henry II – wisely – decided to hire the best business talent going, including a group known as 'the Whiz Kids,' a young bunch of ten ex-Air Force officers who all held degrees in economics and business management. They would become the bedrock of Ford's senior team for the next two decades.

Next up, Henry II hired former GM Vice President Ernest Breech as his assistant to revamp Ford along the management principles of GM. Wasting no time, hard-nosed Breech brought in a series of executives, including 120 ex-GM engineers under the control of Harold T Youngren, the former Chief Engineer from Oldsmobile. But the biggest coup that Breech pulled off was bringing in his

golfing buddy, industrial designer George W Walker on a $5 million consultancy wager to design the new '49 Ford Sedan that the company so desperately needed.

Walker and Gregorie were now in a head-to-head contest to win the styling of the '49 Ford, with Walker's model gradually gaining ground with the product committee that Ernest Breech had introduced to select all future styling proposals. This team consisted of Henry II, his brother Benson Ford, Breech and Youngren, plus a couple of other executives. Finding his authority undermined and going through a difficult divorce, Gregorie decided to throw in the towel, quietly resigning in December 1946. With the '49 Ford design successfully signed off, Walker's consultancy was terminated. Youngren swiftly hired two designers from GM – Don DeLaRossa

1949 Ford with distinctive spinner in the front grille, designed by Joe Oros. Seen here in coupé guise, the '49 Ford became the template for the British Ford EOTA Consul being designed at this time.

and Gene Bordinat – to help run the studio, which remained chaotic and rudderless for the next year or so, although it was organised into the specific studios of Ford, Lincoln, Mercury, advanced design, and colour and trim that we would recognise today.

Around this time, plans were put in place to construct a major new engineering research centre around Oakwood Boulevard in Dearborn, a project that would take until the mid-1950s to complete, but today still forms the core of Ford's product development facility in Detroit.

In early 1948, Breech decided to rehire George W Walker Associates as design consultants to lead Ford Design into the next decade. Tall and strongly built, Walker had originally been a professional football player, but had redirected his talents via Cleveland Institute of Art and set up an illustration studio for industrial products during the 1920s. Walker's greatest assets

were his ebullient personality and wide smile. During the 1930s, he steadily built up his office in Detroit, gaining clients such as International Harvester, Packard and assorted automotive suppliers through relentless networking of business associates he met through his numerous country club memberships.

According to historian Michael Lamm, Walker brought in several of his favourite assistants on lucrative consultancy deals, including Gil Spear and 'the gold dust twins' – Joe Oros and Elwood Engel. Dedicated but somewhat humourless, Oros came from a humble Detroit background, and, like Walker, had attended Cleveland Institute and gained an internship at GM Styling. Engel was more easygoing, and was popular with the clay modellers for his jokes. Both would become Walker's right-hand men in Ford over the next decade as the design activities of Ford worldwide expanded massively.

Chapter

2

Postwar and the Briggs studio

1948 was a pivotal year for Ford of Britain. General Manager Patrick Hennessy was promoted, and took over from Percival Perry as Managing Director. More significantly, Ford took steps to set up a proper engineering and design function in the UK. At a meeting with Henry Ford II and Graeme K Howard, head of the new Ford International Division, it was decided that "The introduction of a Chief Engineer, as well as a Body and Styling Engineer in Dagenham ... Action is necessary." When asked by Hennessy for even more engineering support, Henry Ford II replied "Look here, Pat, you'd better take care of your own problems." That started a big shift in emphasis for Ford of Britain, with the remit to go ahead and develop its own models rather than continually rely on American support.

In that same year, Ford of Britain introduced a new policy of graduate recruitment, in marked contrast to rest of the British motor industry where an engineering apprenticeship and accompanying practical skills was considered the only entry route into the industry. For example, Jaguar only hired its first university-trained engineer in the mid-1960s. Likewise, BMC's management was almost exclusively 'home grown,' which undoubtedly led to its decline by the 1960s as the leading car producer in the UK, when the management skills to manage such a complex business became more demanding. Herbert Austin was famously quoted as saying "The university mind is a hindrance rather than a help," thus giving a clue to the typical attitude to higher education in engineering and design that prevailed in many British companies right up to the 1970s.

Two early graduate recruits were Terence (Terry) Beckett and Sam Toy. Beckett joined in 1950 and was a university-educated engineer and economist – a rare combination indeed. Both would go on to become key figures in the story of Ford of Britain, becoming Chairman of Ford in the 1970s and 1980s respectively.

Initially, the engineering department was expanded to just 15 staff. This was to cover both cars and trucks and included development engineers, draughtsmen and clerks. Three senior engineers covered car development, two engineers covered all trucks, with both activities under the control of a Chief Engineer and an assistant chief, with the remainder of the staff allocated to whichever projects were most pressing that month. As well as a new saloon car, Ford urgently required a replacement for the old 7V truck, resulting in the ET6 truck, which was the first major project for the British Ford engineers over the period 1947-'49.

It should be noted that Ford of Britain had far greater autonomy than did Vauxhall under GM at that stage, with better continuity of management too. Ford also had great advantages in logistics compared to BMC or Rootes Group, being centralised around Essex rather than spread out around the country.

The EOTA Consul and George Snyder

With such tiny UK engineering resources, it was decided that the all-new 1950 Consul – codenamed EOTA – could only be designed and

This photo shows the large group of Briggs Motor Bodies engineering and styling staff in summer 1953, just after the Ford takeover. It was taken in the styling garden of the new Odeon facility in Chequers Lane. The young apprentice recruits in the front row include Maurice Ginn (fourth from right), and Charlie Thompson (ninth from right). All the female secretaries and tracers are seated in the middle row, together with senior staff.
(Courtesy Maurice Ginn)

engineered by the US parent. Ford International Division had just been set up to coordinate the activities of its overseas subsidiaries, such as the UK, Germany, France and Australia, and this British project was one of its first tasks. Luckily, the US engineers decided to use the project to try out many new technologies that were expected to face more internal resistance, and would take more time to push through the combatant Dearborn hierarchy for a domestic program than for this fledgling overseas one. New features included a monocoque bodyshell as developed by Briggs Bodies, oversquare and overhead valve engines and MacPherson strut independent front suspension. The use of this British project as something of a testbed for newly-developed technologies was a thoroughly good outcome for the EOTA project, and put Ford of Britain in good shape for the rest of the 1950s.

Executive Chief Engineer George Halford headed up the delegation of British engineers who were sent over to Dearborn in early 1948 to liaise with their colleagues on the new EOTA project. Body engineer Fred Hart and Briggs body engineer Andy Cox formed the main contingent for body engineering and the EOTA project was notable for being the first chassis-less monocoque body that Ford had ever attempted to put into production.

The Chief Styling Engineer chosen to lead the British styling studio was George Snyder. He had been involved in the clay model development of the EOTA project in the Dearborn studio during 1948 and was sent over to finalise the design of the British car with Briggs in Dagenham and to lead the styling for the next new project – the 'Light Car.' Snyder had begun his career at Brewster in the 1920s, together with Bob Gregorie, moving to GM where he worked on the 1938 Buick Y-Job concept before becoming studio chief at Oldsmobile before the war. He was thus a thoroughly good designer, but, according to author and historian Michael Lamm, very moody. In fact he was fired from GM by Harley Earl, who found him difficult to work with, but was soon picked up by Harold Youngren for the new Ford team.

As in 1937, Hennessy once again accompanied the final prototypes to Detroit for sign-off. The production start was scheduled for summer 1950, with a launch at Earls Court in October 1950. The first cars were delivered in January 1951, the initial production being focused on the four-cylinder Consul for the first few months, with its 100in wheelbase. The larger Zephyr – codenamed EOTTA – used the same basic body as the Consul, but with a 4in (100mm) longer wheelbase and bonnet to accommodate its six-cylinder engine. This was a new market for Ford, which, apart from selling a few Pilot V8s, was best-known for producing cheap, minimal models such as the Prefect and Anglia. The price of the 1.5-litre Consul at launch was £544 – the same as a very basic sidevalve Hillman Minx. Not surprisingly, the Consul proved the best-selling variant, with 231,481 built up to 1956.

Ford Consul and Zephyr on the production lines at Dagenham. The 13in wheels were a new feature for such a large car, as were pendant pedals and 12V electrics. The 1508cc 47bhp four-cylinder Consul had a 4in shorter bonnet and simplified grille.

The flagship Zephyr Zodiac model from 1954 retained the new 2262cc six-cylinder engine from the Zephyr, but with power boosted to 71bhp, and extra equipment.

The EOTA Consul project took design cues from the latest American Ford sedans, such as this 1949 Ford Club coupé.

The EOTA/EOTTA Fords were launched with the tagline 'Five Stars Motoring.' This stood for the five main features of the cars: all-new OHV engines with oversquare cylinder dimensions; monocoque body construction; MacPherson strut independent front suspension; hydraulic brakes on all four wheels and 'centre-slung' seating for passengers sitting within the wheelbase.

Once launched, the team did not waste time introducing further developments. Following customer feedback, the rather stark IP was swiftly redesigned for October 1951, while the exterior team was straight onto its next project, the new 'Light Car.' Also at Earls Court Show in 1951 were two convertible prototypes, one Consul, one Zephyr. In summer 1951, Ford approached Carbodies in Coventry to develop a convertible version of the EOTA as a rapid six-week project. It appears there was not much direct styling involvement by Snyder, and it was left largely to Carbodies' engineers to make the necessary body changes, with longer doors and new rear fenders. Carbodies used its expertise gained on the 1948 Hillman Minx convertible, and, in fact, the Ford convertibles used the same hood frame layout.

The 2.3-litre six-cylinder Zephyr was joined in 1954 by the more upmarket Zephyr Zodiac model, which had all the Zephyr extras fitted as standard, including whitewall tyres, two-tone paintwork, twin fog lamps, and leather trim. This set a trend for upmarket executive derivatives, with Vauxhall following up with the Cresta E in 1954 and BMC with the A105 Westminster Vanden Plas during 1955.

100E Anglia and Prefect

The 'Light Car' project began in early 1951 with two different exercises. The first was a continuation of the E494A Anglia concept of a very simple, utilitarian model to sell at a minimal price. The second direction was for a more modern interpretation of a basic car that used smaller or simplified versions of the technology and features developed for the EOTA Consul. Prototypes of both cars were developed during 1952, with the more modern car known as the '1600' – this being developed into what we know as the 100E. Photographs of a damaged prototype of the utilitarian model show a car with a simple pressed front panel and integral grille, a bonnet with external hinges, the spare tyre mounted externally and no trunk lid. It also had simple vertical sliding windows as on the Austin A30. A second model was also made, denoted 'Chavant,' presumably because of the newly-introduced Chavant clay used. This design was more elaborate than the final 100E style, with a Wolseley 1500-style grille and a secondary feature line in the lower doors.

Another proposal was for an amalgam of an Anglia two-door body, with Prefect front wings and a vertical vee-shaped front grille. The inherent crudity suggests this wasn't a project led by the Ford stylists, but rather a hasty proposal by Briggs.

By this stage, Snyder had established a small studio within the Dagenham 'River' factory complex, and had brought over the basic equipment and methods used within the Dearborn studios. However, he still relied heavily on the skills of Briggs Motor Bodies, who had built an extensive team of styling designers and body engineers and had all the capabilities to take a project from sketch to steel prototype, not only for Ford but for other clients, too.

The Chief Stylist at Briggs in Dagenham after the war was Bob Bingman, who led a team of no less than 135 staff, all engaged in styling and body development. The accompanying photo was supplied by Maurice Ginn, who joined in 1950, aged 19, and became a body engineer. He moved to Chrysler in Detroit in 1955, and later to Ford. Ginn stayed in the US until 1966, when he returned to Ford at Aveley, and remained in the design studio until his retirement in 1989. At 85, he is still remarkably sharp, and was able to help the author with details of that period.

Another young recruit was Colin Neale, whose older brother Eric had joined Jensen in 1946 as its first proper designer. Eric had trained with Mulliners of Birmingham, and now, as the designer of the 1950 Jensen Interceptor and Austin A40 Sports, had given young Colin the necessary tips on how to get into car design with Briggs, where Colin arrived in 1950.

An archive film of the 100E's development gives a good indication of the styling studio techniques of the time. Designers are seen

The 100E styling was the work of George Snyder, standing here with modeller Fred Barratt working on a scale clay model of the 100E Anglia. The front and rear ends of the final 100E were designed by young Briggs designer Colin Neale.

A Briggs stylist with a quarter scale model of the 100E. The final design was signed off in April 1952.

producing sketches using conté crayon and charcoal, with gouache and airbrushes used for more finished renderings. Designers themselves are seen working on ¼ scale clay models, with a full-size clay model of the 100E being developed by a couple of modellers using recognisable modelling rakes and tools. However, there does not appear to be a surface plate or modelling bridge, simply large inspection angles and height gauges in the cramped workshop. The full-size clays were built over a wooden armature, with lathes added to bulk it out and form a keying surface for the warm clay. Smaller parts were generally made of epowood, with a lot of spokeshaving and sanding of parts involved. In those days before polystyrene foam, a lot of time was spent producing wood and canvas interior bucks to investigate the package as it was developed, with the engineers and modellers adjusting the bucks as they evolved.

Snyder's early Ford Design team had surprisingly diverse backgrounds, reflecting the wide net that was required to recruit competent industrial designers and modellers in those days. The modellers were led by 'Little' George Saunders, aided by Fred Barratt and New Zealander John Frayling. There was also an Australian modeller, Jan Smits, who lived in Earls Court's 'Kangaroo Valley' alongside fellow designer Vister de Wit, a large South African who reputedly wore a thick black overcoat, even in summer. De Wit was a prodigious pipe smoker and famous for regularly setting fire to the waste paper basket, full of his discarded sketches.

Several designers had originally come from Rootes in Coventry, including Ron Bradshaw, Brian Powell and Horace 'Non' Crook. They were undoubtedly colourful characters, too: 'Non' Crook had a hazy background in show business, sporting an impresario's goatee beard and bowtie. Eric Archer had also come from Rootes, having started his career at Dunlop Tyres doing sidewall patterns, and was known for initiating 'Sartorial Days' when the designers would come to work in their finest clothes. Quite what the blue-collar guys on the Dagenham production lines made of them parading down Chequers Lane, and the comments they received, one can only imagine!

For the 100E Anglia, Snyder's small team came up with a simple full-width body style, which took some of the styling cues of the larger EOTA and shrunk them to fit the 87in (2209mm) wheelbase. These included a bold indentation relief line to break-up the slab sides and lightly flared flat-topped wheelarches. Doors were one–piece pressings with a quarterlight in front and a single large pane of glass for the rear door – the same layout as for EOTA. At the front the sidelights were grouped under the headlamps in a separate stamped surround – body colour on the Anglia, a bright finish for the Prefect. Likewise, the four-door Prefect had a more elaborate grille and bonnet ornament. At the rear, vertical rear lamps in small fins were designed to meet forthcoming 1954 lighting regulations with twin stop/tail lamps and a pair of red reflectors. Monocoque body construction and MacPherson strut front suspension were employed as on the EOTA. Although the engine used a new block, it remained a traditional sidevalve design, this time 1172cc.

1953-'55 Ford manufacturing expansion

From 1951 onwards, Sir Patrick Hennessy began to worry about the future body supply situation from Briggs Motor Bodies, once Walter Briggs died. Briggs' largest customer in the US was Chrysler, and there were concerns Chrysler would buy Briggs Motor Bodies (indeed it did) and thus control the supply of Ford bodies.

With the production of the 100E coming on stream, Ford of Britain was desperate to secure the body supply for this crucial high-volume model, which would form the majority of production throughout the 1950s. Therefore, in March 1953 Ford made an offer to buy out the share capital of Briggs Motor Bodies Ltd for £5.6 million and to use the body facilities for its

Dagenham production lines, mid-1950s. Seen here is a Zephyr Zodiac convertible for export. The convertible body was made by Carbodies in Coventry.

exclusive use, becoming known as Ford Body Division (although the name 'Briggs' was still used by many Ford employees for another decade or so). Most of the Briggs UK facilities were subsequently used by Ford, including all 6000 Briggs staff, and the Southampton and Romford plants.

The Briggs Doncaster plant had been built mainly to produce bodies for Jowett in Bradford, but sales had collapsed by 1953, and the company ceased to produce cars by 1954. At the time there was some public belief that the Ford purchase of Briggs caused the collapse of Jowett, but that is not strictly correct. Jowett was in huge financial trouble before Ford bought Briggs, and large stockpiles of Javelin bodies were accumulating around Bradford. In the end, Ford continued to use the plant at Carr Hill in Doncaster to outsource production of the Popular from August 1955, and later on the 105E Anglia estate and Thames 300E 5cwt van.

Purchase tax on new cars was reduced on 15 April 1953, from 66.66 per cent to 50 per cent: this triggered a surge in demand for new cars on the UK market and all manufacturers responded with plans for increased production in the latter half of the 1950s.

To meet this new level of demand, in 1954 Ford instigated its first five-year plan. A £75 million investment was targeted on Dagenham to increase production floor space by 50 per cent. Plans for a massive new £10 million Paint, Trim and Assembly (PTA) plant were started, which finally opened in April 1959 – just in time for the production start of the new 105E Anglia. This expansion was wisely financed by reinvesting profits rather than increasing borrowings. From 1947-'56, Ford retained 79 per cent of profits as opposed to 68 per cent retention at BMC, thus ensuring it could meet this level of sustained investment.

Ford also continued to place great emphasis on product planning, finance and marketing, in contrast to many of its rivals. In 1955 John Barber joined Ford from the Ministry of Supply, becoming Finance Director in 1962. Barber accelerated the hiring of graduates, particularly into the finance departments in Ford, again in marked contrast to BMC. To oversee this rapid growth, Hennessy was promoted to Chairman of Ford of Britain in 1956.

To put the growth in perspective, in 1946 Ford built 31,974 cars, increasing to 93,499 by 1952. By 1959 production was 314,793, with profits of £32.2 million, compared to BMC's profits of £21.4 million. Ford had achieved its goal: it was now the most profitable car company in the UK.

Senior Ford designers in the Briggs studio, 1956. (Left to right) Eric Archer, Roy Haynes, Colin Neale (with bow tie), Ed 'Walt' Disney, and Tom Firth.

The launch was September 1953. The package of the car was far superior to that of the old E494A Anglia with its cramped interior. The biggest difference came from repositioning the occupants further forward in the body, and a much lower roofline – some 3.75in (95mm) lower than before, with a low floor that required the occupants to step down over the sills. Despite the 3in (75mm) shorter wheelbase, the interior of the 100E was roomier due to the use of wider tracks and a 3.5in (88mm) increase in body width to 60.5in (1536mm).

The design of the 100E interior was admired by *The Motor* when reviewing that year's new car trends: "On the less expensive cars, much more could be done in creating an air of quality by carefully matching the colours of interior components. The Volkswagen, for example and the Simca Aronde are very good examples of what can be done by simple basic pastel colours extended to the steering wheel, instrument panel and interior trim. The new small Fords from Dagenham are easily the best British examples, with pleasing colour harmonies throughout the interiors of both Anglia and Prefect. In view of their exceptionally good appearance both inside and out, it is interesting to note that the styling was done by an American brought over from Detroit, who unhappily died when the job was completed. Thus, not for the first time, it has been shown that a skilful designer, steeped in the flamboyant shapes and heavy ornamentation of the American car, can design a European small car which exhibits the most admired characteristics of European style." Indeed so. George Snyder had sadly died of cancer within two years of coming to

Engineering and design expansion

Ford of Britain gradually gained its engineering and design independence during the 1950s. With the go-ahead from Dearborn for more independent product development, Ford of Britain needed to recruit more experienced staff in all areas of engineering and design but this proved less easy than envisaged. After 1949, the truck and passenger car teams in engineering were split into two divisions, with one senior engineer delegated to each. When interviewed, many candidates cited the poor conditions and surroundings of Dagenham as reasons to reject an offer to work at Ford, and this prompted the company to relocate engineering to a new facility in Rainham in 1950, where they had acquired a lease on a disused three-storey factory that was refurbished to offer better accommodation.

A further step was in 1952, when the Birmingham Research Centre was established, in the former Soho Glass works at 112 Lodge Rd, Winson Green. This was chosen to be near Midlands suppliers and the new MIRA testing facility, also to tap into engineering talent from other car companies that was still resistant to move to Essex. The Birmingham site needed extensive redevelopment, and it took until 1955 until it was fully functioning, with new buildings opened that year totalling 7700sq m. The centre ultimately employed 200 engineers and was headed up by one of the truck engineering division's senior engineers, with an initial task to develop the 400E Thames 12cwt van and the 'New Popular' 195-X light car project.

Hundreds more engineers were recruited in Essex too, with groups based not just in Rainham but in Romford, as well as Dagenham. For development testing on the EOTA and 100E, Ford initially used an old USAF site at Matching Green but from 1955 they acquired the Boreham race circuit – just outside Chelmsford – that became the main testing facility for Ford in Britain up to the late 1980s, particularly for commercial vehicles.

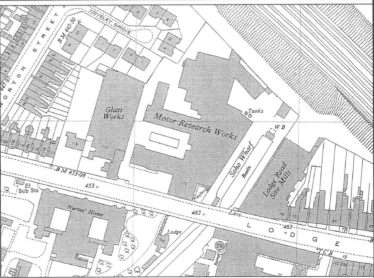

Ford Lodge Road site, 1954.

Ford's Birmingham Research Centre in Lodge Road also included a small styling studio, with Colin Macgregor and Norman Terry as resident designers. The facility grew from 5400sq m to 7700sq m. Engineers conducted various FWD projects in the late 1950s, and were aware of the BMC Mini and BMC 1100 developments in nearby Longbridge. (Courtesy Ordnance Survey)

England, but had laid the foundations for a design department that would grow considerably over the coming decade.

At this point, the new 1172cc sidevalve engine was fitted to the old 'sit-up-and-beg' E494A Anglia, and renamed 'Popular,' under the codename 103E. It continued the strategy of offering basic motoring for the masses, selling for just £390 14s 2d – the cheapest British car by some margin. It had a single vacuum-powered wiper, no heater, vinyl trim, and very little chrome; even the bumpers were painted, and the Bakelite dash of the Anglia was replaced by a flat steel panel.

In 1955, production of the 103E Popular was moved to the Briggs Jowett plant in Doncaster, with chassis and engines sent up from Dagenham rather than bodies being sent down to Essex. The four-door 100E Prefect gained proper wind-down rear windows after 1955, rather than the crude sliding type, and the Squire and Escort estates were added: they were based on the 300E Thames 5cwt van introduced in 1954, but with a snazzy split rear tailgate arrangement rather than twin rear doors. This was a burgeoning area of the market at the time, with rival models such as the Austin A35 estate, Standard Pennant, Hillman Husky, and Morris Minor Traveller all proving popular with young families – those cars were the precursors to today's hatchbacks.

204E Consul Mk II

1953-'54 was the design period for the next project, the second-generation Consul/Zephyr. This time, Ford was able to react to customer feedback on the first generation following three years of sales. Most significantly, the car became larger, with the width and tracks increased by 3in (75mm), length up by 10in (254mm), and more powerful engines fitted: a 1702cc 59bhp four-cylinder for the Consul, and 2553cc 86bhp six-cylinder for the Zephyr, providing 90mph performance.

On the Mk II, the wheelbase was lengthened to 104.5in (2654mm) on the 204E Consul, with a further 2.5in (63mm) for six-cylinder models. As before, the body rear of the A-pillar was similar, with the 206E Zephyr and Zodiac gaining different bonnets and front grilles to provide model differentiation. In fact, the distance from the centre line of the rear axle to the rear face of the flywheel was identical on all models, the only differences occurring forward of that point.

With the Ford takeover in March 1953, Chief Stylist Bingman returned to Briggs in America and the Ford styling team was able to make use of the new Briggs styling studio to start on the 204E project, with more space, proper modelling plates, and a presentation room to show models to management. Following the untimely death of George Snyder, Colin Neale emerged as the lead designer for the styling department, and took on the role as project leader for the new car, even though he was just 27-years-old. Neale was encouraged to visit the Dearborn studios to soak up the latest Ford Design ethos, and, to save time, the full-size clay models were done in the Dearborn studios during 1953, with Neale staying over to direct the modelling team.

By the mid-1950s, the Ford studio had adopted all of the techniques used in the American studios. Seen here is Bob Saward, executing an excellent full-size airbrush rendering of the 204E Consul.

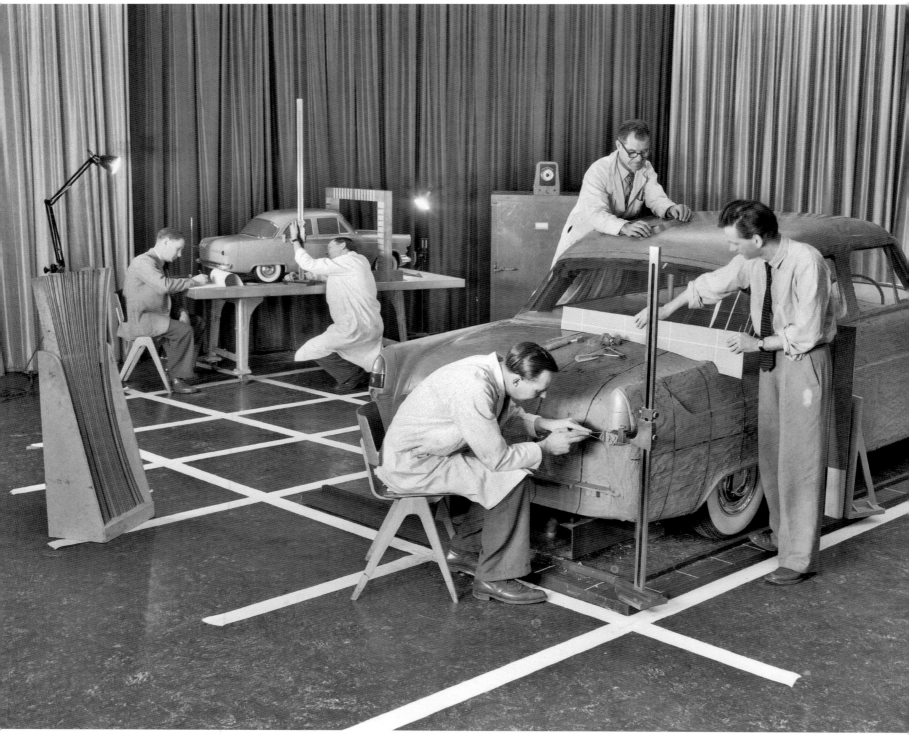

Clay model refinement on the 204E. Modeller Arthur Russ offers up a template, while Ted Aldiss works on the roof. This shows the original high roof style. Due to delays on the later 213E models, the Mk II range was given a rapid face-lift during 1958, launched as the 'Lowline' range in 1959. This included a flatter roof pressing, revised exterior trim, and seats that were repositioned to maintain headroom.

Styling for the '55 model year US Fords was frozen in spring 1953, and these provided something of a template for the British design. The '55 Fords were all-new, and introduced a number of latest design motifs, including a fuller shoulder, more barreling in the bodyside, broad rear fins, flat-topped wheel arches, and hooded headlamps. The four-door Fairlane became the basic template for Neale's 204E design, with the Consul taking the rear lamp style of this latest model, as did the new Thunderbird sports car.

During the model stage, the greenhouse theme for the 204E was taken complete from the '55 Fords, including the front screen. However, at a very late pre-production stage, the '55 US Fords were given full wraparound screens and vertical A-pillars when word reached Dearborn that GM was introducing this latest feature on the '55 Chevrolets and the design was hastily modified accordingly – an expensive modification at that late stage. In a similar vein, the

Canadian Ford subsidiary model, the Meteor Rideau, was also closely styled along the lines of the '55 US Fords, complete with wraparound front screen.

The British model stayed with a single-curvature screen and conventional A-pillars, mainly because Triplex in the UK had not fully developed the technology to produce such extreme curvature for windscreens at that time, plus (wisely) the feature was seen as too transatlantic for British tastes. By 1957 Triplex had perfected the technique with help from Vauxhall, who duly went ahead and introduced the wraparound screen for the 1957 Cresta PA. The full wraparound screen was deemed to be a key GM feature to be applied worldwide to all models but it was seen to be a dated fashion by the end of the PA's life in the early 1960s. Ford of Britain was lucky to avoid this fad.

The new Fords were billed as 'The Three Graces.' Here, the three versions are launched to the press in the auditorium of the Briggs Odeon presentation room, in January 1956.

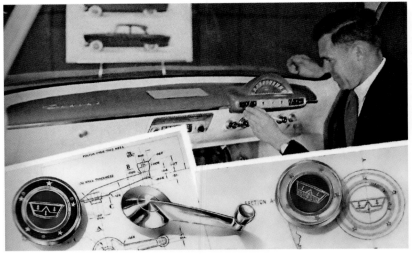

All details were drawn and fully mocked-up, including instrument graphics and badges.

Dealer launch of the new Fords in the 'Odeon.' Note the five stars above the stage: part of Ford's advertising signature throughout the 1950s. Built in the early 1950s, the Odeon was used for all styling and launch presentations. By the early 1960s, it had simply become an office for the typing pool.

A staged shot showing Terry Beckett and Eric Archer discussing samples, while Doreen Archer and Tom Firth kneel by the 3/8 scale model of the new Zodiac.

Briggs Chequers Lane design studio

Following the death of Snyder and the acquisition of Briggs, the Ford Dagenham styling team moved up the road to Chequers Lane where a new styling studio had just been completed by Briggs, known colloquially as 'The Odeon,' due to its impressive stage and proscenium arch in the presentation room. The entrance was in the corner of the private viewing garden and the main studio was downstairs, opposite the stage area. The facility even came with its own part-time butler, George Makepeace Casey, who wore a yellow and black striped waistcoat around the studio.

Terry Beckett was initially asked to head up this new styling facility from 1954-'55, and the team was expanded with the arrival of Roy Haynes, Tom Karen and Eric Archer. Other young designers included Peter Kennedy and Charlie Thompson. Kennedy joined Briggs as a trainee stylist just prior to the Ford takeover, while Thompson was a Briggs apprentice training to become a body draughtsman. Thompson was approached by Neale in 1955 to see whether he'd like to join styling, but had to complete two years national service first. He finally joined styling in late 1957, his first full project being the Mk III Zephyr, working under Colin Neale.

Although Beckett had no formal design training, he had impressed Hennessy with his sound judgement on styling matters once he started to attend styling reviews as Hennessy's assistant. This experience as a styling manager stood him in good stead later on, since he could offer useful guidance for models, and was fully conversant with the design process.

Colin Neale took over from Beckett in 1955, when Beckett was given the task of setting up the product staff department – later called Product Planning. Beckett initially set up three groups to plan a range of small, medium and large cars through the latter half of the decade. It must be said that Product Planning did not have an easy time during the 1950s, being a new department staffed by ambitious young graduates with a remit that ran right across the established functions of Sales, Manufacturing and Engineering – all of which were reluctant to cede any authority to this raw upstart group. However it had one trump card: the support of the all-powerful Finance department.

The Briggs styling studio was located at the top end of Chequers Lane, Dagenham. Known as 'The Odeon', the facility was tucked into the sprawling arrangement of older Briggs buildings to the north of the main press shop. The date of the map is 1962. (Courtesy Ordnance Survey)

The Briggs studio had a tiny styling garden, seen here being used for presenting the Three Graces in spring 1956. On left sit designers 'Walt' Disney, Tom Firth and Eric Archer. On right in front row is Andy Cox (legs crossed) and Sir Patrick Hennessy, while Colin Neale sits behind, with arm draped on chair.

Like GM, both Ford Engineering division and Design Chief George Walker had a series of diktats on many areas of car proportions and design, including the requirement that front screens should be orientated so that they always lead the eye to the centre of the front wheel. Indeed, this can be seen on many Ford models from this era, from the 1949 Ford Sedan onwards. Thus, the A-pillar on the Consul leads straight to centre of the front wheel, whereas on the longer Zephyr, it is the centreline of the curved windscreen that satisfies this Ford design rule.

Once the clay models were approved in Dearborn they were shipped back to Dagenham for final rework, as the design was productionised by ex-Briggs body engineers. The first UK prototype was a black Zephyr Six, completed in December 1954 and driven around the Engineering car park at Rainham, watched by a keen group of engineers and designers. Two further prototypes, a Consul and a Zodiac, were finished in mid-January 1955 and used for endurance testing in southern Germany and Kenya during that spring.

Main styling studio, 1957. Every designer had a drawing board and anglepoise lamp, while canson paper and gouache were the main tools of the trade. Eric Archer is seen nearest the camera.

Designers were often asked to produce advanced artwork, too. Seen here is a fantasy vehicle on the cover of a 1956 *Ford Times* magazine signed by Tom Karen, who joined in 1955, and later went on to run the Ogle design consultancy. (Courtesy Neil Birtley)

The Ford Thames 400E forward control van was introduced in 1957. A refined piece of styling by Eric Archer and 'Walt' Disney, it was far more accomplished than rival vans from Bedford, Commer or BMC. Originally made at Dagenham, from 1961, production of the 400E was moved to Langley, together with the Thames Trader truck. (Courtesy Peter Lee)

This was a cover to a 1950s brochure published to explain the styling process to Ford dealers. The imaginary styling studio sketch was done by Non Crook, yet bears a surprising resemblance to the Dunton facility of a decade later.
(Courtesy Neil Birtley)

Ford had a well-developed colour and trim section by the mid-1950s. Professional displays to explain ideas at styling reviews became standard practice, as in Dearborn. Here, Doreen Archer demonstrates the Zephyr convertible interior colour strategy.

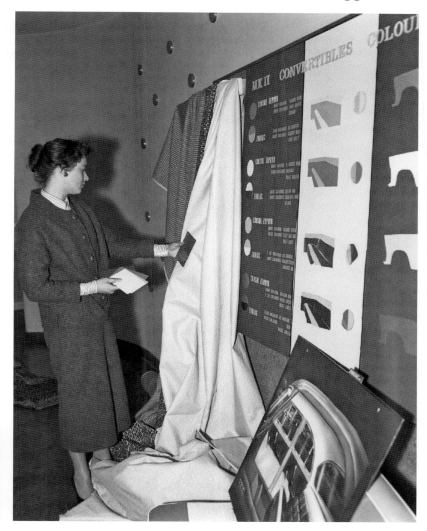

109E Consul Classic

With the Mk II Consul growing to a 104.5in (2654mm) wheelbase and 1.7-litre engine, Ford realised it needed a mid-range model to plug the yawning gap between the 100E Prefect and the new model, something closer to the original EOTA Consul. Emerging details about the new Vauxhall Victor FA, to be launched in March 1957 with 1.5-litre engine and 99in (2514mm) wheelbase, were seen as something of a target for Ford to aim for in terms of size and market positioning for this new mid-size model.

The resulting 109E Ford Consul Classic was a result of four years of development. Approval for the project was given in autumn 1956, as soon as the Mk II Consul project was completed. The original design requirement was for the 109E project to cover a full model

Doreen Archer was one of the first women ever employed in a UK car design studio. Seen here with fellow designer Tom Karen.

range to take Ford into the new decade, comprising two-door, four-door, estate and coupé variants. The styling exercises were mainly undertaken in 1956 under Colin Neale's direction, and it was the last project undertaken by Neale before he left Dagenham for Dearborn in 1958. As before, the US Fords being styled in Dearborn provided something of an inspiration for the British project, with the new Lincoln Premiere and sister Mercury Montclair receiving more flamboyant styling at this point. A new Ford brand – Edsel – was due to be launched in 1957, and the somewhat baroque design for these models influenced the 109E model. The '59 Fords were also being designed in the studio, and featured twin headlamps in a tight grouping above a full-width grille, similar to the latest Thunderbird style. This look was adopted for the front end of the 109E, and at its launch in 1961 the eventual Consul Classic became the first popular British production car to offer twin headlamps.

The most controversial styling feature was the reverse rake rear window, part of a line of development that Ford in the US were pursuing, being introduced on various models at that time, including the '58 Lincoln Continental.

In addition to the two-door and four-door saloons, the 109E project included a dashing two-door coupé derivative, codenamed 'Sunbird'. This started as a small morale-boosting project by Neale's team conducted over about a week in 1957, with little or no reference to management, after sawing off the roof of the recently-approved two-door Classic clay model.

The 'Sunbird' styling was led by Neale, with sweeping lines incorporating a pillarless coupé roof, thin C-pillar and a vast trunk. The trunk used the existing Classic saloon long trunk lid, which made the greenhouse proportion rather shorter than ideal. The designers proposed a longer cabin with decent rear headroom and proper rear seats but the extra cost of retooling for a shorter trunk lid was rejected, hence the slightly unbalanced look and package of the rear end.

Fortunately, Hennessy loved it when he saw it, plus it coincided with the ideas of Sir Horace Denne, Ford's Sales Director, who wanted a 'co-respondent's car' to add glamour to the product line. In the UK, the Sunbeam Rapier had shown how a pillarless coupé hardtop based on the Hillman Minx lower body could prove highly appealing in the marketplace, and Ford was keen to emulate the success of this Rootes model. Launched as the Consul Capri, it retained the 99in (2514mm) wheelbase and took design elements from the Ford Galaxie Starliner and the latest Ford Thunderbird. But it was a whimsical project, not based on any thorough product plan, and the severely compromised rear seat arrangement further restricted its success.

The first 109E prototype was running in January 1958. The car was engineered to be robust, in order to capture sales in overseas markets with rugged conditions – so-called 'Safari spec' to Ford engineers. The original aim was to introduce the car in 1959 or 1960, a few months after the Anglia, but was finally delayed until June

Reverse rake windows

The idea for a reverse rake rear window had first been shown on a Packard concept car in 1953, called the Balboa-X, described by Packard as a 'canopy top with picture window'. Here, the rear window followed the angle of the rear seat backrest and the window could be wound down to aid ventilation. Other advantages were said to be the reduction of optical distortion and the accumulation of rain or snow, plus it avoided the perceived danger of loose articles on the parcel shelf – simply because there was no such shelf!

Two years later Farina showed a Fiat 600 coupé at the Turin Motor Show featuring a reverse rake window. This small saloon caught the eye of Patrick Hennessy who was visiting the show and the feature was suggested by him to be incorporated in the styling for the new compact projects being developed in Dagenham. This was also in line with Ford's policy in the US, for they were pursuing the 'Breezeway' retractable rear window for the '57 Mercury Turnpike and a similar reverse rake rear window for the '58 Mk III Lincoln Continental.

To underline Ford's commitment to the reverse rake window, the extraordinary La Galaxie concept was displayed in 1958, styled by Ford's rising star designer, Elwood Engel. He later gave instructions to carry out basic wind tunnel tests to better understand the airflow around that area for production cars, the results also being used for the British projects with that feature.

For Ford of Britain, the reverse rake rear window offered several advantages. First, it was low cost, avoiding the need for curved glass. Second, it allowed a long trunk lid with excellent access to the trunk and spare tyre and also provided a long roof with good headroom for rear passengers. Lastly, it kept the rear glass commendably dirt-free, due to the clean airflow around the C-pillar.

1958 Lincoln Continentals with the reverse rake 'Breezeway' rear window that could roll down behind the rear seat.

The 1958 Ford La Galaxie concept showed Ford's commitment to the 'Breezeway' rear window. In production form, it featured on the 1957 Mercury Turnpike, 1958 Lincoln Capri, and 1960 Lincoln Continental.

Publicity illustration for the Consul Classic 109E. At the time, brochure illustration and styling studio techniques were similar; chiefly employing gouache and crayon. The 109E was available in two-door or four-door form, and in Standard or De Luxe trim. This De Luxe model is finished in two-tone paintwork, with optional whitewall tyres.

1961, allegedly due to engine shortages – every engine was directed towards the Anglia, which was proving a runaway success in the marketplace. In truth, there had been a complete rethink about the strategy for a mid-size model which resulted in the Cortina, covered in the next chapter.

Realisation that the 109E Classic was likely to become something of a stop-gap model for Ford led to the unusual decision to employ Kirksite body tooling, produced by Pressed Steel Company in Oxford. This type of tooling is generally used for pre-production or low volume runs of bodies, rather than the hardened steel dies normally used. Pilot build for the car commenced in May 1961 in the new PTA plant at Dagenham, with the Consul Capri launch coming a few weeks later in July 1961.

105E Anglia development 1957-'58

It should be explained that two projects were under way in 1956-'57 – the 109E Consul Classic and the 105E Anglia. Following the Suez Crisis in October 1956, the priority of these two projects began to shift, with the smaller 105E Anglia project gaining more urgency. Furthermore, the Birmingham Research Centre began to confirm the (correct) rumours of new compact cars from Standard Triumph and BMC (the Herald and Mini respectively), with prototypes seen being tested locally at MIRA. Life was about to get a lot tougher for Ford in the compact car market, and it needed to react – and fast. In 1958, work on the 109E Consul Classic was put on hold and the 105E project was accelerated, with a planned launch for summer 1959. The rumour mill went the other way, too: Triumph was tipped-off that its 'Zebu' project (an early Triumph 2000 mock-up) with its novel reverse rake rear window might be beaten to the market, and would be seen as simply copying the new Fords ... Triumph duly abandoned this feature in 1958, opting for a more conventional rear window treatment.

The engineering layout for the new Anglia was not a foregone conclusion. Whereas the Essex engineering team retained responsibility for the larger 109E Classic project, the Birmingham Research Centre was given responsibility for this smaller 'Light Car' project, also codenamed 195-X. The Birmingham team was initially

The Fiat 600 coupé by Pinin Farina was inspiration for the British Ford designs being developed at the time, such as the 109E Consul Classic and the 105E Anglia. (Courtesy Stephen Wickham)

The Anglia, seen here in early 3/8 scale model form in 1955, when it was known as project 195-X.

working on possible FWD layouts, but finally settled on using the existing known layout of a longitudinal engine and RWD with leaf springs at the rear and MacPherson struts at the front. Fred Hart was Executive Engineer Light Cars, with engineer Roy Lunn heading up the Birmingham team.

Colin Macgregor was a Briggs designer who had been requested by Terry Beckett to move up to the new facility in Birmingham in 1955, to start work on styling for this 'New Popular' project, which began as a basic utility concept but eventually led to the 105E Anglia. Macgregor's first model followed the theme and proportions of the Fiat 600 coupé again, but this time for reasons of production simplicity, not just styling. The reverse rake rear window allowed a simple roof pressing and flat glass rear window, offering big cost savings. It also had the useful advantage that it allowed a wide trunk opening and left the rear screen clear from road dirt.

This initial model was produced quite quickly in 1955, and took the cost-saving approach to extremes. According to Neale, "It was very spartan inside," with a pod instrument panel containing just a speedometer and fuel gauge, no heater, and hammock-type canvas seats, not unlike a Citroën 2CV. Inner door panels were simple vacuum formings, and there was some investigation into using GRP body panels. Some of the features of this utility car model were taken up by the 109E project team, but the main development shifted somewhat, with the utility approach being abandoned in favour of a more comprehensive specification, including a thoroughly modern all-new short-stroke OHV 997cc engine with 39bhp, a 4-speed gearbox, and top speed of 77mph – sufficient for cruising on Britain's new motorways.

Photos of 3/8th scale models from July 1955 show the 195-X project at that stage. The reverse window is evident, as are the hooded headlamps and low bonnet of the final design. Colin Neale led the overall design for the 105E project, but his proposal for the bodyside treatment wasn't initially accepted, although a similar style was later adopted for the final car. He moved to Dearborn in 1958, where he teamed up with Elwood Engel in the advanced design 'Stiletto Studio' (mainly so-called because it was long and thin, but also because its remit was to offer up 'dig-in-the-ribs' alternative proposals for the other Ford studios). Neale enjoyed the wider opportunities offered to him, and decided to stay in the US. He eventually moved over to Chrysler with Engel in 1962, where he stayed until his retirement in the 1980s.

Dearborn's international studio constructed Anglia proposals too, including models for a van and estate car design. As the program developed, Project Engineer Roy Lunn was transferred to Essex as Product Planning Manager to follow the project – by now called 105E – into production, although by 1958 he too had followed Neale to Ford in Dearborn as Chief Engineer in the advanced studio.

One car that had a significant influence on the 105E was the Austin A40, launched in October 1958. This was the first production car styled by Battista 'Pinin' Farina for Austin, as part of a change of direction for the British company to update its image by using Italian styling. The A40 was notable for its clean-cut looks, crisp, squared-off greenhouse, and good luggage space. It offered a 948cc 34bhp OHV engine, 4-speed gearbox with short lever on the floor, an optional heater, and low maintenance design with few grease nipples. The A40 also offered a hatchback layout in 1959 – the first mainstream British car to offer this feature. As a bench mark for the Anglia, it raised the game considerably.[1]

Just prior to the new Anglia launch in May 1959, the existing Prefect 100E was updated, using the new overhead valve 997cc engine and 4-speed gearbox, together with minor revisions to styling, including optional two-tone paint and chrome side strips, becoming the 107E. The aim was to retain a small four-door model in the line-up, seeing as the new 105E Anglia would be sold as a two-door model only, but the update of the new engine and gearbox gave a useful few months of learning to iron out any last-minute glitches before production was ramped up for the new Anglia.

Production of the 105E Anglia started in September 1959 in the new PTA plant, linked by a 725 foot (220m) overhead conveyor over Kent Avenue from the Briggs body plant. That month coincided with the public launch of the BMC Mini and Triumph Herald, both all-new designs from competitors. That trio of crisply styled and up-to-date cars for Britain's motorway age would go on to become key rivals throughout the 1960s.

1. Coachbuilder Abbott's subsidiary, Friary Motors, developed a hatchback Anglia for sale in June 1961. Called the Anglia Touring, the roof profile was similar to that of the Austin A40, and was available for £89 12s 6d as an aftermarket conversion.

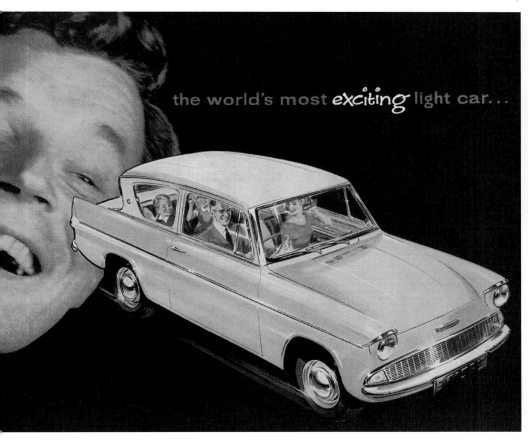

the world's most *exciting* light car...

Publicity for the Anglia centered on its fun-to-drive appeal, ease of maintenance, roominess, and vast trunk. Prices for the Anglia started at £589 in Standard form.

The all-new Anglia 105E used a 90.5in wheelbase, 3½in longer than the outgoing 100E but, surprisingly, some 3in narrower. Like the 109E, it was available in Standard or De Luxe forms, with two-tone paintwork a popular option for the De Luxe.

Full-size chalk and airbrush renderings for the
Anglia in the styling studio, 1956.

Chapter

3

Roy Brown and the Aveley studio

The period 1958-'59 was a time of confusion for the Dagenham styling studio. As mentioned in the previous chapter, Colin Neale was seconded to the USA in 1958 to work in Dearborn's 'Stiletto Studio' with Elwood Engel, and at this point Ford management in the UK made it clear that new leadership was needed for the British studio, in order to take it forward into the 1960s with a host of new projects. This lead to some jockeying of position within the studio staff, with Bob Saward and Tom Firth both vying for a potential promotion against Australian designer Maurice King. However, in early 1959 it became clear they were not going to be offered the top job, which was likely to go to an American designer. Hence, Saward and Firth both decided to leave Ford to go to Rootes in Coventry, taking lead modeller Fred Barratt with them.[1]

Other departures during the late 1950s included Ron Hickman, John Frayling and Peter Cambridge, all of whom were poached by Colin Chapman to establish a design section for his fledgling Lotus company. Frayling developed Peter Kirwin-Taylor's sketches for the Elite into a decent 3D model, while Cambridge became the main interiors designer. Hickman had started as a clay modeller but left in 1958 and remained at Lotus until 1967, when he established his own design consultancy – most famous for the Workmate DIY workbench.

1958-'59: Turmoil and disruption: Zephyr III

In the midst of this disruption, the 213E Zephyr Mk III project was struggling to make headway. Originally planned for a 1961 launch, the model was deliberately positioned more upmarket, to become a genuine flagship for the Ford line up, since the role of the Consul would be taken up by the new 109E Classic (and subsequently the Cortina). However, given all the other new projects and capital outlay going on at the time, Ford decided to retain the basic platform from the six-cylinder Mk II Zephyr, with a 107in (2718mm) wheelbase for all versions. Marketing decided that the Consul nameplate would be dropped for these 213E models too, even though the smaller four-cylinder engine remained, being known as the Zephyr 4, with the six-cylinder models being known as the Zephyr 6 and Zodiac.

The first full-size clay model for the 213E project had been completed in late 1957, with input from American designer Elwood Engel, as part of his regular visits to the UK studio. This continued some of the themes from Neale's 109E Classic design, including the wing-type rear fins that ran well forward with a distinctive undercut shoulder line. When shown to the UK management, it

---

1. *This Ford team was responsible for introducing clay modelling into the Rootes studio, replacing the older technique of Plasticine ¼ scales and wooden 1:1 mock-ups that had previously been the typical method used in the Coventry studios. It was also credited in bringing Ford's slicker sketching and presentation techniques, according to Rootes designer Roy Axe. For Tom Firth it proved a short-lived sojourn – by 1961 he was persuaded to return to Ford. Bob Saward went on to design the Hillman Imp.*

was considered 'too American.' Some months later, Colin Neale was requested to return to the UK to do a further proposal, dubbed 'Breakaway' in early 1958. This also had some 109E Classic overtones with a torpedo fuselage-style bodyside and a reverse rake window, although the front end with four lamps set into a wide grille provided the basis for the look of the eventual Zodiac Mk III. Neale returned to the USA when that model was subsequently rejected.

At this point, the studio struggled to find a new direction for the 213E project. According to historian David Burgess-Wise, Hennessy wrote to Neale in Dearborn soon afterwards, commenting that "We are still in trouble with our Mk III. For one thing it seems difficult to meet the Galaxie type of roof to the design below the belt line. We have tried a number of variants yet are not happy."

Pietro Frua proposal for Mk III Zephyr, 1958. This was based on the floorpan of the existing Mk II Zephyr, and introduced a Chrysler-type theme of a clean bodyside that ran into slanted vertical fins at the rear. Note the vertical A-pillars and stepped grille that were revised for the production car.

Zodiac prototype in Aveley showroom, probably late 1960. The six-light Zodiac was particularly handsome, with a roofline that was some 3in lower than the old 'Lowline' Mk II. The 213E Zodiac had twin 5¾in lamps, while the Zephyr stuck with single 7in headlamps.

Unusual prototype 213E Zodiac that utilised the four-light cabin from the Zephyr. During development, the front end was widened considerably, giving a somewhat under-tracked look compared to the original Frua model.

Hennessy then decided to commission a model from Pietro Frua in Turin. In the late 1950s, Italian design was being heralded as the way forward for a number of British car companies. BMC had engaged Farina in 1955 to become its main design consultant, and Standard-Triumph had turned to Michelotti in 1957 to design its next range of cars, commencing with the Triumph Herald. Rootes was also dabbling with Turin, setting up a joint venture with Touring to develop a special version of the Humber Sceptre, called the Venezia. Having taken the Farina Fiat as a template for the Anglia and Classic, it seemed natural that Ford might look to Turin once again for inspiration for its next big design direction.

This Frua model was based on the floorpan of the existing Mk II Zephyr, and introduced a Chrysler-type theme of a clean bodyside that ran into broad vertical fins at the rear. The greenhouse was notable for its six-light construction, with very slim pillars used all round, while the front end introduced four headlamps arranged in a slanted vee-shape, not unlike that used for the '58 Thunderbird. This model was well received by the UK management when shipped to Dagenham, but was felt to lack sufficient Ford design cues to be fully approved.

Zephyr 6 launch illustration. The Zodiac was launched on 13 April 1962, with the Zephyr 4 and Zephyr 6 arriving two weeks later.

The interior of the Zephyr used a number of new materials, including 'Saronweave' seat fabric and ICI 'Novon Ten' printed wood decor inserts.
In a nod to safety, the IP gained a padded top roll.

Roy Brown (left), with John Fallis (standing) and Maurice King. King was head of the styling studio for a few brief months, in 1959.

The Lincoln Futura concept was originally designed by Roy Brown, but was later modified by legendary customiser George Barris for the TV series of *Batman*. Ghia was contracted to build the original car in 1955.

Hennessy appealed to Dearborn to help with finding a new Chief Designer who could lead the studio. "I want a designer with a lot of enthusiasm to come over here and build us the finest design department in Europe," he said to George Walker. Walker duly sent Roy Brown, who had recently been heading up the Edsel studio. The Edsel brand had been launched to great fanfare in 1957, but its spectacular flop led to the abandonment of the entire venture in autumn 1959, leaving Brown without an immediate design position. Others have commented that Brown being 'banished to the UK'

was a kind of punishment for the Edsel fiasco, but that is less than fair to Brown, and a misunderstanding of the situation in the UK. His secondment was actually Walker's attempt to give him a new opportunity to which he could respond, and help him regain his confidence as a design manager.

Roy Brown was born in Ontario, Canada in 1916. He studied Industrial Design at Detroit Art Academy, but had also worked as a dance-band crooner to supplement his income as a youngster. He worked at GM in the 1940s as a styling designer, before joining Ford in 1953. One of his first jobs was the 1955 Lincoln Futura concept, later modified by customiser George Barris to become the Batmobile used in the 1960's TV series. Following this he was given increasing responsibility, culminating in his appointment to design the new Edsel range.

On arrival in the UK in late 1959, Brown was tasked with consolidating the Frua model with the desires of the British executives, to come up with something that bore some visual link to other Ford UK products. Over a few months over the winter of 1959-'60 the Frua model was steadily revised, taking the front end of Neale's 'Breakaway' model and blending it into the main section of the Frua design. To achieve that, the greenhouse was given quite a strong taper in plan from the A-pillars, which themselves were raked strongly rearwards, rather than retaining the wraparound screen of the Frua model. To allow the blend, the front end was widened considerably, with the rounded front fender merging gradually into the rear fin along the whole length of the bodyside in a remarkably bold piece of modelling.

Once the new six-light Zodiac style was settled, thoughts turned to the mainstream Zephyr 4 and 6 variants. One bonus of the 213E project was that these Zephyr derivatives were allowed to have a different (and less costly) greenhouse treatment in order to provide more differentiation within the range, rather than simply grilles and two-tone paint as before. In a bid to strengthen the Ford family look, the Zephyr 4 and 6 were given an upright Galaxie-style thick C-pillar and four-light greenhouse treatment, which sat very comfortably upon the Italianate lower body. The design of the doors with separately-welded upper door frames meant that the rear door glass could be revised at relatively low cost, although in the end the trailing edge of the rear door pressing on the Zodiac also had to be modified to allow the large one-piece glass to drop fully into the door cavity, meaning the mating face of the rear fender also had minor differences compared to the Zephyr models.

Curved side glass was employed for the first time on a British Ford to allow for a 3.5in (90mm) increase in elbow room within the same overall body width, albeit using a very small amount of glass curvature. Charlie Thompson was tasked with designing many of the details of the 213E, including much of the front end and grille. On the Zodiac, this was an elaborate pressed alloy component, with a top section of fine vertical bars, to continue the theme of the previous Zodiac.

Another designer who worked on the 213E was John Stark, who arrived at Ford in 1960, part of the rapid staff expansion that was taking place. He was hired by Roy Brown to do graphics for instruments. Stark had been to Glasgow School of Art, then did national service before writing to Ford and BMC: only Ford replied.

Stark's initial work was for the Mk III Zephyr. "The Zephyr had dual tone vinyl seats to match the door linings," he recalls. "We also did Bedford cord for the trim, made a good job of it too. It was great, a step forward – known as Saronweave. The Rover P5 was the bench mark car for the Mk III, they wanted it at least on a par with the P5." As before, Connolly leather was optional on the Mk III. "Sir Patrick Hennessy would come to viewings, he insisted on that."

Metallic paints were not offered on the Mk III at launch, but a good range of 12 solid colours were developed, including maroon, grey and dark blue. "Ambassador Blue – the dark Prussian blue – was very popular, you still see examples," says Stark. Ford management wanted metallics on the Zodiac as a flagship model, and, with the arrival of the top-of-the-range 'Executive' model in January 1965, two metallic paint finishes were finally developed. "The first two metallics were Venetian Gold and Silver Fox. They were basically copies of Jaguar colours of the time," confirms Stark.

"The Zodiac had twin exhausts – bliss! It was nice. The promise of something really fancy," recalls Stark. Indeed the Mk III Zodiac quickly resonated with many buyers who appreciated its transatlantic modern looks compared to the stodgy offerings of BMC, Humber or Rover. To add to the glamour, drawings for a drophead Zodiac were made with Carbodies but were not finally pursued due to high unit costs. However, Abbott estate versions were developed in conjunction with Ford during 1961-'62 and launched promptly in October 1962. Available in Zephyr or Zodiac form, these were very stylish cars that cleverly utilised the Zodiac rear door on all models, with the top corner of the upper frame modified so the roofline could run straight through.

Project Archbishop: Cortina Mk I

Before the Zephyr Mk III was launched in April 1962, Ford had another more urgent project, one that would go on to change the whole company and reinvent the British car market into the 1960s. Talking to author Graham Robson, Terry Beckett recalled the genesis of this important model – the Cortina: "We were building a new framework, organisationally, and in terms of people as well. It was a change of culture, and I have to tell you that by the time we came to plan the Cortina, the difficulty was that we had been through two models that had got badly out of control [these were the Classic 109E and the Zephyr 213E]. We had to get control of our costs. We weren't trying to control the cost of everything in the car, we were going to control what we called the 'key parts.' If we could control those, we were already in control of about 90 per cent of the car."

"We also triangulated the cost of these from existing Ford parts which were similar, and with the best of competitive practice. I had endless examinations of all our competitors' costs; we examined every detail to see if we could learn anything from them in terms of manufacturing processes, design, customer benefits etc. We were able to triangulate the key parts – about 500 of them – and we put them in what we called the Red Book."

By 1960, Product Planning had learned from previous mistakes and had a clear vision of what was required for the new decade for their new mid-size car range to bridge the yawning gap between the Anglia and the forthcoming Zephyr/Zodiac Mk III. In fact, the gap was so large it would lead to two new models, the Cortina and the Corsair. The concept for the former was extremely tough: a medium car for a small car price. Larger than the Anglia but lighter than the Classic, it also needed a large boot and to be more profitable than any previous Ford.

Then there was Ford of Germany. It was planning a replacement codenamed 'Cardinal' for the P2 Taunus, and was pushing ahead with a radical FWD package that had been under development since late 1958. Ford US was also supporting the FWD 'Cardinal' project, seeing it as a useful new compact model to tackle the VW Beetle and Chevrolet Corvair. The $43 million 'Cardinal' plan included a second production site in Kentucky, with transaxles shipped over from Germany (which at the time was a low-cost labour country).

1960 Ford Falcon. The basic design theme was used as a template for the Cortina project, including the C-pillar, trunk, rear fenders and wheelarches.

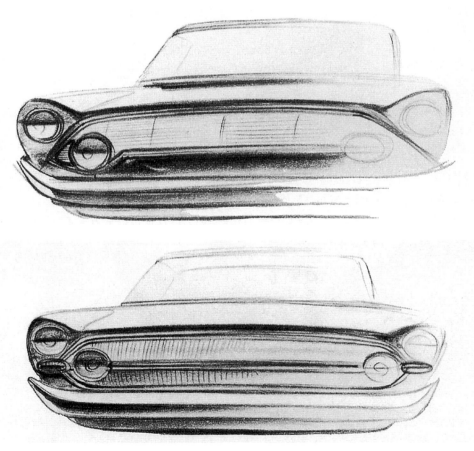

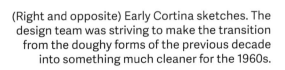

(Right and opposite) Early Cortina sketches. The design team was striving to make the transition from the doughy forms of the previous decade into something much cleaner for the 1960s.

Ford of Britain also saw the new BMC Mini as a big threat, particularly to the Anglia. With the basic model listed as £497 including purchase tax, the Mini stole Ford's pitch as offering the cheapest car in the UK market, and would put Ford under huge pressure to reduce the cost of the Anglia. The well-worn story of how Beckett's department costed the Mini, and could not see how it made a profit, warrants full explanation here.

The department actually made three attempts. The first was a simple look-over by Beckett a matter of weeks after the Mini was launched in September 1959. He spent a couple of hours examining a new Mini on a parked car transporter, and made notes while the driver had his lunch in a café. Simply by examining it externally by eye he could observe the complexity and costs, and roughly calculated that there was no way BMC could be making a profit on it. The Birmingham Research Centre had recently completed a FWD light car prototype so he understood exactly what the detailed costs would be for such a layout. Two weeks later he arranged for his department to buy a Mini for a complete strip down. Being

Cortina 113E two-door model, ready for sign–off in Aveley studio. John Bugas of Ford International rejected the slanted tail lamps proposed here in January 1961. Circular 'Ban the Bomb' style lamps were hastily designed for approval, similar to those used on the new Falcon.

Cortina model September 1960. Note the Falcon-style bodyside line.

dissatisfied by the alarming results, the team repeated the exercise, this time right down to its spot welds. "We examined every part of it – and there wasn't any way they could be making money."

At this point Sir Patrick Hennessy reputedly phoned Sir George Harriman, BMC's managing director, informing him that Ford had undertaken this exercise, and that it wasn't in either of their interests for BMC to offer a car at such an uneconomic price – not only would BMC go bust, but, in the meantime, Ford would be forced to slash costs and risk jobs and profitability to compete. Harriman arrogantly assured him that he knew what he was doing – "I am, after all, a production engineer by training, old boy ..." That was the end of the matter as far as BMC was concerned, but other sources also confirmed that it was losing £30 on every Mini.

Surprising as it may seem now – the Cortina and the Mini are vastly different in terms of size – at £639 for a two-door Standard 1200 model, the Cortina split the difference between the two-door Mini De Luxe at £537, and the basic four-door Morris 1100 at £675. As a comparison, the Hillman Minx started at £702, including tax.

Ford of Britain was not consulted about the 'Cardinal' project, which incensed Hennessy, not least because it would give it a harder time in European markets, where Ford dealers displayed and sold models from both Ford Germany and Ford UK – the so-called 'two fishing line approach,' whereby the customer could be snared by an alternative product within the Ford offering if the German model didn't suit. To be honest, Hennessy was probably too powerful and autocratic a figure at that point to be brought into a joint venture with either Ford US or Ford Germany, so had been left out of the discussions.

Hennessy decided he would fight back. In spring 1960 he instructed Fred Hart, Terry Beckett and Roy Brown – newly arrived from the US – to commence work on a totally new 'Archbishop' project, to be launched at the same time as 'Cardinal' in summer 1962. That was going to be extremely tough: Cardinal had already been under development for a year, and that gave them just two years to complete the UK project. "But we did it," confirms Beckett. "We took just 21 months from first full size clay to 'Job One,' which was an all-time record for the industry, and certainly for Ford."

Chief Engineer Fred Hart confirmed to Hennessy that the only way they could engineer the car in time would be to use mildly developed components from the existing Anglia 105E drivetrain. Thus, the initial package was designed around a 98in wheelbase with a generous trunk, so the first clay models could be started immediately. The Anglia's new 997cc OHV engine was enlarged to 1198cc with 50bhp and the gearbox revised to offer synchromesh on all four gears.

The body was the most radical piece of engineering in the project. Calculated to be as light and stiff as possible using aircraft stressing principles, the body engineering was led by Don Ward, Chief Body Engineer, assisted by engineer Dennis Roberts, who had learned his trade at Bristol Aeroplane Company before arriving at Briggs Motor Bodies. Roberts reduced the number of body pressings by 20 per cent, and actively designed parts to double up their function. For example, the trunk had no conventional floor, but was simply a perimeter frame with the top of the inset fuel tank acting as the main trunk floor. Chief Engineers had to sign off each component in the Red Book as it was designed, to ensure it met with the full specification regarding cost, weight and performance. In the end, the car ended up weighing 300lb less than the Classic at 1725lb (781kg).

According to Stephen Wickham of the Ford Classic and Capri Owners' club, Don Ward had jealously guarded body engineering, and insisted that styling report through him to board members, and that this was one of the key reasons that Neale left for the US. Brown's first achievement was a very early showdown soon after his appointment, in which he wrested styling control back from the engineers.

The move to the new Aveley studio in summer 1960 added disruption to this tight program for Brown, yet the team managed to get the two-door clay model ready for approval in November 1960, followed by the four-door in April 1961. In all, five clay models were produced, with the final selected design having a tapering flute along the flanks – an extension of the motif used on the Anglia. Beckett considered it the single most important feature on the car, making people appreciate its length, breaking up the mass of the body, generating a sense of movement, and having a functional role in that it stiffened the body panels.

An estate model was also planned, with

A modeller works on a clay Cortina door handle in Aveley studio.

Final Cortina 113E. Job One was available on 4 June 1962, exactly as per schedule.

the full-size clay approved in September 1961. The Cortina estate had unique tail lamps and alterations to the rear door upper frame to allow a straight-through roofline – the first British Ford wagon to have such full investment, reflecting the growing importance of this body style by the early 1960s. The estate was launched in De Luxe and Super estate versions in early 1963. The Super used American-style 3M Di-Noc wood-effect film on the bodysides and tailgate, edged with mock-wood GRP mouldings, all a bit overwrought for European tastes: it was dropped after a couple of years.

The sporting 1500 GT model arrived in April 1963, using an uprated

bodyshell. This had been conveniently developed for the Australian market, which demanded stronger suspension mounting points and uprated suspension components to cope with the rigours of the bush, so to utilise it for the 1500 GT was a useful spin-off.

The Cortina interior had to accommodate a standard column gearshift or an optional floor shift using a very long wand-like gearlever. The original IP design at launch was extremely austere, comprising a painted metal panel with a small anodised panel containing the key slot, a simple ribbed top pad, a strip-type speedometer and two-spoke steering wheel. It also featured a unique single cast column stalk with a flipper on the end for the indicators.

This IP was hastily revised in September 1963, adding a separate binnacle with large round instruments within it. This proved a short-lived design, for in October 1964 came yet another IP design, when 'Aeroflow' ventilation was added, with swivelling eyeball face-level vents at the ends of the IP – a first for a family saloon in Europe.

In the end, Beckett and the design team certainly got their costs under control. Development costs for the Cortina came in at £13 million – £50,000 under the investment target, with the car costing 16 shillings (20 new pence) under its target pricing.

Aveley styling studio 1960-'67

When Roy Brown arrived in autumn 1959 he was tasked with a whole host of new projects into the 1960s, and therefore much larger styling studios would be necessary to carry out the work. Hence, in August 1960 – right in the middle of the 'Archbishop' project – the styling team moved out from Dagenham to the new Aveley site.

The Aveley studios were not actually in Aveley itself, but rather in nearby South Ockenden, Essex. In April 1957, Ford had acquired a 30-acre (12ha) site in Arisdale Avenue, South Ockenden, for use as a parts distribution depot to supply the fast-expanding operations and 1000-strong UK dealer network that had been established. The £1.6 million building eventually came to be a huge 120,000sq ft (11,150sq m) warehouse employing 600 people, complete with its own narrow gauge railway branching off the adjacent Upminster-Tilbury line. In early 1960, an extension was added to the north end of the vast parts warehouse to accommodate the fast-expanding engineering team, as one of several sites around Essex for the relocation of engineers at Dagenham. One of the main functions of the Aveley engineering site was for prototype builds of new projects, but it also housed 'Leo,' the first computer employed by the British motor industry, used for preparing the parts ordering paperwork.

Engineering and styling occupied this new extension at the northern end of the site, which comprised about one third of the total space at Arisdale Avenue. Styling had roughly 1400sq m in total, comprising an exterior studio, interior studio, a colour and trim studio, a small advanced studies studio and a small outdoor viewing courtyard measuring no more than 20m x 8m. There was also an indoor showroom with one turntable, an engineering support and packaging drawing office, workshop and stores.

"The styling studios were simply on one end of the main parts distribution warehouse," recalls designer Neil Birtley. "The main Ford publicity photo studios were just across the road at the opposite end to styling in a former Dexion shelving factory. Canterbury Sidecars were just opposite on Arisdale Avenue [they produced sidecars and motor caravan conversions]. Down the road was Aveley village itself, a London overspill council estate and a flooded gravel pit opposite. It was quite a bleak place on the windswept Essex marshes."

Expansion of the design staff, Eric Archer's school

After the move to Aveley, the design team rapidly expanded in the early 1960s. Following the Ford US buyout, more American designers arrived from the Dearborn studios, often seconded on 18-month stints. Two early arrivals were Charlie McHose, a Californian, and Tom Land, a son of the Land-Polaroid camera family. Claude Gidman was sent over soon after to look after truck design, including the Transit and new D-Series range. In December 1964 Phil Clarke arrived from the US – just after the departure of Roy Brown when the studio was under a lot of pressure to deliver – where he worked for John Fallis on projects such as the Cortina Mk II, Escort, and early Capri work. More local new arrivals included Tom Firth (who rejoined Ford from Rootes) and Dave Reece, who transferred from Vauxhall.

By the early 1960s, the colour and trim section was being run by Non Crook, with John Stark, Pierre Yates and Doreen Archer on the team. "When I started Eric Archer was engaged to Doreen, in the colour and trim section. A very glamourous lady, I was bowled over by her, I hadn't met many such women," recalls Stark. Meanwhile, the Lodge Road studio up in Birmingham had Norman Terry as a designer, mainly working on the Ford electric Comuta car project.

Finding it hard to recruit young stylists, and with no real training for automotive designers in the UK, Eric Archer was delegated by Brown to set up a small apprentice school in 1961 at the defunct Chequers Lane studio. He recruited a small number of apprentices for design training, with a view to offering jobs within styling at the end of their tenure. One such apprentice was Neil Birtley, then at school in Durham. "I read in a magazine that Ford had a styling studio, at that time nobody mentioned styling, it was all technical engineering. I just wrote a letter to Ford head office, and after two weeks got a reply from Mr Archer saying would you like to come down to have an interview. I joined in Easter 1962."

"Eric's school had four, later five, apprentices housed upstairs in what had been the design engineering office. After 18 months we all moved over to Aveley and they closed the training school. I became a fully-fledged stylist!"

Eric Archer and wife Doreen discussing trim samples with Roy Haynes (kneeling).

The Lincoln Continental had the same lightly 'puffed' bodyside edged in chrome that was a hallmark of the Corsair: as did the Taunus.

Sailing along – the 'Buccaneer' Consul Corsair development

The next big project was the 120E, codenamed 'Project Buccaneer,' allegedly in celebration of the seafaring tradition of Liverpool, where the new car would be built. More likely, it was a nod to the Blackburn Buccaneer fighter plane that had become operational in late 1961, and it was an exciting name that was in the headlines at the time.

The aim was to capitalise on the market that the Consul and the 109E Classic had established, with key competitors comprising the Hillman Super Minx, Austin Cambridge, Morris Oxford and Vauxhall FB Victor – true 1.5-litre D-sector cars. Originally sold as the Consul Corsair, the emphasis was on refinement and style in a bigger package than the Cortina; particularly rear seat and trunk space. 'Project Buccaneer' utilised the entire Cortina underbody, but with a 3in (75mm) insert in the floor pressing just ahead of the rear seat pan. The Corsair also shared the basic windscreen, A-pillars, and door inners of the Cortina, plus many inner panels, including the engine bay, scuttle, and bulkhead.

The design team was led by Roy Brown as Chief Stylist, supported by John Fallis, Executive Stylist Exterior and Maurice 'Morrie' King, Executive Stylist Interior. As with the Cortina, it was a fast 21-month program, beginning in January 1962, with a target launch of October 1963. In the early stages the project was done in the advanced studio at Aveley, and was then transferred to the main studios for development. Eight full-size models were produced to cover the exterior and interior development, and it seems the design proceeded very smoothly through the various committee stages, with no real sticking points, in contrast to many other projects. Brown's maxim was 'Keep it simple ...'

The theme for the car was a big departure from previous designs, being heavily

View of the exteriors studio at Aveley, looking south. Designers were housed along the western side of the studio, with the model plates adjacent. In the foreground is Neil Birtley, and seated behind is John Pritchard.

influenced by the latest American Fords. Colin Neale had worked with Elwood Engel on the 1961 Lincoln and '61 Thunderbird in the Stiletto Studio, where Neale came up with a neat rear end for their Thunderbird proposal. This two-door model was subsequently revised to become a full-size four-door design that was developed into the famous '61 Lincoln Continental, with its lightly puffed body section and chrome framing to the panel edges. That whole theme strongly influenced the British team, and the idea was promoted to Roy Brown and John Fallis by Engel on his trips to Aveley around 1960-'61 to try it in downsized form for the forthcoming 'Buccaneer' project.

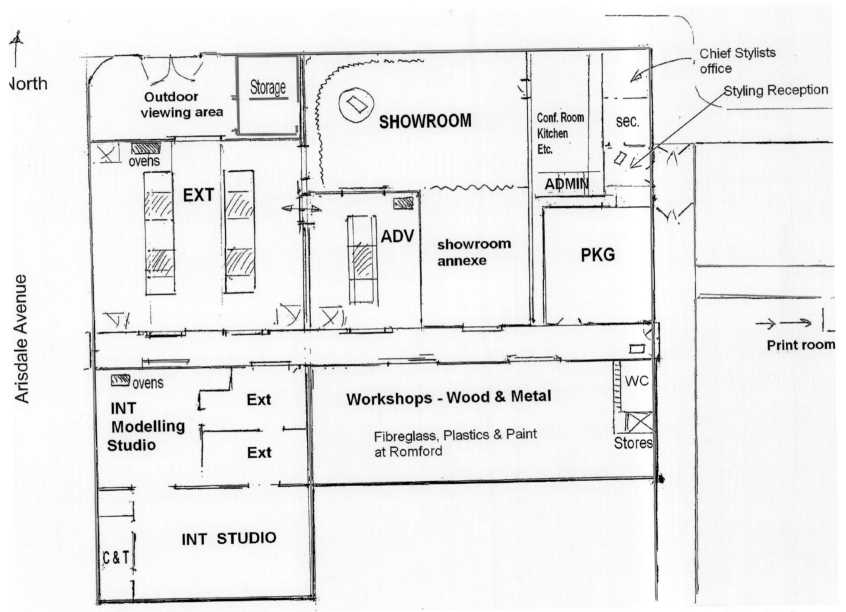

Layout of the Aveley studios, drawn by designer Neil Birtley. The studios had an area of around 1400sq m and included a small advanced studio, a presentation showroom, and a tiny viewing yard outside. The facility housed roughly 20 designers, including the colour and trim section. Around 20-30 modellers were employed at that time. (Courtesy Neil Birtley)

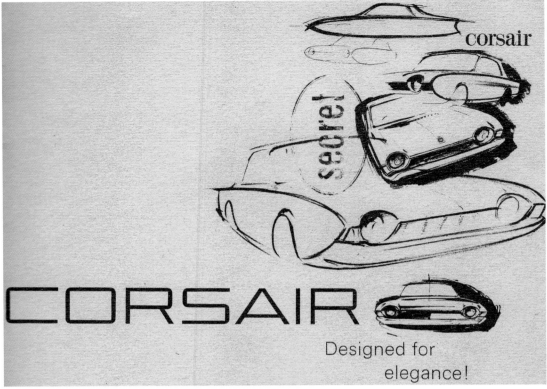

Sketches from the Corsair launch brochure show the elegant bullet-shape profile that was inspired by the Ford Thunderbird.

The Corsair interior saw the use of new trim materials from ICI, such as 'Vulkide' vacuum-formed plastic sheeting for rear trim panels, and 'Vynair 15,' a breathable PVC-coated material used on seats. This shows the revised interior from 1965, with a round rather than 'quartic' horn ring.

The resulting Corsair was notable for its very clean styling and neat detailing, such as the single chrome line along the shoulder that incorporated the door handles. The pointed front end was also clever in that the bumper and chrome sidelight finisher provide the line for the sharp spear profile, whereas the actual front end is more bluff and conventional than you would think. The sill and lower edge of the body have a pronounced curvature to them, and the effect helps to generate the sharp profile of the car.

John Fallis was quoted as saying that "it looks as if it's moving when it was standing still" – possibly the first use of this over-used phrase in UK parlance. Following the Classic, both two-door and four-door body styles were developed, with Charlie Thompson producing sketches for a Corsair coupé too, although this was never progressed.

The original plan was to utilise the Cortina doors unchanged, thus with the concave spear running through them. At least two models were built with that configuration, but later rejected in favour of tooling new outer door skins. Door upper frames and glasses were carried over, however.

As with the exterior, the interior also had a clear theme. Here, the elongated binnacle sat on top of the IP, finished in brushed aluminium. A lower panel indexed with this upper binnacle to create the impression of a padded IP that bisects through these two parts. "For the Corsair, the instruments were in a long strip," explains John Stark. "I did all the lettering – remember, this was pre Letraset days too! I drew them full-size, for mock-ups for management to review for approval."

The colour-keyed steering wheel sported a 'quartic' horn ring to allow vision through it to the strip speedometer, which also utilised a printed circuit board attached at the rear – one of the first examples of its kind. GT models featured a floor gearshift mounted on a centre console – the first UK Fords to feature such a floor console (although the console design was shared with the Lotus Cortina announced in January 1963). This

Battles in Dearborn

Over in Dearborn, the styling division had recently gone through a major upheaval, with Gene Bordinat Jr replacing George Walker as Vice President of styling in June 1961. Bordinat had not been the first choice, Walker having groomed his two protégés Elwood Engel and Joe Oros to succeed him – the so-called 'gold dust twins'. According to Michael Lamm in his book *A Century of Automotive Style*, Walker himself favoured Engel to get the top job, but allegedly Engel was caught double-billing Ford for a business trip to Aveley in spring that year so was immediately out of the race. Next, Oros was nominated to take over the vice presidency by Walker but William Clay Ford strongly intervened, favouring the more measured personality of Bordinat over Oros. Ford top management agreed that Oros didn't quite cut the mustard either, so – surprisingly – Bordinat was named as the eventual successor.

Bordinat was hardly an outsider for the job though, having been one of Walker's favoured design managers over the previous decade. In fact, he had been known to Walker since childhood, having gone to school with the Walker children in Pleasant Ridge, Detroit in the 1930s. Although he initially joined GM as a designer in 1939, by 1947 he was recruited by Walker at Ford, initially heading up the advanced studio.

Bordinat expanded the design staff and doubled the size of the workspace in Dearborn so that more full-size models could be produced. He also encouraged deeper involvement with Ford in the UK and in Germany, sending designers over on international secondment for two to three years to help run the programs. From 1964 he introduced the weekly system of design sub-committee (DSC) shows across all Ford's studios that existed until his retirement some 19½ years later, in 1980. DSC 'part one' shows were held every Friday morning for top corporate and divisional managers, providing a main weekly update on all programs. These were supported by Monday morning 'part two' approval shows in the main presentation rooms. Around the same time, William Clay Ford assumed responsibility for corporate product planning and design, and in 1957 became Chairman of the company's design committee, a post he held until his retirement in 1989.

In a final twist, Walker was determined to get his revenge on Ford once he retired by pulling a few strings. He arranged for Engel to get the top job at Chrysler design to replace Virgil Exner in November 1961. It cost Ford dearly, since Engel's subsequent designs during the 1960s led to a resurgence in Chrysler's fortunes.

George Walker and his beaming smile. Walker stands with Bill Clay Ford in the new presentation showroom at Dearborn, in 1957. Joe Oros and Gene Bordinat are seated behind, with other design executives.

console provided the location for the two extra instruments mounted at the front, together with an armrest and cubby box behind.

Marketing for the Corsair was more sophisticated than for the Cortina. Personalities employed in promoting the Corsair included racing driver Jim Clark, fashion model Jean Shrimpton, actress Samantha Egger and Jocelyn Stevens, editor of *Queen* magazine.

At launch, press reaction to the Corsair was highly positive. The initial *Autocar* test of October 1963 for the 1500 De Luxe noted that "There is a hint of Taunus and Thunderbird about the styling, which many people regard as Dagenham's best for some time." Similarly, "Headroom is unusually good: business men can travel without removing their bowlers." This sartorial reference seems surprising as late as 1963! They were more critical of King's interior however: "The interior décor appears to be the work of a stylist instead of a designer, although it is practical and not unduly garish … Fussy door trimming is out of place on an otherwise tasteful interior."

In October 1965, the Corsair was revised with the addition of the V4 engines from the Transit and a revised IP, with a straightforward 'plank'-style incorporating four round dials. Soon after, in March 1966, the estate was added, being developed and manufactured to special order by Abbotts of Farnham. This was a clever amalgam of the volume-produced Cortina estate greenhouse with the Corsair lower body, utilising the entire roof, door glasses, rear quarter window, C-pillar and D-pillar pressings from the Cortina estate. The rear fenders, tail lamps, rear bumper and rear panel were unchanged Corsair, meaning the stepped GRP tailgate had to make up the difference in length. It proved an extremely smart conversion, probably the best-ever made by Abbotts, even if the price was high at £1218 – some £142 more than the Cortina GT estate.

The expansion of commercial vehicles: D-series truck and Transit van

In 1961 the Ford parent company decided to purchase all of the remaining share capital of Ford of Britain for £150 million, to exert greater control over the fast-growing subsidiary. After that point, more American managers were seconded to the UK in all areas of the company, including Engineering and Design. Dearborn was unconvinced that Ford of Britain had sufficient capacity for product development in either cars or trucks. In truth, the product development experience with trucks was limited to the Thames Trader alone, since previous truck designs were based heavily upon US designs.

Ford's UK management was also not particularly focused on commercial vehicles, rather preferring passenger cars as its main priority. In addition, warranty claims on the Trader had been particularly high, often due to misuse and overloading by operators, a practice that was rife in that unregulated industry at the time. Nevertheless, the American view was that if Ford UK wanted to compete in the commercial vehicle field, it should do so with fully-developed, class-leading products rather than remaining an also-ran in this sector. To that end, the parts depot west of London at Langley was transformed into a proper commercial vehicle manufacturing facility in 1961.

A new advanced design team was set up within the truck engineering division, with a clear remit: achieve market leadership. Period. The Bedford TK was a particularly strong competitor, which launched in 1960 and quickly achieved a leading position in the market. Featuring a tilt cab, it was definitely the truck to beat in the early 1960s. A new truck engineering centre at Gants Hill, Romford, was established around 1962 to house this truck work, although initial program planning had started earlier at Aveley and Rainham.

The new truck layout began to take shape, featuring a forward control cab to achieve maximum float length together with a tilt cab. New construction and use regulations were planned for 1964 that allowed maximum weight to increase from 24 to 32 tons, together with a legal speed raised to 40mph. These new operating conditions favoured foreign trucks, such as Mercedes and Scania, which were already designed for higher loads and speeds in Europe, and Ford was obviously keen to incorporate these requirements into any new truck design.

The new cab, designed by Claude Gidman and Ed 'Walt' Disney, reflected the house style that was emerging with the car projects,

The D-series was launched under the slogan 'Snake Supple, Rhino Tough' in November 1965. Load capacity was denoted by the first two figures after the letter D – eg D0810 = 8 tons. D1614 = 16 tons. Excellent servicing access was given to the engine and other components via the tilt cab.

Early pre-production D-series flat bed, with non-standard extra kerb window mounted in the passenger door. The cab offered three-abreast seating as an option.

D1000-series trucks were differentiated by use of a chrome front bumper and an extra chrome grille above the main panel, to distinguish them from the smaller models.

such as the Mk II Cortina and Mk IV Zephyr, with single round headlamps flanked by sidelights set within a horizontally-grooved front panel. This lower front panel was painted white, with the FORD name set out in bold letters across the front.

Phase 1 of the D-series program covered 2 tons to 8 tons, launched in 1965, while phase 2 covered the heavier derivatives of 10 tons upwards and was designated D1000 series, not launched until 1967. This included trucks, tippers and artics from 15 tons to 28 tons GTW to compete with the heavier Bedford KM series.

The advanced truck design team started planning on the Transit van, too. A proposal for a forward control replacement for the Thames 400E had been on the cards around 1959, but in January 1960 the decision was taken to go ahead with a 'common van' project for Europe to replace both the 400E and the German Taunus FK van using the latest Ford Econoline van as a starting point.

Product planner Arthur Molyneux took the lead in establishing some key attributes for this van, soon known as 'Project Redcap.' As with the D-series, these centred around making it a class-leading product and avoiding the misery of existing vans such as the BMC J4, Standard Atlas or Commer FC – all 10/12cwt light vans that were slow, poor handling and crude to drive. Other attributes included a

SVO operations

To prove out the numerous derivatives of engine and chassis, 100 pre-production D-series were built in a variety of configurations. A new Special Vehicles Option department (SVO) was established at Langley with its own engineering and marketing for non-standard D-series and Transit derivatives. Its remit included all engineering releases and purchasing for special fittings. This was an extension of the existing RPOs – Regular Production Options – that were listed in catalogues eg radio, sliding doors, laminated windscreen etc.

To support SVO, a Special Vehicle Engineering division (SVE) was also established. Following Ford Dearborn naming policy, this is the actual engineering team that is designated to design and develop the features planned by SVO, particularly ones for fleet or military customers. Ford was keen to keep this specialist expertise in-house rather than let it go to outside specialists, and it meant that the Ford warranty was still retained – a vitally important aspect for many commercial customers.

decent driver's seat with ergonomic back support and sliding doors for safe access in busy streets. Volkswagen held the patent for sliding van doors, but Molyneux noted it was due to expire in 1963, so Ford decided to proceed with using it unhindered.

In 1961, US product planner Ed Baumgartner was installed as

project manager for this £10 million program, with Vernon Preston as chief vehicle engineer and Vic Hammond responsible for styling, supported by Non Crook and 'Walt' Disney as designers. Talking about the problems he encountered, Baumgartner said "You can't imagine how separate the British and German teams were at the start when I came over to join the team. They just did not want to have anything to do with each other, so my initial task was a combination of coach and referee. The British loved tormenting the Germans, and the Germans loved tormenting the British!"

With the forward control layout of the existing 400E and Taunus FK being abandoned in favour of a semi-forward control layout with the engine mounted ahead of the cabin, the new van would have to be longer than the existing models, or else sacrifice load capacity. Thus the decision was taken to make the vehicle much wider than previous vans to regain the potential loss of load-space volume. Two wheelbases were agreed upon, 106in (2690mm) dubbed LCX and a 118in (3000mm) LCY version to cover the full range of payloads and capacities.

Initial styling models were produced in Dearborn and shipped to the UK in early 1963, but from then on the design was done in Aveley and Gants Hill. "Dearborn sent over a fully finished GRP van they'd done called 'Redcap,' done in the colours of Marlboro cigarettes –

red and white," recalls Birtley. "It was big and beefy, wider and longer than was needed for the UK project, but containing the basic theme of the later Transit. It needed resizing, but the basic styling theme was there. We used a V4 engine, whereas Redcap had a V8."

Body engineering was headed by Don Ward assisted by Dennis Roberts, following the completion of work on the Cortina. With payloads covering a wide range from 12cwt (610kg) to 35cwt (1777kg) plus a requirement for monocoque construction panel vans and a separate chassis frame for chassis cab derivatives, the design of the body and chassis was critical. Roberts cleverly engineered the chassis members so that the main U-sections were common to all versions, being welded to the underneath of the body on panel vans and boxed-in for chassis cab derivatives with a separate exposed frame behind the cab.

The new layout had several advantages. The first was simpler maintenance and accessibility for the engine, provided by the wide engine bay. The second was safety, with the drivers feet better protected in an impact, and the third was much better drivability and handling. One by-product of the wide track was that the load floor and rear doors were designed to accept a standard 4ft x 8ft flat sheet of plywood or plasterboard – the first time this had been attempted in a British van.

This early clay model proposal for a new Thames 400E, by Vic Hammond's team, had overtones of the Commer FC van. (Courtesy Peter Lee)

Pre-production LCX Transit with sliding doors. The first running prototype was built in January 1964, with the final launch in October 1965 – the same week as the Corsair V4 launch. Prices started from £542 for the SWB LCX petrol van.

The design detailing was good, too. The headlamps were raised and housed in squared-up pods with silver bezels, making the lamp more in scale with the width of the front end and giving the van a distinctive 'face.' Likewise, the wide-mouth grille that wrapped around the sides and was painted white as on the Trader and D-series used oversized round sidelights to complete the picture. "I did details such as the headlamp bezels and the 'Transit' emblem for the rear door," recalls Birtley.

Demand for a diesel engine led to the fitting of the Perkins 1759cc unit, which was longer than the V4 units being developed for this project, and demanded a 4in (100mm) longer front end. In the end, only the bonnet and front grille panel were changed, and initial diesel Transits were distinguished by this different 'bull-nose' front end. Other petrol engines were the V4 Essex units of 1.7-litre and 2.0-litre capacity, with powerful V6 Essex units available later on, which utilised the longer bull-nose front end.

First prototype LCY Transit undergoing tests at Boreham. The LCY Transit with 'twin bogie' 14in wheels looked strong and powerful – it was what every young van driver in 1966 desired.

Interior shot of an early prototype Transit. Although the cabin seems stark by today's standards, it was a revelation in comfort and ergonomics compared to the Thames 400E.

Early prototype diesel Transit with the longer 'bull-nose.' Note the prototype curved bumper – not used in production.

Although it was a 'common van,' the German and British versions were actually quite different. The British version used imperial measurements and Lucas-sourced electrics, while the German version used metric bolt sizes, Bosch components, and their own range of V4 engines. There was a clever modular approach to the numerous derivatives, however. Vans could be ordered with hinged or sliding doors, with or without a side loading door, while rear doors could be twin slam doors or a large top-hinged tailgate.

The big change was in terms of proportions. The 'short & wide' format was very different to traditional British vans. It should not be underestimated just how visually appealing the Transit was when launched in October 1965: here was a van that not only offered class-leading payload and new practical features, but looked – and proved – fun to drive, too. The wide stance implied great stability, which was borne out by the first driving experience, with car-like controls and light steering.

Despite the use of 14in wheels, it did not look under-wheeled either. In particular, the LCY versions looked simply great; those 'twin bogie' rear wheels set wider than the body were like some advanced vehicle from the latest *Thunderbirds* children's TV series, or a Syd Mead rendering. Every schoolboy wanted the school minibus to be a 17-seat LCY Transit Crewbus, and all young van drivers wanted to be seen behind the wheel of a Transit, not the offerings from Bedford or BMC. The sexy image was helped later on when the Transit became the selected vehicle for British rock bands – there is no way that David Bowie or Rod Stewart would have looked cool turning up to gigs in a Commer FC …!

Like the D-series, the Transit was produced at Langley, which already built the Thames 400E. Bodywork was pressed and assembled at Southampton until 1972 when all final Transit assembly moved to the Southampton plant to allow expansion of truck production.

The use of the Transit name actually came very late. Up until pilot build in April 1965 the plan was to call it the 'Transit' in Europe and 'V-series' in the UK. However, this was soon overturned and 'Transit' emblems were hastily added to the UK photography examples being prepared for publicity that spring. Despite that, Job One was bang on-target – 9 August 1965.

Dearborn influences: Project Panda

With Dearborn exerting stronger control on its European operations, the International Division started to send staff in considerable numbers from 1962 onwards. The British management that had grown under the leadership of Sir Patrick Hennessy was uneasy at first, but most concerned seemed to accept that the advantages, in terms of greater experience of the US staff and the huge resources that could be drawn upon, were a price worth paying to see Ford achieve market leadership in the UK.

Although the 213E Zephyr/Zodiac range had only been launched in spring 1962, planning on its successor commenced that same year

Ford expansion and Warley

In addition to Dunton, Ford made some massive investments in the UK in the early 1960s. The biggest was the addition of a second manufacturing plant at Halewood near Liverpool, which opened in March 1963 at a cost of £30 million. The new plant was capable of producing 1000 cars per day from the 328-acre (133ha) site, initially producing the Anglia and the new Corsair. Halewood later produced the Capri, and became the main plant for the Escort: a model it was to produce for the next 30 years, until 2000, when Escort production came to an end. It was then transferred to Jaguar as a plant for the new X-type, and today it remains under JLR ownership, producing the Range Rover Evoque and Discovery Sport models.

In another bid to free up space at Dagenham, the former Hawker Hurricane factory west of London at Langley was acquired and transformed into a proper commercial vehicles manufacturing plant in March 1961, initially producing the Trader truck and Thames 400E van.

It wasn't only more production capacity that was required. Dagenham was bursting at the seams without sufficient office space for engineers and other senior management. Thus in 1964 a new headquarters building was constructed at Warley in Essex to accommodate some 2000 central office staff, at a cost of £13 million. Warley housed the sales and marketing departments and senior executives for Ford UK, but from 1967 it also became the headquarters for Ford of Europe. Despite this, Ford still maintained an impressive office in central London in Regent Street for senior executive meetings.

Finally, tractor production was shifted out of Dagenham to a new 100-acre (40ha) site at Crane's Hill, Basildon in March 1964. Construction of the new plant with its distinctive onion-shaped water tower, had begun in 1962 as part of the '6X project' plan to integrate the US tractor operations and the Ford UK tractor operations, which up then had been largely independent. This new plant was set up to produce the latest 'Thousand Series' tractors, which replaced the Fordson Major and Dexter models, the range comprising the 2-, 3-, 4- and 5000-series models. Ranging from 37hp to 65hp, the tractors ushered in a new era for Ford as they were completely new from the ground up with brand-new engines and transmissions and a fresh livery of blue and light grey, replacing the former blue and orange Fordson colour scheme. On 15 May 1964, the first Ford 4000 tractor rolled off the factory production line at Basildon. Since then approximately 1.6 million more tractors have left Basildon to work on farms around the world.

Architect's photo of Warley headquarters, soon after completion in April 1965. The penthouse suite on the roof was built as accommodation for Henry Ford II on his visits, but was almost never used.

under the codename 'Panda.' In the US, Ford was on a relentless challenge against GM in terms of design leadership, and that same thinking was brought to the UK with GM's Vauxhall division, despite the fact that Vauxhall was a far smaller operation – and far less of a threat – in the UK. Word that the new flagship Cresta/Velox model was to be replaced on a three-year model cycle for 1965 rather spooked Ford into pushing ahead with a challenger, even though there was no desperate need to replace the 213E, which was selling strongly, and was well-regarded by dealers and customers alike.

Rumours that the styling of the new PC Cresta would reflect the latest GM styling encouraged the Ford team into believing that a similar transatlantic look was required for the UK 'Project Panda.' Hence the styling followed a similar theme as Ford's latest hit, the '64 Mustang, with its characteristic 'long-hood, short-rear-deck' look, and a hint of kick-up in the belt line. Indeed, the Mustang was seen as a something of a touchstone for Ford styling worldwide following its runaway sales success in America, with designer Joe Oros promoting that look on his regular visits over to the UK.

It wasn't only the styling of Panda that was heavily US influenced. The new Engineering Director was Harley Copp, brought over to head product development, with support from British Engineering Chief Fred Hart. Copp had recently led several Lincoln projects

and was convinced that the Panda should become a "fine car for Europe," a kind of new Lincoln for Britain. In August 1965, Dearborn also appointed Stan Gillen as the first US Chief Executive for Ford UK, a clear signal that the decades-old ruling under Hennessy was coming to an end.

Project Panda was the last purely Ford UK project undertaken. It used a newly-designed underbody with much larger dimensions than the 213E. The wheelbase was now 115in, some 8in (200mm) up on the old car, with tracks pushed out to 57in front and 58in rear, the latter incorporating independent rear suspension for the first time on a British Ford, running on 13in wheels as before. The biggest change was for the engines, which used the new 60-degree V4 and V6 Essex engines developed for the Transit and Corsair.

Length was increased by just 4in (100mm) but much of the increase in size was due to the 'fill the box' philosophy promoted by Aveley's new studio design chief, Don DeLaRossa, who had been sent over by Bordinat to replace Roy Brown in late 1964. The idea was to push the corners of the car out with very little plan shape front or rear to give a more impressive presence on the road. To today's designers, weaned on the idea that plan shape needs to be used as much as possible to visually reduce overhangs, it seems an odd notion, but it was a popular fashion of the time.

This four-door Mustang model, dated July 1963, became the inspiration for the Mk IV Zephyr/Zodiac series. The Mustang, designed under Joe Oros, proved a runaway success for Ford, and elements of it went on to influence both the Cortina Mk II and Capri.

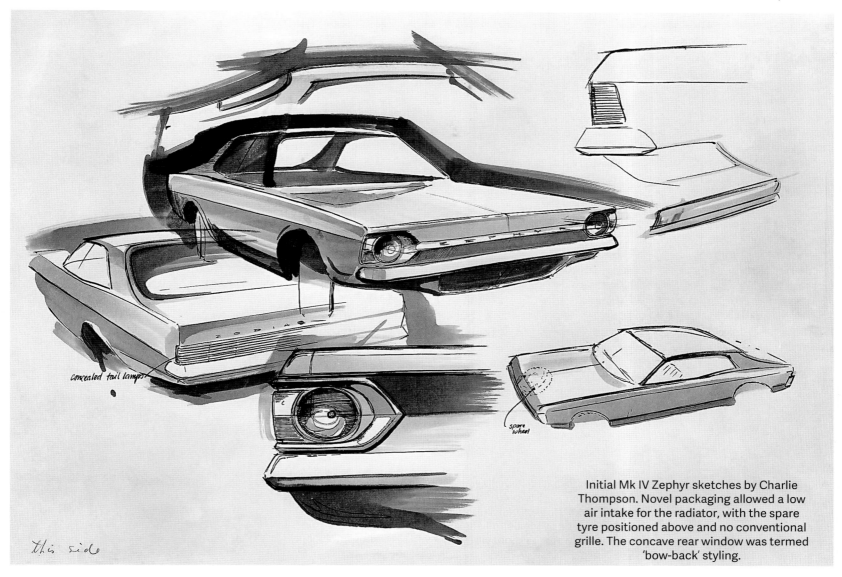

concealed tail lamps

this side

spare wheel

Initial Mk IV Zephyr sketches by Charlie Thompson. Novel packaging allowed a low air intake for the radiator, with the spare tyre positioned above and no conventional grille. The concave rear window was termed 'bow-back' styling.

One of the initial 1:1 clay models of the Mk IV Zodiac from April 1963. Approval for the £28 million program was given in December that year.

Bertone proposal for the Mk IV. The Italianate greenhouse bears some similarity to the Jaguar XJ6, ironically, being developed around the same time. In total, 12 full-size models were done for 'Project Panda' – a colossal effort for what was to prove a fairly lacklustre model for Ford of Britain.

Ron Bradshaw and Charlie Thompson were the main designers for the exterior, with Thompson's model being the theme that was finally selected at program approval in December 1963. To make some sense of the huge 'aircraft carrier' bonnet, the spare tyre was mounted at the front of the engine bay, with the radiator mounted below. This meant there was no functional need for a conventional grille above the bumper, something that was used as a design opportunity to distinguish the lower grade 3010E Zephyr V4 and Zephyr V6 models from the top range Zodiac.

As with the exterior, the interior also had an American feel to it. The generous dimensions meant the cabin could genuinely seat six passengers when the bench front seat was specified, trimmed with soft vinyl in a buttoned armchair style. The IP was an impressive affair, with the instruments and switches all housed in a large hooded binnacle, and no centre console for models when fitted with the column gearshift that was still offered.

The Mk IV was launched in April 1966. Abbotts of Farnham was given early access to the new car so that it could prepare a handsome estate conversion, which duly followed in October 1966 and was one of the largest estate cars available at the time.

However, unlike previous large Fords, the Mk IV series failed to connect with the British executive buyer. Ford had underestimated how the market had shifted after 1963 with the arrival of the very tasteful Triumph 2000 and Rover 2000. These models in particular had a great appeal, with their combination of neat styling and sporty image within fairly compact dimensions that provided lithe handling and strong performance, in contrast to the stuffy old Humbers or Wolseleys of before. These new models were perceived as drivers' cars rather than luxury limousines, and the excessive bulk and somewhat-vulgar American styling of the Mk IV was seen by many as a reason to reject the car, not to mention the rough V4 engines or the sloppy handling noted by many road testers.

It is arguable that, in hindsight, if Ford had made the Panda more like a sporty four-door Mustang and less a barge-like Lincoln, it could have hit a sweet spot in the UK executive car market, which instead eluded them in the late 1960s.

More Cortina – the Mk II

By the mid-'60s, Ford UK was on a roll. The Cortina and Zephyr models were on a four-year replacement cycle, following American practice of the day – a fairly punishing schedule for the design and engineering teams. Vauxhall was likewise on a slightly ridiculous (and ultimately unsustainable) three-year full-model replacement cycle for the Victor, Viva and Cresta models, with a face-lift after just 18 months. Hence the Cortina Mk II was scheduled for its second generation redesign for 1966, with work starting in late 1963, as soon as the Corsair was out the door.

Modeller Graham King on a quarter-scale clay of the Cortina Mk II.

Clay modelling in the 1960s: modeller Jack Bish enjoying his work on the front end of a Zephyr clay model, 1963. Bish later became Interior Modelling Manager.

This second redesign was, in fact, a complete reskin that kept the entire underbody and platform largely unchanged, as were the engine and drivetrain. Exterior styling followed that of US Fords such as the Fairlane, with its crisp greenhouse, thick C-pillar, and full-width grille. A slight 'W-form' was added to the front and rear in plan view to increase the appearance of width, part of the 'fill the box' philosophy promoted by DeLaRossa and Oros.

The exterior design was led by Roy Haynes, aided by Harris Mann as Principal Designer. Although it retained the same platform and internal pressings as the Mk I, the body was 2.4in (61mm) wider, with tracks widened 3in (76mm) at front, and 1.5in (38mm) at the rear to provide more shoulder room. To help that aim, curved side glass was used, having first been introduced on British Fords with the 213E Zephyr in 1962.

Cortina Mk II sketches by Alan Jackson. These were done for an article in *Style Auto* magazine in 1966, so were probably 'after the event' sketches. After one year on sale, engines for the Cortina were revised in 1967 with a crossflow cylinder head and new strokes to give 1300cc and 1600cc – known as the 'Kent' engine. (Courtesy *Style Auto*)

Styling was done in parallel with the Mk IV 'Panda' and followed a similar theme with a hint of kick-up in the belt line. Several full-size clay proposals were produced, some following the more baroque style being developed over in Germany for the new Taunus 20M that was being designed at the same time. As before, an estate version was also developed in-house, with slim vertical tail lamps framing the wide tailgate aperture. The somersault-type rear seat fold was retained as on the Mk I, to give a class-leading load length of 74in (1880mm).

An alternative model for Cortina Mk II, being worked on in the showroom at Aveley, looking towards the exterior studio. Don Brooks works on the trunk, Derek Mirthwaite (with beard) on the bodyside.

Clay model for the Cortina Mk II in Aveley studio. A number of different front ends were tried out for this project.

The original Cortina was proving a massive success, with over one million produced up to September 1966. It had stormed ahead of the traditional D-sector models such as the Morris Oxford and Hillman Minx, and was generating 50 per cent of Ford UK's profits by this point. Hence the caution taken with the successor model and the careful control of the project by all areas in the company. Talking to author Jonathan Wood some years later, Terry Beckett – promoted to Marketing Chief in 1964 – recalled that Product Planning made sure the designers weren't given too much free rein: "My belief is that a designer or stylist works best when he's faced with a series of tightly constrained objectives," he commented. "With the Cortina, these included the tumblehome of the windows, the height of the roof and its flat contours and the shaping in the bonnet." Whether the designers would have agreed with him is another matter!

The two-door and four-door saloons were launched at the Earls Court Motor Show in October 1966 under the tag line 'More Cortina,'

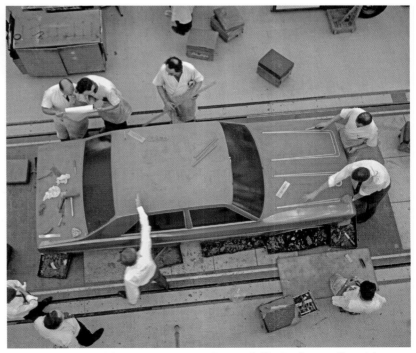

Overhead shot of another Cortina clay model in Aveley studio, with an unusual twisted shoulder line.

Cortina 1600E in Amber Gold. The 1600E looked stunning in some of the fabulous colours offered, such as Light Orchard metallic or Aubergine – perfect for the Carnaby Street crowd of the late-'60s. (Author's collection)

with prices starting at £669 for a two-door 1200 De Luxe. The estate followed in February 1967, with the Lotus-Cortina Mk II arriving in March. This latter was built with all-steel panels on the main line at Dagenham, and proved very popular for the first year, being made in higher volumes than the Mk I.

By this stage, the Cortina was very popular with the fleet market in the UK, Ford having become extremely adept at tweaking the model line-up and trim levels to provide a clear hierarchy of models to suit the job grades within British companies. In early 1967, product planner Howard Panton worked closely with Design to propose a new four-door luxury version, using a mix of existing Lotus Cortina and GT parts, with coachbuilder Hoopers commissioned to do a full wood and leather interior. This followed the same formula as the 'Executive' version of the Zodiac announced in October 1966, and the Corsair 2000E, which offered a fully trimmed interior and full options as standard. This prototype was favourably viewed by the product committee, and subsequently developed to become the Cortina 1600E, launched in October 1967.

Here, the Executive formula received a new sporting twist that buyers found irresistible. In addition to the 1600GT engine and Lotus suspension, the exterior was dressed up with a matt black grille and rear panel, spotlamps at the front and Rubery Owen's latest 5.5in chromed 'Rostyle' wheels that enhanced the car perfectly. Inside, Ford decided to mimic the successful Rover 2000, styling the rear seats as two separate chairs with a large centre armrest. The Jaguar-style trimming of an outer hoop and fluted centre panels with piping on the edges was retained, although leather was eventually dropped on production cars in favour of a new deep-embossed 'Ambla' PVC from ICI. The 1600E was hugely successful, and carried a remarkable cachet that belied its mass-market roots, practically inventing the luxury sports saloon in Europe that later became defined by BMW.

Ford also had the best paint colours of the time. Top colour choices for the Mk II were Blue Mink and Silver Fox, representing some 40 per cent of Cortina sales in 1967. Saluki Bronze (a soft brown metallic) was also highly popular. These were some of the first metallic paints available in the UK, having previously only been available on expensive Jaguars and Mercedes models. Ford was proud to have beaten Vauxhall to the market, which only managed to offer 'Starmist' metallics from 1970, as did Chrysler UK. However, this early Ford paint technology later proved to lack durability and under prolonged exposure to sunlight the top laquer coat tended to fade and peel off, often within just two years.

Late 1960s

Chapter

4

Ford of Europe and the start of Dunton

In 1965, Ford of Germany Managing Director John Andrews was appointed Vice President of the new European Group Operation – a loosely termed attempt to co-ordinate sales and co-production of some Ford models. On the commercial vehicles side there had already been the 'common van' Transit and the D-series truck projects, but these Ford co-operations had been purely on a project-by-project basis.

It took until 1967 for Henry Ford II to finally commit to creating Ford of Europe. A few days prior to the 1967 Le Mans race he summoned Andrews, Stan Gillen and Walter Hayes to the Plaza d'Athenée Hotel in Paris where he was staying. "What we need is a Ford of Europe, to knock a few heads together and make things happen faster," he said. "And it's no good looking to Dearborn, they have enough on their plate. You have to do it yourself. Make Ford of Europe." Hence Ford of Europe Incorporated, a wholly-owned subsidiary of Ford US, was announced a couple of weeks later in June 1967, based at Ford UK's Warley headquarters. John Andrews was initially installed as President, but was soon replaced by Gillen, after Andrews was sadly diagnosed with leukaemia that summer.

Ford of Europe (FoE) was set up as a co-ordinating organisation with few staff and no dedicated manufacturing sites. Its first concern was to plan future model programs as pan-European projects between Merkenich and Dunton, with the next Taunus/Cortina as the first complete project, and the Capri as an initial target for manufacturing and sales planning co-operation, seeing as the British design had already been signed off and prototypes were already under test.

Duplication of functions was eliminated where possible, leading to a shake-out of many local senior managers in 1967-'68. In addition, Ford International Division sent 'Foreign Service Employees' overseas to work for Ford of Europe, typically on a three-year secondment with American staff replacing British managers as heads of every department of Ford UK. In Design, Damon Woods was brought in during 1967, as the first Vice President to oversee both the UK and German studios. Gil Spear was Chief Designer at Dunton, with Jim Sipple now Chief Designer in Merkenich. It did occasionally go the other way though. Having proved his worth in Planning and Marketing, British manager Terry Beckett was promoted to Vice President of Sales Operations for FoE, with Sam Toy replacing him in UK Marketing.

The new Escort was another Ford of Europe program, although this remained a project that was designed in the UK, with initial production from Halewood and Ford's Genk plant in Belgium. It was offered for sale across Europe from early 1968, but it took until January 1970 to get production started at Ford Germany's new Saarlouis plant as an entry model, something Ford Germany had sorely lacked up to that point.

After Hennessy finally retired in 1968, Leonard Crosland took Chairmanship of Ford of Britain, which he held until 1972. At the same time, Bill Batty replaced Barke as MD of Ford UK and Stan

Merkenich design centre

Just as Ford UK was planning Dunton, so, too, was Ford Germany planning a proper Engineering and Research Centre, based at Merkenich in Cologne, just north of the main production plant in Niehl. The new facility was slightly smaller than Dunton, but mirrored its layout and facilities, comprising styling studios, engineering offices and product planning.

Construction work was completed in 1968, with the facility being dedicated in 1969 as the John Andrews Engineering Center, named after the recently-departed Chairman of Ford of Germany at the time.

The design team in the styling studio at Merkenich was initially led by Wes Dahlberg, who had designed the 1960 Taunus P3 'Badewanne.' Despite his German name, Dahlberg was an American Ford designer from Dearborn, who had run the German studio since the late 1950s. One of his first recruits was Uwe Bahnsen, who joined Ford in 1958, working closely with Dahlberg on the Taunus range, including the 17M P6 model, which was the first Ford design led by Bahnsen himself.

From 1965, the old Niehl studio started recruiting more designers including Claude Lobo, Hans Muth, Walter Rhein, Tilbert Bode, Helmut Schrader, Horst Seigner, Mattias Neumann and Wouter de Vries, together with two English designers – Graham Symonds and Jim Hirons. These latter two both later transferred to Dunton when the two studios worked closely together on the TC project. Dahlberg returned to the US in 1968, and was then replaced by Jim Sipple.

Ford Merkenich site in the 1960s. By 2010, more than 2500 engineers and designers were employed at the site.

Gillen took over as FoE President, retiring completely from Ford in 1971.

With the creation of FoE, the need for regular flying of many staff between the two main sites in Germany and the UK became commonplace. Thus FordAir was established, Ford's dedicated airline, flying from Southend or Stansted to Cologne-Bonn airport. FordAir operated a mix of Gulfstream turboprops and BAC 1-11 jets, with a total of 20 pilots and ten stewardesses. Later on, FordAir used a pair of Boeing 737-700s, which by the 1980s were updated to the Airbus A319. Carvair air ferries were also used to transport cars and prototypes between the sites, chartered from British Air Ferries.

Replacing the Anglia: Escort

Although work began before FoE was established, the Escort was another pan-European project, and it was decided to continue the front engine, RWD layout of the Anglia, complete with leaf-sprung rear axle and MacPherson struts up front. The Birmingham Research Centre had constructed a lot of prototypes and experiments with various powertrain layouts – including rear engines, and FWD in both transverse and north-south installation, as on the Renault R4 – but these were rejected in favour of a thoroughly conventional layout. The engineers at Ford Germany were a bit disappointed after their innovative FWD Taunus ... Whereas the Anglia had been the work of the stylists and engineers at Birmingham, the 'New Anglia' project went through the full product planning process, resulting in clear engineering and cost targets for this £20 million program.

Careful cost analysis led to such features as the use of smaller 12in wheels and tyres (a 13.5lb weight saving), and deletion of swivelling quarter vents. But it also introduced decent rack and pinion steering (around a £1 cost saving) and a one-piece bodyside, ensuring accurate door fits.

Harris Mann was a lead designer on the project, under John Fallis. "Ford had the Red Book where each new model would have cost objectives against every item, based on the biggest competitor. For Escort it was Vauxhall's HA Viva, all the costings were based on that car. For example, doorhandles: Viva £x, Escort £x. Every single aspect was given a cost and a design objective. Whatever you were designing had to hit that cost."

By 28 May 1965, four full-size clays had been prepared at Aveley for selection. One had a very upright rear window, with a Thunderbird-style rocker treatment; one was coupé-like, another was very plain, with a straight belt line like a small Datsun.

In 1966, Vauxhall replaced the HA Viva with the larger HB model, which proved a bigger threat – it was not only better than the Anglia, but the 'Coke bottle' belt line was very similar to the new Escort, still two years away from launch. It also used the latest Lucas 7in x 3.75in rectangular headlamps, also planned for introduction on the Escort.

Designer Neil Birtley takes up the story: "I remember us getting the HB Viva at Ford, everyone was rather shocked that it contained lots of features we were about to put on the new Escort. There was a very hurried revamp, to 'defrill' the Escort, which actually spoiled it a bit – a pity. The grille was made less like the Viva and the bodyside didn't have as much 'Coke bottle.'"

Hence, the characteristic 'dog bone' front grille was added, at quite a late stage. Up to then the styling had the bonnet dropping down between the squared lamp surrounds, with a straight lower edge and high bumper. Then the bumper was pushed down, which

Sketch proposal for the Escort. The drawing style demonstrates the predominant technique of the late-'60s, using thin layout paper with a roller ball pen for the linework, and marker pen. (Courtesy David Ginn)

In 1967, there was a plan for the Escort to be sold in the US as a sub-compact model, hence various fastback coupé models were produced, not unlike the Opel Kadett Olympia. (Courtesy David Ginn)

This two-door coupé proposal shows an interesting transition to the Cortina Mk III, in terms of the body section and doors.

Base model Escort interior. Note the narrow seats with plain vinyl covers. September 1970 brought nylon cloth trim as an option, a safety steering wheel, and eight new body colours.

allowed the numberplate to be mounted direct to the front panel, above the bumper – which also allowed a further cost saving!

Harris Mann agrees. "Just before the Escort came out, the new Viva was launched with an increase in price. Thus, the Escort could be priced slightly higher accordingly – a big chunk of extra profit overnight. Ford undercut the price marginally as the Viva was slightly bigger but they were onto a winner straight away."

Ford Germany was initially involved in this ECC project (European Common Car) but then had to concentrate on its Taunus P6 12M/15M development. It only became re-involved in the Escort in 1967, when some late changes were made – such as the addition of the four-door version, which lacked the one-piece bodyside pressing.

Several models were also made in 1967 of an Escort coupé, for possible introduction by 1970. There was a plan to export it to the US using 1.6-litre and 2-litre engines, but final approval of the Capri project made this unnecessary.

The interior design used a simple metal IP pressing with a padded PVC top crash pad. Basic versions had just two dials in the instrument binnacle, with a 110mph speedometer and combined water temperature and fuel gauge. The 1300GT got four minor dials in an extended pod that was offset to the right of the steering wheel, showing battery, fuel, oil pressure and water temperature. A simplified 'Aeroflow' ventilation layout was used, with just two centre rotating vents, but at least it featured proper air extraction through vents under the rear window, unlike the Anglia. The Escort continued the beautifully light controls of the Anglia, and combined it with an excellent gearshift, making it an easy car for drivers to enjoy. Colour keying of plastic components was also a notable feature on the Escort; better than most rivals. Basic versions still used rubber mats on the floor, but at least they were colour-keyed to match the upholstery!

A deep-dished, phenolic plastic three-spoke steering wheel was used at launch,

The 1969 Escort four-door GT sported a matt black grille, and was fitted with the latest Lucas rectangular headlamps, as on the Capri and Vauxhall Viva HB.

The Escort was the last major project completed at the Aveley studio, with program approval in 1965. Seen here is an early production Escort 1100 De Luxe – the Escort in its simplest two-door form, with round headlamps and plain hubcaps.

but replaced in October 1968 with Ford's corporate safety wheel, also used on Capri and Mk IV models. At the same time, safety door handles and window winders designed to break off in an accident were introduced across the Escort, Cortina, Mk IV, and Corsair ranges.

Job One was achieved on 17 November 1967 at Halewood, and the car was launched on 17 January at the Brussels Motor Show, with the slogan 'The New Escort. The Small Car That Isn't.' Prices were £635 for the basic two-door, and £666 for the 1100 Super version.

The 743kg weight target for a standard two-door saloon was met, within 2kg.

An Escort van derivative was also developed, made available in 6cwt (304kg) and 8cwt (400kg) payload versions. This improved on the old Thames/Anglia 307E van, with a useful loadbed of 71in and 72cu ft capacity. One surprising cost-saving approach was the carry-over rear doors from the Thames 307E van, and these were cleverly incorporated into the styling, with very few people even noticing the feature.

Escort van used carry-over rear doors from the outgoing Thames 307E van. (Author's collection)

Dunton Research and Engineering Centre

By the early 1960s it was becoming apparent that Ford's scattered research and engineering facilities needed reorganising. Apart from the styling and prototype build departments based at Aveley, there was the Birmingham Research Centre, employing over 200 engineers, plus facilities in Rainham, Dagenham and Boreham. The trucks division was split between Gants Hill, Romford and Langley, west of London. Plans were put in place in 1964 to build a dedicated engineering and design centre on a new 268 acre (108 ha) site at Dunton Wayletts, Essex. It was maybe not totally coincidental that Vauxhall had just invested £2.25 million in a fabulous design and engineering centre, opened that year, giving it the best facilities in the UK at the time. Ford was keen to not be outdone, plus it needed to attract more engineers.

The Dunton Research and Engineering Centre was constructed by George Wimpey for a contracted build price of £6.5 million, with the initial cost totalling £10.5 million. Wimpey broke ground on the site in July 1964, and completed work in January 1967, although some staff were installed on site from April 1966. It was officially opened by the then British Prime Minister, Harold Wilson, on 12 October 1967.

Architect's model of Dunton Research Centre, 1964. The four-storey block would house the main engineering offices, with the single-storey Design block to the left.

Aerial view in 1967 with contractors still on site. The styling block is the nearest building. The executive offices for design were in the two-storey part, overlooking the large viewing yard. Note: the track in front is not the start of the looped test track – that came later – but simply contractors completing levelling of the surrounding fields.

Aerial view of Dunton soon after opening in 1968, viewed from north-east. The design block was separated from the main engineering block by a flying walkway. The top part of the yard has been fenced off as a storage yard. Note the full line-up of Transits in the yard on this day.

Dunton drawing office, 1967. Typical of the many drawing offices in Dunton at the time, each engineer was equipped with a large parallel motion board and set squares.

Dunton exteriors studio, first day after moving in, 1967. Neil Birtley sits alone at his drawing board in the sparse surroundings. "It was like the Eastern National bus garage!" says Harris Mann.

Ford UK's Managing Director Leonard Crosland described Dunton as "The largest and most comprehensive facility in Europe for the development of future Ford cars and trucks. It marks a significant step forward in the evolution of vehicle design and testing, from drawing boards to laboratories and, ultimately, to computers." Chairman Sir Patrick Hennessy followed up by saying "We have come a long way in the last 50 years. More than half those employed in industry today are producing goods that did not exist 50 years ago. And 90 per cent of the scientists who ever lived in the world are still alive today. Here at Dunton we have given designers and engineers the finest of new tools to face the challenges to come."

Dunton originally had 28,762sq m of office space and 33,000sq m of workshops, making it the largest engineering research centre in Europe at the time, employing around 3000 staff. The layout comprised two offset blocks joined by an overhead walkway, with the design centre block being the northern-most building, nearest the A127 Southend road. The 3000sq m single storey design block housed the styling studios, workshops, offices and presentation room for styling reviews, with a large outside paved yard, some ten times bigger than the little courtyard at Aveley. Upstairs were two departments: Product Planning and Program Timing, with a staff of around 60, headed by Alex Trotman.

At the time of its opening, Dunton had teams covering engine, chassis, transmission, electrical, body and vehicle engineering, as well as design. When first opened, the design feasibility team comprised just three engineers, working under Dennis Chellingworth, one of whom was Gordon Royle. "It was a bit basic at first, and the occasional bird, enjoying the wide open spaces in the studios, often made its own addition to a designer's sketch!" he comments. Proper GRP models were possible too. "Before then we had to use clay models for all our management reviews and customer clinics. The finish of the GRP models is equal to the competitive production vehicles positioned alongside our models, and are, of course, far more durable and easier to transport."

Harris Mann concurs: "Dunton was typical Ford costings. Not like GM's studio with nicely tiled floors that looked immaculate for years after. No, it was just dry concrete floors and exposed pillars. My first impression of the Dunton studio was that it was like the Eastern National bus garage: very sparse with high frosted windows! When the air-conditioning started up there was concrete dust blown everywhere through the fans. It'd churn out dust everywhere, covered the clays in dust for months. They had to sort that out pretty quick. Then it was tiled out, but only with lino tiles, not ceramics like GM. But I learnt a lot there."

The 'Colt' project: Capri

In the wake of Ford's 'Total Performance' orientation from 1962 with a new focus on motorsport, planning of a new 2+2-seater coupé began in late 1964. This followed the template set by the Mustang,

Dunton opens – and staff leave for British Leyland

The imminent opening of Dunton had led to a huge recruitment drive for engineers in spring 1967. However, this coincided with the creation of Ford of Europe that summer, with the responsibilities of planning and engineering now being split with Ford Germany in Cologne. Surprisingly, Ford now found itself with too many staff, and no sooner had these bright new engineers arrived at Dunton than they were faced with calls for redundancies, with each department being asked for a 10 per cent headcount reduction.

This also coincided with BMC actively recruiting staff for the new amalgam with Leyland that would become British Leyland in spring 1968. Walter Hayes – soon to become Ford of Europe's PR director – wrote in despair to Dearborn about the Ford brain drain: "Ford of Britain has, in the past day or two, lost four good senior management people to the new British Leyland group, including the Manager of production planning and control … Obviously when these men are established in their new positions they will take other men from here."

Indeed so. Designer Roy Haynes departed for BMC in September 1967 to head up a new styling studio. Harris Mann was soon recruited: "Roy got in touch with me and others and encouraged us to leave and join him. 'It'll be a great opportunity,' he said, 'lots to do, loads of projects, a new set up at Cowley. What d'ya think?' He offered me a good position there. I wasn't one for sitting around, I wanted to get on, learn more."

Haynes had just led the design of the Cortina Mk II, and eventually recruited about nine people from Ford, including Mann, John Stark, Paul Hughes, packaging engineer Jim Puddifat, plus a couple of clay modellers. "He planned to take Phil Clark too, a brilliant guy, American," says Mann. "He'd trained at Art Center, very creative, and was reputed to have done the original Mustang concept car. He was planned to head up the whole department at Cowley, but fell ill with leukaemia and sadly died. I then basically filled his position within the new setup."

Mann confirms that BL had no effective product planning function, nor any grip on cost control. 'That was a big difference then. Roy had a good product planning head, had knowledge of industry, of engineering. And a flair for design. Roy and Engineering Director Harry Webster just didn't see eye to eye at all, they really didn't. Roy got really uptight about it and after one year decided that's it – and quit."

"That was another area where he fell out with the BL management. Roy wanted to get BL into profit, create a challenger to the Escort. Soon after that up at Longbridge they started to strip cars and cost them. Before, they'd stripped them to see how they were built, to assess new features, but never for cost analysis. All in all it was a big learning curve for BL."

In the end, British Leyland was wrong-footed by Ford, as by the time the Morris Marina came out in 1971, the Mk III Cortina, with its larger body and 2-litre engine, had been launched. The Marina struggled to compete, caught between the Escort and Cortina throughout the 1970s.

which was launched to great acclaim in April 1964. This new program, dubbed 'Colt,' was initiated in Dearborn, and was planned to use an existing platform, with engines, suspensions and transmissions that were already developed for other models. This reduced the level of investment required for a niche model, with the majority of the money going on a new bodyshell and ambitious marketing campaigns.

The compact 2+2 coupé format was fairly unusual in Europe, previously being the preserve of Italian specialist marques such as

Alfa Romeo and Lancia. In the UK, the Sunbeam Rapier had proved popular since its introduction in 1956, and demonstrated how this format of a sporty body based on humble Hillman Minx underpinnings could succeed. Whereas the Rapier was a single model, the Ford Colt project comprised one basic body style but with a multitude of engines, trim options and dress-up packs to suit every pocket. It aimed to offer something that would appeal to young family men who wanted something sexier than a plain two-door saloon.

Ford in the US took the lead in the packaging. The Dearborn engineers soon homed-in on the Cortina/Corsair platform as being the best starting point for this new model. The forthcoming Anglia replacement – the Escort – would be too narrow, plus the engine bay could not accommodate the full range of anticipated engines from 1.3-litres to a full Essex 3-litre V6. Experience of the Cortina GT and Lotus-Cortina performance models also convinced Ford's British engineers they could produce a decent sporty car from these same components.

After much deliberation it was decided to use the Corsair underbody. The 101in wheelbase (3in, or 75mm longer than Cortina) would allow passengers to sit suitably lower with legs spread out. Front tracks were pushed out from 50in to 52.5in, rear tracks from 49.5in to 51in. To be precise, the new Colt was actually closest to the Corsair two-door GT in terms of dimensions and components.

Regarding styling, Gil Spear was running the Advanced Vehicle design studio in Dearborn at this point and was tasked with producing some initial sketches and models. Design Vice President Gene Bordinat and assistant Bob Maguire decided to ship a couple of the Colt models over to Europe to see if the UK or Germany would be interested in developing them. Once the British had showed an interest, Spear was then seconded to the UK to develop the Colt clay model, although a few other alternative clays were produced by Aveley.

This Ford International studio model by Steve Sherer was shipped to Dunton for 'Project Colt.' Photographed here in 1965, this model encompassed the overall theme for the project, but with larger dimensions than the final Capri. "John Fallis, our jolly Irish design executive, made the two-seater become a four-seater," comments Patrick le Quément.

Tape drawing was a new technique introduced after 3M developed flexible black crêpe tapes for use in photographer dark rooms. Car design studios quickly adopted it as a fast method to develop bold graphic images that could be easily modified as the design developed. Here, designer Ron Bradshaw perfects his technique.

Sketch for a speculative Capri cabriolet.

Two GRP hard models were completed in early 1966, dubbed 'Flowline' and 'GBX'. These were shipped to the US for initial approval in April that year. Following this, an extensive series of customer clinics were run in the spring of 1966, in London, Brussels, Milan, Cologne, Hamburg, Geneva, and Amsterdam. The results proved generally positive, except for reservations about the rear side window and lack of visibility for rear passengers. The GBX was generally preferred.

In July 1966 at a Ford UK board meeting, Stan Gillen and Henry Ford II approved the 'Colt' program for production, with a budget of £20 million. The original aim was to launch at Earls Court in October 1968, with cars built solely at Halewood – the same as the

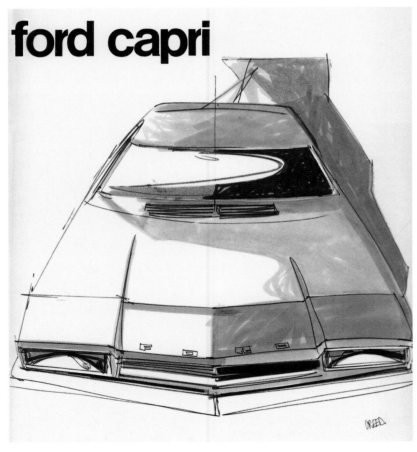

Sketches for the Capri by Trevor Creed. These were drawn for an article in the Italian magazine *Style Auto* in 1969, and were done as 'after-the event' illustrations. They are typical examples of the more vibrant sketch techniques using Magic Markers. (Courtesy *Style Auto*)

Capri engines spanned from a 1.3-litre, 52bhp up to a 3-litre V6 with 128bhp. The 3000GT was launched later, in October 1969, and included the bonnet bulge used on all German V6 models. Modellers Brian Walters and Alf Ash are seen here claying up the revised bonnet panel for the 3-litre Capri.

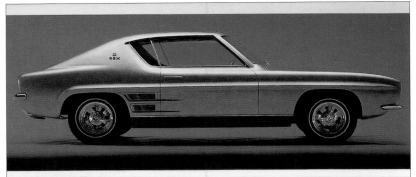

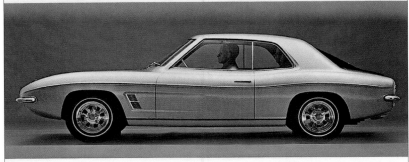

The two contenders for 'Project Colt'. Top is GBX, bottom is Flowline. The twin dummy fender vents and pronounced bone line through the centre of the door were themes common to both proposals.

Sign-off for the 'Project Colt,' April 1966. Only around ten prototypes were made before pre-production build – staggering by today's standards. John Fallis was the exterior design manager, John Hitchman was overall project engineer. Rear tail lamps were shared with the Escort – a sign of the tight cost control for the project.

Corsair. First prototypes were built in autumn 1966 using Corsair platforms, although the final body was not simply a reskinned Corsair. In reality the Capri bodyshell evolved to become more unique during its development as each panel required alterations to suit the wide range of engines, gearboxes and options that were planned for it.

One late change was to the C-curl rear side window in 1967, when most other skin tooling was already commissioned. The final model approval was therefore not until October 1967 in the new Dunton showroom, with Job One starting in November 1968 and the car launched finally at Brussels Motor Show on 24 January 1969.

The original UK engine line-up was:
- 1300   52bhp Kent engine
- 1300GT   64bhp Kent
- 1600   64bhp Kent
- 1600GT   82bhp Kent
- 2000GT   92.5bhp Essex V4

From autumn 1969, the Essex 3-litre V6 engine with 128bhp was added as a powerful top model. This was distinguished by the addition of a bonnet bulge to clear the bigger engine.

Ford Germany became involved at a fairly late stage in the Colt project, once it had gained program approval. In addition to the decision to fit the Taunus V4 and V6 engines it was also decided to double up the manufacturing and produce the Capri in Cologne as well as Halewood using duplicated sets of tooling. Production in Saarlouis was also added in 1970, at the recently-opened Escort plant.

A big part of the original Capri marketing and appeal was the five 'equipment packages' that were offered on top of the basic engine range: these comprised X, L, R, XL and XLR. In theory, combinations of XR and LR were available but not many were built.

- X-Pack was basically a dress-up pack for interiors. The £32 cost included reclining front seats, a shaped rear seat, handbrake warning light and extra interior light. This also featured twin horns and twin reverse lamps at the rear.
- L-Pack was mainly exterior styling. £15 got you bumper over-riders, dummy air scoops on the rear fenders, brightwork wheeltrims, lower bodyside bright trim strips, and a locking fuel filler cap.
- R-Pack: Rally Pack, for GT models only. £39 gave you smart 5in Rostyle wheels, a black grille, matt black paint on the bonnet, rear panel and sills, fogs and spot lamps up front, map reading lamp on a flexible stalk on passenger side, and leather steering wheel.
- XL and XLR Packs were offered and proved very popular. XLR was the one to have on your drive, complete with matt black bonnet, side scoops and Rostyle wheels!

For the interior, two versions of the IP were offered. Low-line models had just two dials, one of them a combined unit and a rev counter. The high-line version had six dials, fitted to GTs and engines of 1600cc upwards. There were four horizontal rocker switches on the IP, with slider controls for the heater and an integrated DIN-sized space for the optional radio above. A new style of safety-

A German Capri 1700 GT XLR. German market versions had slightly different treatment of the matt black bonnet that extended around the side windows. Ford popularised the use of the Rubery Owen Rostyle wheel: a new deep-drawn steel wheel design from the mid-'60s.

padded three-spoke steering wheel was first seen on the Capri, too, which would later become a standard fitment on the Escort and Mk IV models.

The whole equipment package program meant a huge amount of input from the design team, to develop all the various options and variations across the whole Capri range.

When launched under the slogan "The Car You Always Promised Yourself," the Capri proved a runaway success, both in the UK and Germany. The car continued without much change until receiving a face-lift in September 1972 when larger headlamps and tail lamps were fitted.

Interestingly, the Capri was by no means a sure-fire success when it was planned. "Ford UK were more or less told by Detroit they had to build the GBX," recalls Neil Birtley. "UK Product Planning and Marketing said that any kind of mass market coupé would never sell in the UK or European marketplace, possibly based on the disastrous sales of the old Classic-based Capri. Just about everyone in the studios said it would sell like hot cakes, but it was decided to program it in as a low-volume build, with production costs cut to a bare minimum so it had to fit in alongside the heavily-prioritised Escort at Halewood.

"However, orders went through the roof within a few months of announcement, and shifts were doubled to meet demand. A major effort then had to be made to get enough panels pressed to build them. Luckily they had been astute enough to build on – essentially – a Cortina platform, of which they could make plenty. By the time the face-lift model was introduced it was correctly identified as a priority premium product!"

Ford was one of the first British car companies to try to explain car styling to the general public. This humorous layman's guide to the styling process was produced in the 1960s. (Courtesy *Ford Times*)

The Comuta electric vehicle of 1968 was developed in the Lodge Road research centre.

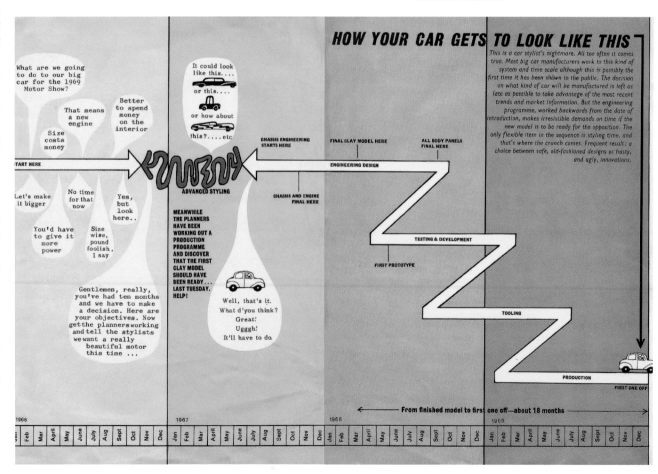

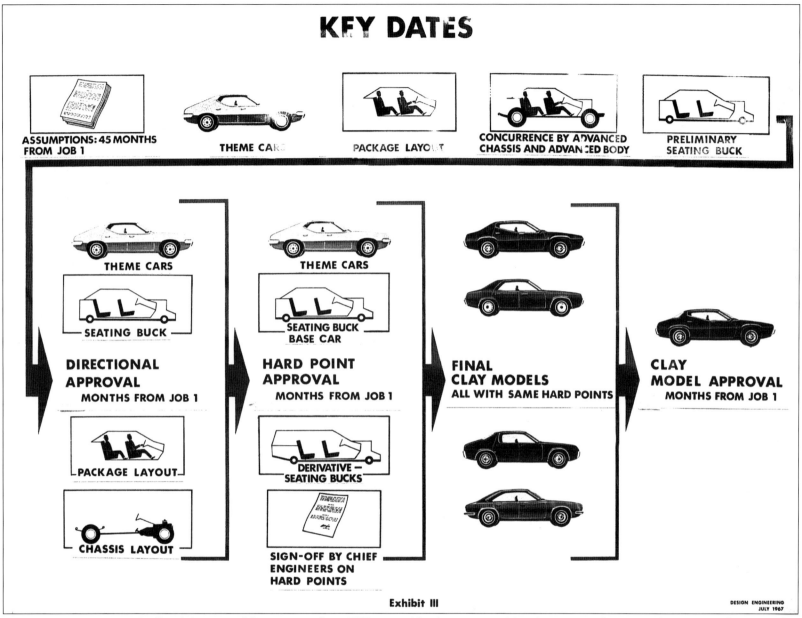

KEY DATES

ASSUMPTIONS: 45 MONTHS FROM JOB 1

THEME CARS

PACKAGE LAYOUT

CONCURRENCE BY ADVANCED CHASSIS AND ADVANCED BODY

PRELIMINARY SEATING BUCK

THEME CARS

SEATING BUCK

DIRECTIONAL APPROVAL
MONTHS FROM JOB 1

PACKAGE LAYOUT

CHASSIS LAYOUT

THEME CARS

SEATING BUCK BASE CAR

HARD POINT APPROVAL
MONTHS FROM JOB 1

DERIVATIVE – SEATING BUCKS

SIGN-OFF BY CHIEF ENGINEERS ON HARD POINTS

FINAL CLAY MODELS
ALL WITH SAME HARD POINTS

CLAY MODEL APPROVAL
MONTHS FROM JOB 1

Exhibit III

DESIGN ENGINEERING
JULY 1967

Meanwhile, this was Ford's official design workflow process from 1967, as used for the Escort and Capri programs. The timescale was typically 45 months to Job One.

The arrival of Joe Oros and Cortina TC

With Ford committed to a four-year model cycle policy for the Cortina, the third generation Cortina was duly announced in autumn 1970. To meet the strict timing, planning for this Mk III version had started in 1967 under the codename TC – standing for Taunus/Cortina – just as soon as the Mk II had been launched. As a Ford of Europe program the former rifts and rivalry that existed between Ford UK and Germany under the Cardinal and Archbishop days were deemed to be a thing of the past, although in practice that was not

yet the case … For Ford UK the aim was replace both the Cortina and the Corsair with a single model that would compete squarely in the D-segment against the Vauxhall Victor FD, Hillman Hunter and imports such as the Fiat 124/125 range. For Ford Germany, it would replace both the Taunus 12M and 15M ranges and be marketed under a single Taunus nameplate.

The basic engineering layout was initially led by Chief Engineer Harley Copp, based at Dunton. However, Copp returned to the US in 1968 to head-up Ford's crash testing program, and thereafter development was led by Fred Piziali. The TC was the first all-metric car program for Dunton, with engineering drawings using metric-only measurements, rather than imperial measurements with metric equivalents added afterwards, as had been the case with the Transit, Escort and Capri projects beforehand. As the program progressed, it became evident it would also share some suspension and components with the forthcoming Granada, another FoE project that was on the drawing board.

Design-wise, the TC project did not have an easy start. In winter 1967, Damon Woods was tragically killed on a return visit to Dearborn, when his car skidded one night on the freeway driving to Ann Arbour. The position of FoE VP was left open for some months, until Joe Oros was seconded from Dearborn to take up this position in summer 1968. At that point the exterior styling of the TC Cortina had already been signed off, but there were major problems with feasibility of the front end, particularly the fenders, which he needed to sort out – and fast. In his Ford oral history interview, Oros reported that "A lot of the sheet metal detailing should not have been approved because there were flaws in the dies and in the highlighting of the sheet metal. We had to hurriedly change some of the surface detailing … and correct some of the surfaces that were going in production."

Gil Spear led the styling of this new Cortina project, supported by a team of seconded American designers, including Andy Jacobsen, Fritz Mayhew, Toshi Saito, Dave Royer and Dick Petit. "They were on another planet when it came to the quality of their sketches and renderings, and we, the youngest designers, spent much time learning from them," recalls Patrick le Quément, who had joined as a young designer in June 1968 to fill a vacancy left by the exodus of staff to British Leyland. Other British designers were involved, such as Graham Symonds and Jim Hirons, both recently drafted in from Ford Germany.

The basic underframe and inner panels were shared between the Cortina and the Taunus, with the front screen, scuttle panel, A-pillar, and front door glass all being common parts. However, there were deliberate styling differences that the two teams in Merkenich and Dunton were encouraged to pursue to gain their regional board approvals. Or at least, the two design teams still wanted their own input, and were not prepared to compromise everything just yet! The Taunus had a straighter belt line, a more formal greenhouse, with a more upright rear window, and less of a pinched 'Coke-bottle' waist in the rear door and fender than the Cortina. Arguably, it was the better looking car. The Taunus design also had a pronounced 'Knudsen Nose' W-form front end, and different grille shape. Each design team was allowed to introduce some variation in exterior styling, interiors, and engine line-up, and the Taunus would continue with a unique two-door fastback coupé version, too – a body style that was to remain popular in Germany throughout the 1960s and '70s.

Replacing the Cortina Mk II, Corsair and Taunus ranges with one single product was a brave move and required a fair degree

Joe Oros arrived in 1968, and soon brought over a team of fellow US designers to work on the TC Cortina Mk III.

Dunton had a much larger showroom than Aveley, overlooking the viewing yard. It included two turntables and grey curtains. Teething problems with the gutters and drains led to the collapse of the showroom roof just prior to the opening of the facility, meaning that Wimpey had to rebuild it, delaying the official opening ceremony until October 1967. Ford and Wimpey had ongoing arguments over several years as to who was at fault, here.

of compromise regarding dimensions. The all-new platform had a wheelbase of 2578mm (101.5in), 89mm (3.5in) longer than the previous Cortina and slightly more than the Corsair, but was 52mm (2in) wider and no less than 119mm (4.5in) lower. It looked a rather larger car than Cortina Mk II, but in truth it was exactly same length at 4267mm (168in), yet with an interior that offered more space.

The MacPherson strut front suspension that had served Ford for 20 years was dropped in favour of a double wishbone layout (or SLA – short & long arm suspension) and a four-link live axle with coil springs at the rear. There was also a new US-designed 2-litre OHC engine for top models, designated the 'Pinto' engine, while the 1300 and 1600cc Kent engines were given minor revisions to provide more power for the heavier body. In terms of both engineering layout and styling, the TC followed the template set by GM at the time, both the Vauxhall Victor FD (launched in 1967) and sister Opel Rekord, with

Tom Firth sketching. By the mid-'60s, new drawing materials had arrived for graphics work, including Prismacolor crayons and Magic Marker felt pens. These allowed for much more vibrant sketches and renderings than the old gouache techniques.

Early Taunus TC clay model, January 1967.

Cortina TC interior was notable for its extensive use of colour-keyed plastics. The use of a quilted PVC seat style and acres of fake wood on this Olive Green XL interior added to the Transatlantic look.

The TC Cortina saloon range. Single 7in round lamps were fitted on L and XL models, with twin 5¾in round lamps on top GT and GXL versions. Estate versions of the TC Cortina and Taunus differed slightly at the rear, although tailgate pressings were actually common.

the strong 'Coke-bottle' kick-up in the belt line, four-link rear axle, and use of a cogged belt-driven cam for the 2-litre engine.

Like the exterior, the interior was very American-inspired, particularly the IP with its sharply overhanging profile and instruments set in three deeply recessed cans – again, not unlike that of the Victor FD. The oval steering wheel was a deeply-dished safety style with twin vee spokes and different inserts according to trim grade: plain for base models, a three-hole sports design for GT and GXL, and fake wood for upper-range XL models. Instead of

round 'Aeroflow' eyeball vents, air entered the cabin through slot air vents at the top of the IP. As with the Capri, there was extensive colour-keying of interior components, such as steering wheels and handbrakes – more so than other competitors. Uwe Bahnsen was in charge of Dunton interior studio at this point, and his remit also extended to the TC Taunus. The Taunus interior was largely identical, except that the main IP top pad ran straight across rather than dipping down as on the Cortina, and the style of door trim panels and application of wood on top versions also differed slightly.

Highly effective detail rendering in marker pen and Derwent crayon on brown Canson paper by John Pritchard. Script was done by careful application of white Letraset.

Early stages of a clay model in Dunton, 1960s. Standard practice was to keep the upper greenhouse open, to allow the model to become a realistic 'see-through' example for viewings, using Perspex windows. Heavy modelling bridges were used to transfer points for symmetry across the model.

1973 Cortina 2000E, with the revised rectangular lamps. The Cortina was Britain's best-selling car in 1972, '73, '74, and 1975. It was loved by fleet managers, and became the mainstay of many rental fleets, including Hertz, Godfrey Davis, and Avis.

The 'R-module' instrument pack received a Design Council award for automotive products in May 1974, for 'clearly legible graphics.' With its modular construction allowing several different instrument layouts, and white-on-black graphics, the 'R-module' cluster was also used on the '75 Escort Mk II and '78 Transit. (Courtesy Design Council Slide Collection)

In September 1973, the TC Cortina was given a mild face-lift. This included a new front grille, with single rectangular headlamps for GT models replacing the twin lamps as a cost saving. At the same time a new top model was introduced – the 2000E. A new eight-spoke deep-draw steel wheel design became widely used around this time, replacing the more expensive Rostyles. In fact, this popular steel wheel design was used regularly on many Cortina models right up until the final Crusader Mk V in 1982.

Reacting to criticism of the interior, the Dunton team designed a new IP and revised the cabin to give a more 'British' look to it. Round 'Aeroflow' eyeball vents were reintroduced at each end of the IP (but no centre vents as yet). It also featured a new instrument cluster, designated 'R-module,' with two widely-spaced dials for speedometer and tachometer, five rectangular warning lamps mounted centrally at the base, and a central dial containing fuel and temperature gauges.

Granada MH and 'Brenda' Escort

The next project was known as MH, or 'Medium Hummer.' The early stages saw exterior model proposals produced in Dunton, but the production design was handled by Sipple's German design team in Merkenich with Walter Rhein and Tilbert Bode involved. Merkenich also developed a two-door coupé version that was never sold in the UK.

According to Oros this MH program also had a shaky start, being late on its schedule upon his arrival in Europe and needing a lot of determination to get it on track for launch in 1972. "We managed to

Finding new talent: Ford and the RCA

Formal training of car designers in the UK did not really exist up until the 1960s. Following the closure of Eric Archer's apprentice training school, Ford was finding it difficult to recruit designers with the high level of creative and visual skills needed for the studios, which led to discussions with the Royal College of Art in London.

Founded in 1837, the RCA was originally split into four schools: Architecture, Painting, Sculpture, and Design, and these remained largely unchanged until 1948, when Robin Darwin was appointed Principal and instigated a policy of more specialised training for the new profession of industrial design and post-graduate study.

In 1960, Professor Misha Black was tasked with building a new department teaching industrial design under the title of School of Industrial Design (Engineering), or ID (E). By 1962, the RCA had gained a new building on Kensington Gore, next to the Albert Hall, and had enrolled around 50 postgraduate students. It soon became apparent that a high proportion of students were interested in transport design and so a course of further specialised study was investigated, with co-operation and guidance being sought from the car industry. Roy Brown was one of the first to respond positively to the idea, but wanted further commitments from other car companies before agreeing to sponsor the course.

At that point, around 1964, no other company was interested and the course did not go ahead. However, with the completion of Dunton in early 1967, Ford was very keen to pursue this idea again with the RCA, and thus the Automotive Design Section was established, with the first two recruits arriving in October 1967 – Peter Stevens and Dawson Sellar. They would both graduate in 1969 and join the Dunton studio.

Ford agreed to sponsor two students per year, receiving a generous sum of around £1200 per year from Ford and working in the company studios during RCA vacations. Once Joe Oros arrived, support was strengthened, with Ford supplying equipment such as a modelling bridge and clay oven, and materials such as Mylar film, tapes and clay. Dunton manager Ken Nelson was delegated to act as the main liaison with the RCA, together with graduate training co-ordinator Chris Pickard. Subsequent RCA graduates included John Hartnell, and Paul Gebbert (both 1970), and Clive Potter and Martin Smith (1971).

Regarding staff, Ford suggested using two designers who had previously worked at Ford – Tom Karen and Peter Ralph – as tutors to come in on a part-time basis to provide the specialised guidance and tuition for automotive design techniques. Designer Patrick le Quément was also involved, teaching there from 1969-'71.

In 1969, Chrysler joined the program, with the support of Roy Axe and Rex Fleming at their Whitley studio in Coventry, and later on Vauxhall joined the program. However, at this stage there was little interest from any of the British Leyland studios – Austin in Longbridge, Rover in Solihull, Triumph and Jaguar in Coventry – which all preferred to continue with their own apprenticeship schemes, training boys from the age of 16.

The RCA Darwin Building in Kensington Gore was completed in 1962. (Courtesy RCA)

GT70

The GT70 was conceived as a mid-engined rally car, similar in concept to the Lancia Stratos of the 1970s. The idea was dreamt up by Stuart Turner and Roger Clark on the flight back from the Monte Carlo rally in January 1970, with Len Bailey being enlisted to design the bodywork and chassis that spring. An initial model was done as a GRP model in Dunton in October 1970 and a total of six prototypes were subsequently built in the UK.

In September 1970 – just as the TC Cortina was launched – Walter Hayes approached Ford US to ask for the funding to build 500 cars, citing the need for a competition weapon as well as a showroom flagship. He called the GT70 a 'prestige sports car', justifying the need to build it by stating: 'Ford's biggest image deficiency is in the field of engineering reputation. We believe that GT70 would add tremendously to the status of the cars that come out of AVO.'

The car was then restyled, with input from designer Ercole Spada and Filippo Sapino, head of Ford's new Bruino design studio in Turin. This version was displayed at the Turin Show in November 1971, featuring distinctive open buttresses at the rear.

Once the Escort started winning international events – including the Monte Carlo Rally – the case for GT70 started to wane. By summer 1971, Ford was focusing on a host of new model programs – the next generations of Escort, Capri and Taunus, plus the new Fiesta baby car project – all of which required huge amounts of investment and manpower. The GT70 was seen as increasingly irrelevant, the AVO setup was struggling, and GT70 work was completely halted by 1973.

The restyled GT70 by Filippo Sapina. These 6x13in four-spoke wheels were one of the first alloy wheels to be offered by Ford in Europe, and were popularly fitted to RS Escorts and Capris.

make all our schedules," he recalled. "It was a tremendous effort, but the designers in Ford of Europe were extremely capable, and we got things turned around and on target."

Much of this was due to the pattern of travelling between the studios that was established by Oros and continued by the design Vice Presidents for the next three decades. Based in Dunton, he would continue a relentless schedule by airplane for the whole five years he stayed in Europe. "I travelled between the studios every week," recalled Oros. "I was in Germany at least once to three times a week every week year round, and every other week I made a round robin trip to Germany, Italy and back to England."

Not that working with Oros was necessarily easy, recalls le Quément. "During most of his visits in the studio, Joe would stand silently with his trademark trousers half mast and his thick sole shoes, tapping a foot continuously, thinking about his next creative outburst. There resulted an immense pool of undistinguishable models, a bit like a very large family of nine kids, each a little different but none totally unique. Designing for Joe was not very gratifying... you could say that it was close to mental torture for, as soon as a program reached a full-size clay phase, Joe took over."

Le Quément worked on the interior for the MH during 1969. "I participated in the instrument panel contest where four designs were selected, one from Trevor Creed, one from Brian Hughes, another from Bob Hutchinson, and mine. Trevor, who had already been with Ford since a couple of years in the interior design studio, excelled at interiors but, for me, it was not an easy task as I had never designed an instrument panel, nevertheless my project did get to the final two proposals ..." Creed's design was the final one selected by Bahnsen to go ahead for production.

Around this time, le Quément and Creed were both selected as recent graduates for an accelerated management career. "After having been in the company for only a year, Uwe Bahnsen told me that I had been identified as being a high-potential employee, or HPE," says le Quément. "I was offered to be the first ever designer to attend the Danbury Management Center and take an MBA, starting in October 1969. This was a part-time arrangement, 1½ days a week of schooling but I had to work every weekend. This began in the fall of 1969 and lasted till I went to Germany for my first assignment there in October 1971. It was hard work, particularly as I was continuously in competition as a designer, having to meet deadlines but losing 1½ days a week in the process ..." In this respect, Ford was at least a decade ahead of other companies in the UK, who only took up this practice of training designers for management roles during the 1980s.

In 1971, Ford Germany and Ford of Britain were fully incorporated into FoE. Joe Oros and American engineering executive Jack Hooven were given the task of sorting out the definitive structure for design and engineering. At that stage Ford Germany was growing fast, and so Merkenich was given a good chunk of responsibilities, although there was a union agreement to keep 60 per cent of the workload

A fine rendering of the MH Granada. Although the main exterior for the MH was handled by Merkenich, Dunton went on to take charge of the Granada Ghia coupé, with much of the work being done by Ron Saunders.

in the UK. Under their new FoE arrangement Merkenich would focus on exterior design, base engine design, electrical engineering and transmissions. Oros felt that the German studio had superior equipment for doing the final exterior detailing, particularly the model bridges with the latest electronic readouts.

At this point the Dunton studio was led by Ken Nelson and would take care of interior design, colour and trim development, and all commercial vehicles. Most of the Motorsport RS work was centred on Dunton, too, in partnership with Ford AVO at Aveley.

There was another side to this arrangement. Oros confirms he

AVO and Aveley

Once the styling studio and engineering teams had vacated the site in 1967, Aveley was utilised by the new Advanced Vehicle Operations (AVO for short) as a specialist low-volume manufacturing plant from November 1970 to produce the Escort RS 1600. This was soon followed by the Escort Mexico and later, in 1973, by the Escort 1300E and RS 2000. Ford AVO ran successfully for nearly four years, but in October 1973 came the energy crisis. Fuel prices doubled and, like other manufacturers, Ford's car sales plummeted. Once this happened, the mainstream Escort plants found themselves with spare capacity and the writing was on the wall for AVO in Arisdale Avenue.

Ford had also opened a vast new parts distribution centre in Daventry in 1968 to supplement the Aveley parts depot. Thus, by early 1975, the AVO plant had closed its doors for the last time. However, Aveley was kept as a pre-production facility for Ford, and also continued with power products engineering, but was steadily run-down as part of Ford's operations, finally closing in 2004. In 2013 the site was demolished and redeveloped for housing.

AVO production line at Aveley. Daytona Yellow and Olympic Blue were highly popular colours for the RS 1600 and Escort Mexico, produced from 1970-'75.

did this for several reasons: "One was that the Germans had the better equipment, and two, we wanted to make sure that we had a German input into our products, and particularly if those products were to be sold on the Continent so that we could say yes, indeed, these products have been designed and have been handled with our German end of the business here in Germany. So, that was a good political position to maintain." As part of that, he requested Bahnsen to return to Germany and take over the studio now that Sipple had departed for the US.

Although the MH Granada was developed by Merkenich, the Mk II Escort was in fact the first exterior completely designed by the German studio with no great input from Dunton. Product Letter ER-2 on 2 Dec 1972 was the kick-off for the Mk II Escort program, codenamed 'Brenda.' It was a straightforward reskin of the Escort, bringing in bigger 1600cc engines, more comfort and luxury – plus more weight, not least due to the 23 per cent more glass area. Wheel sizes went back up to 13in on all models except the entry Popular model, while trunk capacity was up 10 per cent at 290 litres (10.3cu ft). Final engineering sign-off was August 1974, with Job One achieved on 2 Dec 1974, ready for the launch in Brussels on 24 January 1975.

Dunton's input on the interior was a straightforward update of the previous design, with a new IP and proper round eyeball vents, as on the updated Cortina. Fabric trim was offered on the majority of models, while GL and Ghia models had a centre console for the first time, including a quartz clock and an integrated housing for the radio. Radios were still not standard, and when fitted on lesser models were contained in a simple screw-on housing under the IP. Dunton's colour and trim group became involved in decals and graphics to support the work being done by AVO on developing the Mexico, RS1800 and RS2000 models, something at which they would become increasingly expert for the numerous special editions that would come their way during the 1970s.

Planning for the RS models began in early 1974, just as the production design for Brenda was being finalised. The previous generation of RS models had not needed much in the way of design studio input, but this time around Design VP Jack Telnack and Trevor Creed agreed to provide full professional support at Dunton for the engineers who were developing the cars outside the main Ford program. For the Brenda version of the RS2000 an ambitious new front end was proposed with a plastic 'shovel nose' for better aerodynamics, a new bonnet and rear trunk spoiler.

Mike Moreton was one of the engineers at AVO involved with the RS developments: "It gave us a fright at first; initial thoughts were: how on earth are we going to make that? But we soon recovered and worked out how to produce the large one-piece, moulded polyurethane 'soft' front end." The complete 'nose cone' was developed and sourced from a supplier in Germany, and AVO engineers rose to the challenge of productionising it. "The main concerns were: how to modify the Escort body; mounting the large panel to the rest of it, and matching these two, three-dimensional

Escort RS2000. With a 2-litre engine and 100bhp breathing through a downdraught twin choke Weber carburettor, it was every young manager's dream company car in 1976.

shapes, which was the really tricky bit, especially with one made of metal and the other of plastic, not to mention getting the paint colours to match."

The specification included deep Scheel bucket seats, while the optional Custom Pack offered high-backed sports seats, a clock, and a sports centre console. A new four-spoke 6x13in alloy wheel was available for RS models, too. "The clay model, painted bright yellow with bold black RS2000 decals, was an instant hit, especially with the dealers who were shown it when being introduced to the new Escort," continues Moreton. "When it was proudly unveiled ... they stood up and cheered."

The first production RS2000 was built at Saarlouis on 10 November 1975, and went on to be a huge success, selling around 26,000 over six years.

Escort Mk II sketch by John Pritchard.

A colourful decade

The 1970s were a colourful decade regarding cars. Ford's colour line-up included a healthy selection of greens, purples and yellows, with Daytona Yellow being the top selling Ford colour in 1973. It was offered on every model from the Escort to the Granada, although by the end of the decade bright red would become the number one colour. The popularity of metallic paints continued to grow and Ford introduced high visibility 'Signal' paint colours in 1976 incorporating the latest bright pigments.

Ford also led the trend towards matt black exterior trim for items such as grilles and wipers, replacing the former bright finish that had predominated in the 1960s. Vinyl roofs were a popular fitment, too, with Ford offering roofs in Tobacco or Black on many models.

1970 saw the introduction of the first Bri Nylon cloth upholstery on the Cortina TC and Escort, a start of the long trend away from vinyl seats that had been the norm over the previous two decades. Every model offered four interior colourways, including green and chocolate and Ford was extremely adept on the application of bold colour and trim selections to create differentiation within the model ranges. 'Cadiz' striped flat woven fabric was used on sporty models such as the Fiesta S, Capri S and Escort Sport, using orange, green, tan and grey colourways. Newly-developed velour fabrics were quickly adopted too: crushed velour was used on Ghia models, while a corduroy-style ribbed 'Rialto' velour was reserved for Capri II S and Ghia models.

Throughout the 1970s, plastic wood-effect inserts were popular with Ford designers, being applied on instrument clusters, glovebox lids, centre console trays and even steering wheels. It seems astonishing today that fake wood was so popular then, but was well-accepted at the time, being used on domestic furniture and household products such as TVs and Hi-Fi equipment. The use of fake stitching embossed into plastic mouldings was also widespread. Initially used on door linings, the use spread to other areas, such as the edges of consoles or steering wheel centre pads. By the 1980s these fashions had passed, although fake wood had something of a resurgence again in the 1990s.

Colour and trim chart from 1977 (Author's Collection)

Chapter

5

The Uwe Bahnsen era

A new B-segment car had been mooted for years, to compete with Renault, Fiat, and BMC. Several chopped-down Anglia or Taunus prototypes were produced by various groups, but the verdict was always the same: small car, small profits. Sure, there would be some savings in sheet steel, but the factory would need just as many men, and just as many machine tools. Plus, the layout and packaging were poor. However, the market for small cars continued to expand throughout the 1960s, with the BMC 1100, Peugeot 204 and 104, Simca 1100, and Fiat 128 all launched with transverse FWD drivetrains.

In late 1969, Ford decided on a fresh start for the small car project. Advanced Planning Manager Jim Donaldson was ordered to establish a small team: two research engineers, two production engineers, and four to five assistants. The codename was 'Torino' – to please the new Ford President, Lee Iacocca. No designer was involved, the idea being to get 'just a concept, the style doesn't matter.' By January 1970, the first specification was drawn up. With a cost target of $100 less than the Escort, and a weight of 630kg (1400lb), an initial prototype costing $100,000 was readied for showing in Merkenich in October. Not surprisingly, Joe Oros was somewhat wary of it, since there had been no styling input, even if the packaging appeared okay. The Torino mock-up was subsequently shown to Henry Ford II and Iacocca in the Dunton studio in February 1971, with three quick sketches supplied by Dunton designer Trevor Erskine for support.

The Bobcat project: Fiesta

As planning gathered pace during 1971-'72, the project became a global one under the codename 'Bobcat,' with concept planning and cost analysis work now handled by Dearborn. By this stage, the Fiat 127 was the clear bench mark target, and in summer 1972 Fiat 127 hatchbacks were used as mules for the first running prototypes. Bordinat's studio began work on two styling models, the 'Mini Mites,' one being RWD and the other FWD, while Ghia was commissioned to produce a concept – also based on Fiat 127 running gear – dubbed 'Blue Car.'

These three models were used for extensive customer clinics in Lausanne in December 1972, with 700 respondents from Germany, UK, France, Italy, and Spain flown in over two weekends. Rival models included the Renault 5, Peugeot 104, Fiat 127, Honda's new Civic, and the Escort. Further clinics were held in California and Sao Paulo during January and February 1973. From these exercises, the Ghia 'Blue Car' model emerged a clear favourite.

Tom Tjaarda at Ghia did two further developments of the Blue Car for April 1973, called 'Wolf' – one with a long roof like the 1980s VW Polo or Honda Civic, and another yellow coupé/sedan version. Further models were done by Bahnsen's team in Germany and in Dunton, ready for the product committee meeting of 21 June. At this point in June 1973, Jack Telnack was brought in to direct the

The early days of Ford and Ghia

Carrozzeria Ghia SpA was founded in 1915 by coachbuilder Giacinto Ghia, who produced small batches of luxury cars until the outbreak of the Second World War. Ghia died during the war, and afterwards Luigi Segre took over the company with Mario Boano as designer from the late 1940s, producing a series of Chrysler prototypes throughout the 1950s. Ghia SpA also worked for Ford, Packard, American Motors, Renault and Volvo, with their name becoming widely known after the VW Karmann Ghia project was launched in 1955. After Luigi Segre died in 1963, Ghia changed hands several times, culminating with Alejandro de Tomaso taking control, producing the Mangusta and later the Pantera, powered by a Ford V8 engine.

In the late 1960s, Ford set up a small Italian design studio in Bruino, on the western fringes of Turin, prompted by the desire from Ford President Lee Iacocca to have a foothold in Turin, where Ford had worked with various carrozzeria – not least with Frua on the Zephyr Mk III. In 1969, Joe Oros appointed Filippo Sapino as design manager for the Bruino design centre. "I wanted the studio to be 100 per cent Italian, no other nationalities involved, to ensure we had as much as possible a strong Italian input to our European design. I interviewed the designers and engineers myself in a Turin hotel. We found a food processing plant just outside Turin that we rented and leased," Oros recalled.

Ford then decided to buy an 84 per cent share in Ghia in July 1970, with Iacocca's fellow American-Italian Don DeLaRossa being designated President of Ghia. Never an easy man to work with, Alejandro de Tomaso and Ford parted company in autumn 1972 when Ford bought the remaining 16 per cent share and Filippo Sapino was appointed Design Director of Ghia, with Tom Tjaarda as Chief Designer. The Bruino studio was closed.

While DeLaRossa was selected as President due to his Italian roots, he did not spend much time there, preferring to be based in the US. Ghia worked for all the Ford global studios to produce fast prototype studies, producing over 20 models per year throughout the 1970s. However, the Ghia studio reported directly to Dearborn, and in the initial years DeLaRossa did not use Ghia to its best abilities, the studio becoming mocked as 'Lee's Playpen,' and known for producing frivolous American-influenced concepts. Tjaarda illustrates the mood at the time: "It was a weird feeling being left alone, nobody from Ford turned up. In autumn 1972 I decided to do a radical three-seater touring sports car. I pinned the sketches on the wall and waited. But there were still no visits from Ford. So I thought, why not just go ahead and do a full-size model? The Fiesta was the only other project going on at that moment so there room for something else to do." The concept was eventually shown as the Ghia Coins at the 1974 Geneva Motor Show: "It represents what the Capri would become for 2000," according to Ford's press release of the time.

From 1973 Ford used the Ghia name and emblem on its mainstream European models as a flagship nameplate, starting with the Granada and Capri, but the practice soon spread to every model in the line-up.

Ghia Coins (Courtesy www.allcarindex.com)

Having completed the 'Blue Car' (designed by Paulo Martin) in just 53 days in 1972, Ghia then produced two versions of Tom Tjaarda's 'Wolf' in 1973. One had a long roof profile; the other was more coupé-like, with a dipping beltline and a deep swage along the bodyside. This became the winning theme for the production Fiesta.

Early Fiesta 'Bobcat' rendering by John Pritchard. (Courtesy David Ginn)

competing Dunton model, and to head up the British studio. By now the project had become a huge competition between all Ford's design studios, with no less than 26 see-through models being assembled at Merkenich for final selection by the product committee in October 1973. Naturally, every studio director wanted their car to win.

Writing in *Classic Car* magazine in 2016, Tjaarda said "When Iacocca selected our proposal, this didn't go down too well with the other Ford Design executives. Iacocca got furious when some of these started to fiddle with the Ghia model, even introducing radical changes. People were fired and time was lost, but Iacocca insisted on going back to my design, even if the program was delayed by a few months."

In truth, Dunton was tasked with correcting the Ghia Wolf model.

"The proposal that we received from Italy was way under package. It was quite low and slinky," recalled Oros. "The Ghia studio had taken liberties with the package that neither Germany nor England nor the US took." Once the Ghia/Dunton model was approved, Oros called Telnack into his office to explain what would happen next. "Jack, this model ... now that it's approved, we're going to have to ship it to Germany and have Uwe Bahnsen and his crew do the final production detailing." Not surprisingly, Telnack was angry, feeling he should control the detailing in Dunton. "No Jack, we can't," retorted Oros, "and for two reasons we can't: one, you don't have the right tools. Germany has the best tools of the two areas, and he knew this. Secondly Jack, we have to have a German input into this car, and we have to be able to say that German engineering and German design effort was involved in the development of the Fiesta."

Trevor Creed working on a Fiesta tape drawing, circa 1973.

Final Fiesta exterior being modelled at Merkenich, early 1974. Note the competitor models in the background.

The project was approved for production in December 1973, with Ford's engineering centres in Merkenich and Dunton collaborating on a scale not seen before. The timing was becoming crucial. The Yom Kippur War had just broken out, fuel prices doubled overnight, and small, fuel-efficient cars were seen as a top priority within Ford, not just in Europe but also in America. A federalised Fiesta for the US market was swiftly authorised, to be supplied from Saarlouis.

By this stage the all-new VW Polo/Audi 50 was seen as the bench mark car to beat, although the Fiesta was still felt to be better in terms of its airy interior ambience and bigger trunk space.

To meet the strict cost targets, the car would use a new version of the Ford Kent OHV engine, dubbed 'Valencia' after the brand new Spanish factory in Almussafes, Valencia, developed especially to produce the new car. The Valencia engine was available in 957cc and 1117cc capacities initially, with a 1298cc version arriving later.

Unlike the Renault 5 and Simca 1100 rivals that had torsion bars in their suspension, the Fiesta had coil springs. The front suspension was of Ford's typical TCA arrangement, where MacPherson struts were combined with lower control arms and longitudinal compression links. The standard rear suspension used a beam axle, trailing links and a Panhard rod, whilst an anti-roll bar was included in the sports package. All Mk I Fiestas featured 12in wheels as standard, with disc brakes at the front and drum brakes at the rear.

Although the exterior was an amalgam of Ghia, Dunton and Merkenich, the interior was carried out 100 per cent in Dunton, with designers Alan Jackson and John Hartnell leading the work. "The IP on the Fiesta was a tremendous success, and I felt very good about that," said Oros. The main theme was a large one-piece plastic moulding with a large open tray running across and the instruments contained in a pod in front of the driver, with an attractive four spoke steering wheel aping the style of the larger Taunus and Granada models.

Modellers Ron Binnie (with beard) and John Howard work on the Fiesta interior, 1974.

Dennis Brand working on a Fiesta steering wheel proposal.

Dunton was equipped with large workshops for GRP work. Here, moulds are being taken off the final Bobcat clay model in 1975 to make the see-through GRP model.

During later Merkenich development under Bahnsen's direction, the Bobcat design was cleaned up to incorporate current Ford design themes. The car had good aerodynamic performance through using a couple of newly-developed ideas from the wind tunnel engineers.

One was the aerofoil-section grille where the grille vanes acted as open sections at low speeds, but deflected air up and over the bonnet at higher speeds. First seen on the Capri concept shown at Geneva in 1976, it was to become a signature Ford design cue, fitted on every new Ford model in Europe by the early 1980s, including the Transit and Cargo truck. A second idea was the deep front spoiler incorporated in the steel front valence, which had been developed for the Granada Mk II. Finally, there was the neat kick-up at the tip of the roof, which helped airflow around the rear quarters and added greatly to the character of the design from the rear three-quarter view. In all, these ideas gave the Fiesta a drag coefficient of 0.422, the best of any Ford at the time and excellent for the class.

Ford estimated that Fiesta production would be 500,000 per year, with the investment totalling $1 billion (£400 million). In addition to the assembly plants in Dagenham, Saarlouis and Valencia, a transaxle factory near Bordeaux was also built. The Ford Fiesta went on sale in Europe in September 1976, with RHD UK sales delayed until January 1977.

The Bobcat project was a decisive step in the integration of Ford of Europe: it was not the product of Ford Germany nor the UK, it was a joint effort between the teams throughout Ford, with production being centred at Valencia in Spain and the car being developed for sale not only in Europe, but also for Ford in the US. For Dunton, the Fiesta was the start of its subsequent role as a studio that would focus upon interiors and commercial vehicles. Likewise, Ford of Britain would become less of a manufacturing operation and henceforth its strength would lie in being the dominant partner with the strongest and best marketing operation within Ford of Europe. Whereas Ford Germany's market share hovered around 15 per cent, Ford UK's regularly reached 30 per cent at this time.

Final sign-off on the GRP model in the Dunton viewing yard, 1975. Lee Iacocca and Henry Ford II stand in the centre of the group. During development, journalist Edouard Seidler was authorised to write a book on the project, which came out at the same time as the car was launched. Entitled *Let's Call It Fiesta*, it was the first time such a book had been written on the design and development of a car, and the first time Ford had allowed an outsider such access to confidential material.

Uwe Bahnsen

One of the first recruits to Ford Germany was Uwe Bahnsen. Born in Hamburg in 1930, he studied at the city's College of Fine Arts, becoming an accomplished painter and sculptor. He then worked as a window dresser in a department store, spending weekends at the racetracks, where he became well-known as an amateur saloon car racer in Germany. He joined Ford in 1958, working closely with Wes Dahlberg on the Taunus range, including the Taunus P6, which was the first Ford design led by Bahnsen.

Bahnsen was transferred to lead the interior team in Dunton around 1967, then returned to take charge of the Merkenich studio from 1971. In March 1976 he replaced Jack Telnack as Vice President of Design in FoE, being based back in England, where he remained for the next decade. Dapper and affable, Bahnsen loved the British way of life and the close contact with the RCA in London that his post afforded him, allowing him to speak at conferences or to set up exhibitions, such as the V&A exhibition on the design of the Ford Sierra in 1982.

During the 1970s there was a strategic decision to make Bahnsen more visible as head of FoE design, and to promote Ford as a leading brand for design, particularly in Germany where its image and reputation had been seen as somewhat Anglo-American up to that point. Whereas Opel was always accepted as an original German company that happened to be owned by the Americans (as was Vauxhall in the UK), Ford Germany was in a weaker position, being seen as a purely American outfit, despite the decades of German involvement. Having Bahnsen as a senior figurehead in the crucial area of design was a key asset from a PR standpoint.

Bahnsen's taste in design was typified by the 'Eva' Mk II Granada and 'Erika' Escort: crisp, assured designs that trod a fine balance between the latest fashion and appealing to a wide customer base across Europe.

According to Patrick le Quément, Bahnsen suffered from not having enough visibility with corporate management, particularly with William Clay Ford, who officially visited the European design studios just three times a year. "As a result, Uwe could hardly compete with the Detroit-based execs who saw Mr Ford several times a month and so he developed a plan – a very ingenious plan – that clearly worked. He decided to dress exactly the same way when Mr Ford visited. Black suit, white shirt and black tie with … a BRIGHT red waistcoat. And sure enough, combined with his height and side burns you could only but remember him!"

After leaving Ford in 1986, Bahnsen served as director of the Pasadena Art Center of Design's Swiss-based college in Vevey until 1995. He died in July 2013 at the age of 83. Reflecting on his time with Bahnsen, le Quément comments "I was very fortunate, I believe, to have had the luck of working with Uwe Bahnsen. I think he is probably the pioneer of design management which is in fact a new science, not just the management of creative resources, but one who in fact manages the design strategy of a company."

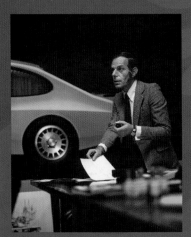

Uwe Bahnsen, shown here in 1975. He enjoyed living in the UK, residing in the village of Stock, Essex for most of the decade he was based at Dunton.

This fine portrait in acrylics was commissioned in 1983 and hangs in the National Portrait Gallery, London. Painted by Alistair Morrison, it shows Bahnsen in typical languid pose with his ever-present cigarette. (Courtesy Alistair Morrison)

Fiesta Ghia, 1976. The Fiesta was awarded a Design Council award in 1977, the first time it was given to a complete car rather than a component or a product.

Cortina TC2 and TC3

Joe Oros had remained as Vice President of Ford of Europe Design for over five years when he returned to Dearborn at the end of 1973. According to le Quément, "Uwe very legitimately hoped to become the next VP for Ford of Europe after Joe Oros left. But as always, it was an American who was chosen to become VP of Design, namely Jack Telnack. Uwe complained and asked Bob Lutz who at the time was in charge of Ford of Germany, what had gone wrong … what could he do if the poker game was loaded?"

Bahnsen was told that, although he had won all the major design competitions, he needed to train a successor if his bid to get the top job was to succeed. At this point he decided to make le Quément his second-in-command, which resulted in Bahnsen eventually getting his promotion to VP in March 1976, once Telnack had returned to the US.

In terms of projects, work on a replacement for the Mk III Cortina and Taunus was started in 1973, in fact before the '73 face-lift for the Cortina was even launched. At that time it was felt the Taunus needed the redesign more urgently to maintain sales than did the Cortina, which was still Britain's best-selling car in 1972, '73, '74 and 1975. Hence the work was led by the Merkenich studio, under the guidance of le Quément.

The main effort for the Taunus TC2 redesign went into the front end, with the awkward W-shaped 'Knudsen Nose' ditched in favour of a lower and squarer design from the Cologne team. Front and rear doors were carried over from the Taunus TC, with only the rear door upper frame being revised with a sharp top corner. The entire rear end, C-pillar and roof were revised with a crisper, more angular look. The result was a much more European-looking car than the 1970 Cortina TC, with its heavy American influences. The new car had 15 per cent more glass area than the TC Cortina and Taunus, with much improved rear visibility as well.

For Ford UK, the initial plan was for a hallway-house design whereby the Cortina Mk IV would receive the new Taunus front end but retain the flowing rear end unchanged. Terry Beckett had become Managing Director and Chief Executive of Ford UK in January 1974 and when this interim proposal was viewed by Beckett, Chairman Sam Toy and Telnack they decided this was an unsatisfactory deal for them and, as the dominant partner in Ford of Europe, insisted that the next Cortina should get the full treatment as a totally new model.

It certainly worked. When finally launched in 1976 the Mk IV Cortina was perceived in the UK as a completely new car rather than a reskin and very few people noticed the fact that the front doors and screen were carried-over from the German Taunus TC. The interior was more of a giveaway, with the IP being the same as the outgoing model, but with improved front seats and revised fabrics, a four-spoke steering wheel for higher grade models and a revised centre console being the key changes.

The decision to commonise the Cortina and Taunus at this point came late however, meaning that the additional tooling required for production in Dagenham would cause the Cortina Mk IV version to be delayed. The new Taunus was announced in January 1976 at the Brussels Motor Show, with the Cortina Mk IV not on sale until October that year.

Cortina Mk IV Ghia, finished in Roman Bronze, with Tobacco vinyl roof. The TC2 saw the introduction of the Ford blue roundel as the brand emblem on the car. Until that point, the 'FORD' name had been variously used as a script on the grille and rear of the car. Bob Lutz was a key protagonist for this change toward brand consistency.

and new bumpers with wraparound black plastic end caps. The front end had a softer look to it than the outgoing model, featuring the corporate 'aerofoil' grille, new bumpers and wraparound side indicators, all part of the desire to project a common design language throughout the Ford range.

The interior set out to correct a few problems that owners had complained about. New seats were mounted 50mm (2in) higher, and the IP was revised by Dunton with a pair of additional centre vents to aid through-flow ventilation.

Cortina Mk V TC3

The final stage in the Cortina story was the Taunus TC3, introduced in August 1979, part of a £50 million investment in the Taunus/Cortina range. Announced as 'Cortina 80' by Ford, it subsequently became known as the Cortina Mk V in the UK.

At first glance this was a very mild makeover of the styling, but in fact it was a fairly extensive retooling of the entire car. The greenhouse was revised, with the door upper frames raised around 25mm (1in) and a flatter roof pressing, an exercise not unlike that done for the Lowline Zodiac range from 1959. The rear window was revised and rear end featured larger sawtooth-style tail lamps

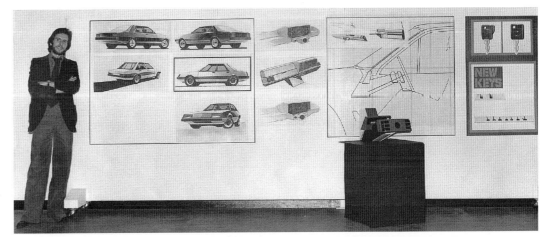

Tony Catignani shows his sketches for the TC3 Cortina, 1975. Tony's father, Alfred, was a clay modeller at Aveley, one of three Catignani brothers who worked as modellers at Ford. (Courtesy Tony Catignani)

The 'Eva' Granada was a skilful update of the original MH. It was updated again in 1981 under the codename 'Gloria,' a £50m development to keep the car fully competitive. The Gloria design changes included a new IP and seats, plus engine revisions and retuned suspension.

Project Eva: Granada Mk II

Face-lifting the Granada was the next priority for design. This was again led by the duo of le Quément and Gert Hohenester in Merkenich. Much of the work was carried out concurrently with the Taunus TC2 program, hence the obvious visual links between the two models that helped shift perceptions of the TC2 as something rather more desirable than the old TC model – particularly in the UK. With Bahnsen increasingly permitted to be the 'face' of Ford Design for the European media, he was able to promote a much more Germanic look to Ford that was in keeping with the mood of the 1970s and a positive change from the former Dearborn-influenced styles pushed through by Oros.

The resulting 'Eva' design developed during 1973-'74 was a clever face-lift of the original MH Granada. It kept the entire underframe, lower doors and basic windscreen from the MH, but updated it with a very crisp rear end and new front from the A-pillars forward. As with the Taunus, the roof profile was made more angular, with a distinct 'turret top' look to it, and very sharp corners to all window frames.

The rear end was particularly attractive, mimicking the angular style of the Pininfarina-designed Fiat 130 coupé by Paulo Martin,

with slim horizontal tail lamps and very sharp creases on the rear corners. Compared to the coachbuilt Fiat, the Merkenich team introduced flat chamfers on the rear fender to soften the corners slightly and allow them to be pressed in steel at Ford volumes. The screen finisher was locally modified to include a sharp lower corner rather than a rounded one, but the basic glass form and A-pillar remained unchanged. Likewise the rear door pressing was only modified at the rear corner to remove the flip-up of the MH style, while the lower door section crease was disguised by use of a thick black door protector strip that carried through the black sections in the bumpers. Careful attention to details such as these allowed the design to be seen by most observers as all-new, even though it retained many carry-over or lightly-modified parts that permitted the project to be carried out for a relatively modest investment.

Dunton's involvement on the interior comprised a completely new IP and revised door panels. A smart soft-feel four-spoke steering wheel also smartened up the appearance of the Eva, which went on sale in August 1977.

Another Dunton project involving the Granada around this time was the RS2800, dating from spring 1974. This was for a low-volume, high-performance version of the original MH Granada to be built at AVO, with a fuel-injected 2.8-litre Cologne V6, alloy wheels, stiffer suspension and Recaro seats. The studio produced a model with a modified front end and additions to the rear fender, which reflected some of the ideas being tried out for the Eva face-lift. With the imminent demise of the AVO facility and the collapse of large car sales at that time, the project went no further.

Changing role for Dunton design studio

Although the car exterior design work for mainstream programs was now being carried out in Merkenich, there remained for many years an exterior advanced design studio in Dunton, albeit small, which was sometimes asked to go beyond the advanced phase if there were multiple programs being worked on.

The Dunton designers also found themselves responsible for developing a number of special edition models that could be produced quickly outside of the main development process. These were usually done by a single designer as an ongoing exercise to

Spot the difference – Ford estate cars

Ford was very thorough at ensuring that design changes were cost-effective and when it came to face-lift time it was careful to avoid totally retooling the body, especially for the estate versions. These typically represented around 10 per cent of UK sales, so investment was always limited compared to the mainstream saloons.

The Mk II 'Brenda' Escort was the most obvious one. This was a neat amalgam of the front grille and bonnet of the new model, and the rear from the original Escort estate. Front fenders were slightly revised to take up the difference, but the entire body aft of the A-pillar was carried over, with only minor changes to rear bumper and badging to bring it up-to-date. Because the basic width between the A-pillar was unchanged, the new IP could be fitted, even with the old windscreen. The same front end-only changes were also applied to the Escort 8cwt van.

The estate version of the Mk II Eva Granada retained the old MH rear doors, roof and rear end unchanged, but the fact that the front door section had been carried over meant that the new front end could be grafted on without any further work.

The TC2 and TC3 Cortina face-lifts were probably the most subtle ones. The TC2 estate was in fact the existing 1970 Taunus TC wagon, with only front grille and fenders updated, yet UK Cortina owners perceived it as all-new. The final TC3 Cortina estate did not get the revised roof and higher door frames of the saloon, hence it continued with the same basic doors and roof pressing as used on the original 1970 Taunus wagon, right through to the end of Cortina production in 1982, although – luckily – few customers apparently noticed.

Cortina TC3 estate.

respond to sales and marketing demands for some limited edition models that could be brought to market within a three month window, either to boost sales during a seasonal lull or to shift stock of slow-selling versions that were building up in the holding compounds – so-called 'white sales' campaigns.

Design changes centred around paint finishes, applied graphics using 3M film decals, special trim or fabric upgrades and different finishes applied to wheels. All of these could be specified fairly quickly without going through the full development process, although all would need full styling approval at the regular weekly or monthly product committee reviews.

One of the first projects was the Fiesta Solitaire of June 1978, a limited edition of 2000 of the standard 1100 L Fiesta finished in either white or black, with a choice of blue or tan Ghia trim. This was followed in October by the Fiesta Kingfisher, featuring a two-tone silver and blue paint treatment, and the Granada Sapphire of May 1979.

Dunton's colour and trim group came to prominence in the 1970s, particularly for rapid creation of special edition models. Here, designers Pierre Yates and Pauline Talou discuss Fiesta special edition colours in 1977.

This latter was an upgraded Ghia 2.8 saloon in Midnight Blue over Strato Silver with S-Pack suspension and Michelin TRX tyres. The 4000-off Fiesta Sandpiper from September 1979 was another two-tone version of the 1100 L Fiesta, this time with Roman Bronze over Cordoba Beige paintwork.

Other special editions included run-out models for the Mk II Escort, including the Linnet, the Harrier and the Goldcrest, all dating from 1979-'80.

The second area of increasing importance for Dunton studio was that of providing styling input for SVE projects. This proved a rich vein of work throughout the 1980s and into the 1990s, and in many ways offset the loss of mainstream exterior design work to Merkenich.

Commercial vehicles design and the Cargo truck

A major area of importance for the Dunton studio was that of commercial vehicles, which absorbed much of the department's capacity in the decade from 1976-'86. Bob Lutz was appointed Head of Truck Operations in 1976, replacing Charlie Baldwin. Lutz had joined Ford in 1974 after a successful career at GM and then BMW, where he had been Executive Vice President of Global Sales and Marketing and overseen their rising success, particularly in motorcycles. Lutz immediately reinvigorated the truck division and made sweeping new plans, comprising a fast update for the aging D-series truck, a similar face-lift for the Transit for March 1978, and a completely new truck, to be launched as the Cargo in 1981.

In 1974 work had begun on a new Transit van – the 'Triton project' (short for 'Transit 1 ton'). But the resources needed for the all-new Cargo truck meant the Triton van work needed to be scaled back, hence the need to press ahead with a face-lift for the aging Transit Mk I.

The '78 Transit face-lift project was led by Graham Symonds. This introduced the new black corporate grille, carry-over square headlamps from the Escort Mk II and new front fenders with bold orange turn signals. The big change was the 112mm (4.5in) longer nose that was now rationalised across all engine types. By now the Pinto four-cylinder petrol engines in 1.6-litre and 2.0-litre

The Mk II Transit gained a longer front end in 1978. The work was led by Graham Symonds.

Modeller John Wall works on the revised aerofoil-section grille that was added for the 1981 model year Transit. The round headlamps were never adopted for production.

capacities had replaced the older V4s, while the York 2.4-litre diesel had replaced the older Perkins type back in 1972. The interior was updated with a new deep-dished three-spoke wheel and an IP that utilised the 'R-module' instrument pack from the Cortina. During the design period in 1977 when the truck team was flat out on the Cargo project, it 'borrowed' a small number of designers from the car team to help out. The result was a particularly successful redesign for the Transit.

Having made his mark with the acclaimed Taunus TC2 and Eva Granada projects, le Quément was then reassigned to the UK in 1974 to lead first interiors, and then the Cargo project, codenamed 'Delta.' This was a vitally important project for Ford to regain its leadership in the truck market, which by the mid-'70s was under threat with the rise of Volvo and Scania trucks, in particular. The Leyland T45

truck was due to be launched in 1980, with a cab styled by Ogle. This was seen as a big step forward in truck design at the time, and gave Ford the push it needed to allow the designers to propose a higher commitment to good design on trucks. "Where Bob Lutz played a key role was to defend the design from the cost-cutters and the engineering side – the 'good enough brigade' who felt we were going over the top," recalls le Quément. Too often the comment at meetings was "After all, it's only a bleedin' truck …"

To buy time, the designers gave the D-series a face-lift in 1978 using the square Escort headlamps and black grille, as on the Transit, whence it was known as the D/N-series. Neil Birtley was a designer on the Delta project: "The D/N-series was tired by then, and was running out of time due to imminent new regulations on head swing clearances and A-pillars, which it couldn't meet. The engineers had already designed a new chassis, and when Lutz gave the go-ahead they quickly fleshed out the rest of the package and hard points to meet all forthcoming regulations'. These included swinging a 1-tonne block into the A-pillar, and much improved driver foot protection."

The Delta project was in full swing throughout 1978-'79. Birtley continues: "The packaging guys had just got their GPGS CAD systems that showed the wire frame of the cab in perspective. To save us time we asked them to print out some pad-sized copies in various views, which then became our underlays. That was the first use of CAD in Design!"

As the Delta developed, the detail design of items such as door handles, steps into the cab, and wing mirror arms were honed, the entire composition of the cab becoming a highly satisfying piece of product design, chiefly executed by le Quément, Birtley, and Alan Jackson. Airflow management and drag reduction played a big part in the process, with the design of a series of air deflectors on the roof, together with an under-bumper air dam. The rear of the cab was also lightly flared to smooth airflow onto the rear container box. In total, these measures reduced the drag figure by up to 25 per cent, with resultant lower wind noise, and improved fuel consumption figures.

Another clever feature was the long windows in the doors, which gave excellent kerbside visibility. The steel door inner panel was still required to take loads from the upper hinge, but the glass was allowed to run flush over the panel. There was initial concern at the cost of another large piece of curved glass, but the designers discovered that the curvature was so slight it could actually be made of a flat sheet of glass, and gently bent to fit by operators on the track at Langley. To mask the inner panel, its outer surface was covered with a black plastic plinth incorporating a label carrying the model designation – all 100 versions had to be drawn up – by Birtley.

During development, there was a push from Lutz to produce something superior

The Cargo was the subject of extensive aerodynamic testing. It was even offered with aerodynamic wheeltrims, although they did not prove popular with hauliers. Headlamps were shared with the Cortina.

Dunton designers, circa 1978. (Left to right) Francois Talou, John Snooks, Jim Hirons, Neil Birtley, Mark Finney (with tee square), Brian Hughes, Bob Hutchinson, John Crutchfield, Graham Symonds, Pete Ballard, 'Walt' Disney, Dave Weston, Peter Kennedy, and John Hartnell. (Courtesy Neil Birtley)

The excellent design work on the Cargo was reflected in its award as European Truck of the Year in 1981. The model designation badge cleverly covered the steel inner door panel.

to Mercedes trucks, together with a clear link to Ford cars in terms of design, particularly the three-plane front end that had debuted on the most recent models. The degree of angle introduced was very small and did not critically affect the length of the cab. "New headlamps were also a concern since there was very little time to develop new units, yet the fashion of the day dictated that round lamps were not on-trend. Hence the decision to carry over the headlamps from the Mk V Cortina, which solved the two problems at a stroke," confirms Birtley.

Another link to Ford cars was the application of the latest Escort XR3 fabric trim, with its red strobed 'Laser' pattern giving a new sporting twist to a truck cab. This was complemented by a red pinstripe surround to all the controls on the IP, and red needles in the dials. Another touch was the use of rubber bellows as a design motif, something that Porsche had used on the bumpers of the 911. On the Cargo it was not just used on the bumpers, but was extended to the connection of the roof air snorkel, the gearshift gaiter and even the column stalk controls, with their red tips. Now the operator could feel like an XR3 driver! As with the original Transit, it made the driver feel good to be associated with the vehicle and elevated the design to a new plateau that was rare in truck design. It was an absolute master stroke.

Another commercial project that was done at Dunton at this point was the P100 pickup, styled by Pete Ballard. This used the

109

outgoing Taunus TC3 front end mounted on a strong box-section chassis frame, with an extended 2870mm wheelbase and heavy-duty leaf-sprung rear axle, giving a payload capacity of 1028kg (20cwt). With a loadbox length of 2.13m it was usefully larger than the Japanese rivals from Toyota and Mazda, which, up to then, had the UK market to themselves. The P100 was made in Ford's South Africa plant, together with a pickup version of the 'Erika' Escort van known as the Bantam, also sold as the Mazda Rustler.

Aero design comes to Ford: Escort, Sierra and Scorpio

Over in Dearborn, Design Vice President Gene Bordinat retired in December 1980 after an unparalleled 19½ years in the job. His replacement was Don Kopka, a leader who would become Ford's corporate champion of aerodynamics. American Fords in the 1970s were uncompromisingly boxy, but Kopka realised that the easiest and least expensive way to meet the CAFE (Corporate Average Fuel Economy) targets was by reshaping the car. "Up to this point the engine engineers had most of the onus for meeting CAFÉ," said Kopka in 1984. "It was almost all on their backs ... they were under the gun. Then the light went on and they began to realise they could get some help ... almost for free by just reshaping the exterior of the car." Early aero efforts included rounding off corners, eliminating projections, and adding airdams under the front bumper which had led to fuel gains of roughly 1.5mpg. Ford calculated these small gains would otherwise have cost around $200 million in engine redesigns, downsizing and lightweight materials. When Jack Telnack returned to the US in 1976, he brought his insight from his European experience with him, and teamed up with Kopka to educate Ford management in accepting the more radical looks of genuinely aerodynamic cars, including the use of flush glass, enclosed wheels and eliminating radiator grilles.

They encouraged Ghia in Turin to conduct research into aerodynamics that resulted in concepts such as the Megastar (1977) and Action (1978). Rising fuel costs in Europe meant that aerodynamic considerations were now taken very seriously, and Bahnsen was keen to get responsibility for aerodynamics firmly under his wing, which was officially achieved in 1977. One early example had been the clever slatted grille on the Fiesta, but the aerodynamicists soon turned their attention to careful management of airflow along the flanks of the vehicle. As we have seen, the design of the Cargo truck benefitted from this work but the cars were the next focus of attention.

Two large rotating and energy-dissipating vortices tend to form at the rear of any car due to slippage of air off the surfaces and the Ford team was the first to realise that it could get these vortices to turn inwards rather than outwards, thus reducing the area they occupy and the resulting drag. It was a major breakthrough in applied aerodynamics for production cars.

Ghia went on to produce the Probe series of concepts to get Ford management and the public used to these more fluid shapes. The 1979 Probe 1 had a Cd of 0.25, but that figure would come down to 0.137 as the series progressed through to 1985 with Probe V.

Project Erika – the Escort Mk III

The first European car project to benefit from this new aerodynamic approach to design was the next Escort, codenamed 'Erika.' At the early planning stages there were hopes of it being a world car, in the guise of GM's T-Car or the Toyota Corolla, but in practice the US and European versions differed considerably, even if the styling was superficially similar at first glance. One big difference was that American body presses were not large enough for the big one-piece bodyside pressings that could be stamped out in Europe.

The workload was split as follows: Merkenich did exterior design, engine and transmission design, and final development proving at Lommel. Meanwhile, Dunton took care of interior design, engine development and chassis engineering (suspension, steering and brakes), with Dunton chief Ron Mellor heading the entire engineering team.

'Erika' was designed to compete with the VW Golf as a FWD transverse-engined hatchback, the established format for cars in this sector by now. The FWD layout gave a superior package within a similar overall length of 3970mm (156.3in), with improved rear legroom, despite the height being reduced by 50mm (2in) – a key part of the objective to not increase the frontal area too much. The wheelbase was similar to the outgoing Escort at 2398mm (94.4in) but the tracks were pushed out by 100mm (4in) to provide better shoulder room in the cabin.

Design work began in October 1976 in both Dunton and Merkenich. The Dunton designers changed the design approach for interiors around this time, abandoning the metal armatures and separate padded top rolls that had been the standard IP construction since the early 1960s with large one-piece plastic mouldings. John Hartnell was one of the senior designers involved, and the new IP for Erika followed the Fiesta in its theme of a low-set shelf across most of its width, with a rectangular binnacle for the driver. Vertical sliding heater controls were mounted high up in this binnacle for easy reach with all the controls grouped around. The radio was mounted high up in the main panel rather than low down as before – part of the growing influence of ergonomics on car design at this stage.

Ford also looked hard at Japanese trim qualities, resulting in three variations of IP. The basic low-cost version was a one-piece ABS moulding as on the Fiesta with no centre air vents. Escort L versions gained the centre vents and a speaker panel. The third version had a thin polyurethane (PU) skin added over the armature to give a soft-touch feeling. This also allowed a two-colour interior to be offered, with the lower glovebox area being in a contrast colour. This higher grade design, offered on the GL, Ghia and sporting XR3 versions, also mated up to an integrated centre console with storage for the

Early Escort Mk III model being clayed up in Dunton. Lead modeller Graham King (with spectacles) inspects the work.

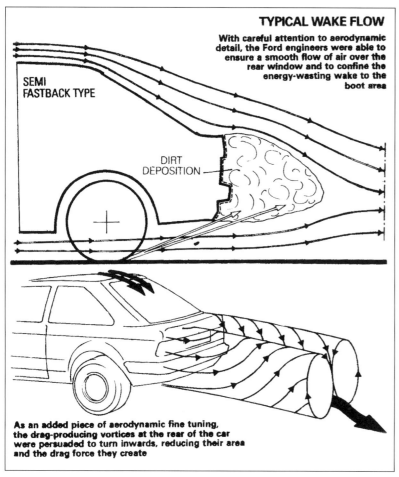

TYPICAL WAKE FLOW

With careful attention to aerodynamic detail, the Ford engineers were able to ensure a smooth flow of air over the rear window and to confine the energy-wasting wake to the boot area

SEMI FASTBACK TYPE

DIRT DEPOSITION

As an added piece of aerodynamic fine tuning, the drag-producing vortices at the rear of the car were persuaded to turn inwards, reducing their area and the drag force they create

Diagram showing the airflow management for the Escort. Wind tunnels at Fiat, VW, Mercedes in Stuttgart, and MIRA were all used in its development. (Courtesy *Motor*)

all-important music cassettes that every owner was acquiring by this stage. The instrumentation for these higher versions included five microprocessor-activated warning lights for brake pad wear, low washer fluid, low oil, low fuel and shortage of engine coolant plus a digital clock.

Rather than being made of hard phenolic plastic, steering wheels were now of a blown PU construction, with three designs being developed for Erika. The basic version and L had a two-spoke design, the GL and Ghia was a four-spoke with soft-feel rim, while the XR3 was a thick-rimmed two-spoke design.

Seats were developed from the design of the new Taunus front seats, comprising a pressed steel frame with a flexible wire mesh diaphragm supported on small coil springs to fine tune the support provided. The main cushion was PU foam with a second 15mm foam layer sewn to the top fabric layers for added comfort. A new innovation was the tall, hoop-style blown PU headrests with an optional pad insert. For the sports XR3, a new flat-woven fabric

called 'Laser' was used with distinctive strobe-effect stripes in bright red, perfectly on-trend for the 1980s. The interior design was approved in December 1978.

As a hatchback, Erika was much more versatile than the old Escort. Trunk space was now 305 litres (10.8cu ft), slightly smaller than the 385 litres (13.6cu ft) offered in the old car, but able to be extended to 1359 litres (48cu ft) when the rear seat was folded down.

As explained, the exterior design was heavily influenced by the need to improve aerodynamics. The Cd figure for the outgoing Brenda Escort was 0.448, the VW Golf was 0.43, and the Erika target was 0.40. To achieve this, a novel 'Bustleback' design was developed that not only improved the slipstream, but gave a more distinctive profile to the car. At quite a late stage the exterior was modified. "We extended the back 'bustle' by 38mm," explained Bahnsen to *Motor* magazine in 1980. "Then, instead of having just a flat rear deck we made of lip of 5mm. Then we froze the back end, and moved to the front. At the front the hood surface was extended 50mm down so that it covers the headlamps." The final Cd figure was 0.385 for the hatch, 0.390 for the estate, which was 65mm (2.5in) longer at the rear.

The Escort Mk III was launched under the slogan 'Simple is Efficient.' This five-door L is finished in Terracotta with India Red trim – bold colours typical of the period.

The Escort XR3 interior featured 'Laser' striped fabric, originally developed for the Cargo truck program.

5000 engineers, and costing £500 million, not including the £500 million investment for the new CVH engine.

The Erika went on to be a big success, being voted European Car Of The Year in 1981 – the first time Ford had gained this award. This was backed up when it received a Design Council award for "elegance of engineering, detail design and low maintenance requirements"in May 1981. By 1982, global production of the Escort was 823,000, outstripping the VW Golf (759,000) and Toyota Corolla (702,000). The XR3 was particularly successful, reaching 9 per cent of UK Escort sales by 1982 and becoming a serious challenger to the Golf GTi.

Over in the truck studio, the Erika van version was being developed, a wholly Dunton exercise. Here, the wheelbase and rear overhang were each extended by 100mm (4in) to give 2.26cu m (80cu ft) of freight and a payload of up to 550kg (11cwt) within a length of 4180mm. During development the designers found that if they used the short front doors from the four-door 'Erika' they could give a usefully longer loadbed length than the outgoing Escort van.

In order to restore the rather restricted over-shoulder visibility this produced, an extra slot window was introduced. This extra window not only gave the van a novel design feature that set it apart from all its rivals, it also gave some extra length in the bodyside to style the potentially-awkward transition between the more vertical tumblehome of the van rear body, yet did not infringe the van regulations for tax purposes. The new model went on sale in February 1981 in two guises: the Escort 35 and Escort 55 van.

Dunton later developed the Escort Combi commercial, launched in May 1986 in tandem with the 'Erika-86' face-lift. Essentially a three-door Escort estate with filled-in side windows, it offered a modest 350kg (7cwt) payload with good performance and better cab comfort on motorway runs for tradesmen who did not need the full capacity of the Escort 35 van. Both commercial models offered a diesel engine for the first time in a Ford light van, in this case a 1.6-litre with 53bhp introduced in 1983.

Unlike the estate and the van derivatives, the XR3 was not considered at first. "We looked at the coupé concept but not seriously," continued Bahnsen. "With the idea of a sports Escort we then got serious. It was not part of the program, but it was not difficult to sell. Everyone recognised the potential in management [for the XR3]."

To keep the Cd figure within target with wide 185 section tyres, the XR3 received a series of striking modifications that gave it a fashionable image. It must be said there was some definite influence from the new Porsche 928 with the XR3 design, including the 'telephone dial' alloy wheels, the large 'tea tray' rear plastic spoiler, the plastic extension to the steel front chin spoiler with spats that extended down to shroud the front wheels, and similar shrouds ahead of the rear wheels. The exterior was signed-off in summer 1978, when the final Cd figure was given as 0.375Cd, with two-door mirrors. An XR-powered XRV sports van was also shown by Merkenich studio, but not finally approved.

At launch in September 1980, Ford announced the Erika project had been a massive 'All the Fives' undertaking: five years, involving

From Bustleback to Aeroback: project 'Toni'

The next project to get the aero treatment was the Sierra, codenamed 'Toni.' This had begun as a project in Merkenich Advanced Design studio in 1977, when Bahnsen appointed Ray Everts – Chief Designer in Cologne at the time – with overall responsibility for the project, with rising star le Quément brought in as support from 1979, once the 'Delta' truck project had been signed off.

'Toni' used an all-new platform with a 2610mm (102.7in) wheelbase, MacPherson struts up front, and a new semi-trailing arm independent rear suspension, like that used by BMW. The Erika's 'Bustleback' shape was used, but developed into a softer form language called an 'Aeroback.' The roof and tail were shaped so that laminar airflow was maintained to the lip of the tailgate. Up front there was no grille. Large grey polycarbonate bumpers incorporated

The team of Merkenich designers that developed the Escort Mk III, Sierra and DE1 Granada models included the group shown here: (Left to right) Wouter de Vries, Y Iijima, Claude Lobo, and Horst Ziegner.

Tony Catignani rendering for the Sierra wagon showing the upright rear doors and large clamshell tailgate. In final production form, the model did not have the blacked-out C-pillar.

Sierra clay models in Merkenich. In 1979, the first digital model bridges had been installed in Ford studios, covered with cumbersome black cladding to protect the electrics from sulphur in the clay. Designers on the project included Klaus Kapitza, Gert Hohenester, Friedl Wülfing, and Thomas Plath.

cooling ducts to take air in through the small slot in the high pressure area below the licence plate. The result was a class-leading Cd figure of 0.34, with 0.32 for the XR4i version.

FoE VP Bob Lutz was reportedly smitten by the car, and backed it fully. The next formidable hurdle was to convince Ford's conservative US board to approve the shape. Although initially horrified by what it saw, Lutz pointed to the rapturous reception given to Giugiaro's concurrent 'Ace of Clubs' and 'Medusa' concepts. This gave the persuasive Lutz the leverage he needed for this $1.2 billion project, inspiring a fundamental shift in Ford management's centre of gravity on style. Radical was in.

Three versions of 'Toni' were designed. In addition to the five-door hatchback, there was an attractive estate version with a 115mm (4.5in) longer rear overhang, and wide clamshell-type rear tailgate. The one-piece rear doors were retooled, too, with a vertical rather than slanting C-pillar. Then there was the range-topping XR4i, a three-door hatchback with unusual Porsche 928-inspired greenhouse treatment, and wild bi-plane rear spoiler. The XR4i used the Cologne 2.8-litre injection V6 with 142bhp, and was meant to add glamour to the Sierra range, and compete against the BMW 323i and Audi coupé, but never quite achieved the success planned for it: the variant was dropped after just two years. A simpler three-door bodyshell came in to replace it in 1985, offered on all engine sizes from 1.3-litres to 2.8-litres.

Just as the exterior was radical, the interior also meant a change of direction for Ford. The big change on 'Toni' was to use a cockpit-style theme, where the centre console area was angled around the driver, an ergonomic design popularised by BMW, which sent out a clear message that this was meant to be a high-tech driver's car; not just another Cortina.

Probe III

The Probe III was developed during 1981 as a way of preparing the public for the imminent launch of the radical Cortina replacement. It was also meant to endow it with a high-tech image designed to disguise the fact that it retained the Cortina's engines and conventional RWD layout. "What makes Probe III the most significant show car yet is the fact that design chief Uwe Bahnsen insisted it should be executed within the bounds of future production viability and customer acceptance," said *CAR*. "For the most part, this objective has been achieved, and Probe III is a full five-seater saloon of standard Cortina-class dimensions."

Exterior design was mainly the work of Tony Catignani in the Merkenich studio and employed various aerodynamic features to achieve the 0.22 drag co-efficient. These included flush glass, a clean underbody, shrouded door mirrors, rear wheel spats, flexible front wheelarch fill-ins and shaped rocker panels. It also previewed the double wing rear spoiler that would be fitted to the Sierra XR4i. However, the most novel feature was the venturi belly pan that could hinge downwards as speed increased to reduce the gap between the nose and the road to create an area of negative pressure ahead of the nose and introduce some downforce.

The interior was designed in Dunton by Wyn Thomas, assisted by Jody Sadler and Martin Burgess. "The Probe was an inside/outside glass fibre showcar with just one opening door," confirms Burgess. "The interior was all-new, unrelated to the 'Toni' interior, very fresh, and very attractive to my eye. Wyn is a fabulous designer, and although everything of consequence on the Probe interior was his, I learned an immense amount by working with this extraordinary designer."

car
USA, CANADA $2.00 GERMANY 5.50DM SINGAPORE $6.50
OCTOBER 1981 75p EIRE IR£1.05 inc VAT

The high-tech secrets of
Ford's '82 Cortina!

This was the headline from *CAR* magazine when the Probe III was revealed at the Frankfurt Motor Show. Shown one year before the Sierra launch to prepare the public for the new aero-look, the Probe III was in fact done after the Sierra design was finalised. (Courtesy *CAR*)

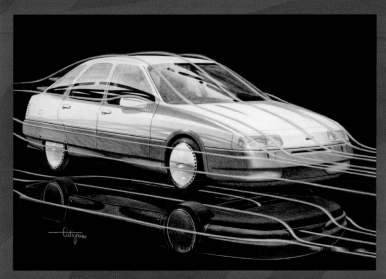

This rendering of the Probe III by Tony Catignani illustrates the smooth airflow around the car to achieve its 0.22Cd. This was one of the first instances of stylists being involved in underbody design, previously the sole preserve of the aerodynamics engineers.

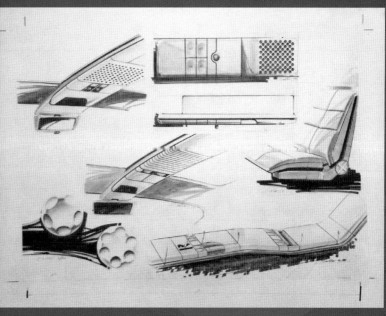

Teaser interior sketches for the Probe III interior by Jody Sadler. The instrument panel used all-digital readouts, whereas the Sierra used conventional analogue instruments.

Ford Design in the UK – 70 years of success

One design newcomer on the Toni interior was Martin Burgess, who had joined Dunton as a graduate in 1980. "Ron Saunders was the courtly interiors design manager for the studio, and he reported upwards to design executive Ron Bradshaw, and further up to the Chief Designer Trevor Creed, and ultimately to the VP of Design Ford of Europe – Uwe Bahnsen," recalls Burgess.

"Reporting to Ron Saunders in the studio was the belligerent, funny, and immensely tactless Jim Hirons. His role in the studio was called 'the grade 9' – that was a supervisory position below the manager, and in charge of the designers," he continues. Burgess confirms that the following designers also worked on the interior: Wyn Thomas, Simon Bury, Cliff Jones, Bryan Burt, Brian Osman, Alan

Thorley and, on foreign service from the US, Tony Frassetto ('the Italian Stallion'). "That's 10 designers, all in one studio, which is not something seen latterly at Ford!

"When Brian Osman, Tony Frassetto and I joined the Toni studio, the IP was already well under way. Jim Hirons had been influential in its design and I thought it was a rather 'busy' concoction and lacking freshness and a clean, clear, design statement.

"Well it just shows what I know. It emerged from market research clinics as a total triumph. People loved it, and Jim Hirons wisely credited this to its 'muchness.' 'Give people muchness and they'll feel they're getting a lot for their money,' said Jim."

Hiron's design split the IP into four zones. The primary zone

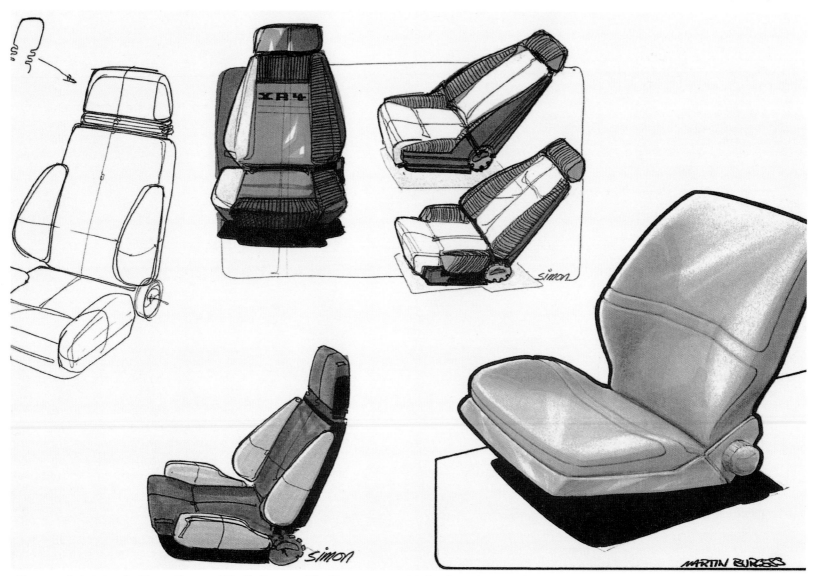

Sierra seat sketches by Simon Bury and Martin Burgess. The Sierra was notable for the softer seat forms employed, and the way that seat graphics were broken up in new ways.

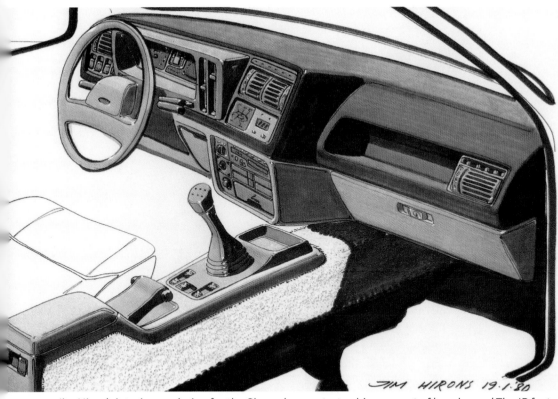

Jim Hiron's interior rendering for the Sierra demonstrates his concept of 'muchness.' The IP featured ergonomic driver zones, a fully integrated radio/cassette with speaker balance joystick, and a comprehensive array of switches – even in the roof.

One of many alternative Sierra IP models. Frank Barker is the modeller.

housed the main instruments in a black plastic pod that jutted from the main IP surface. Zone 2 housed switches for ancillary fog lights and rear wiper on the outboard side of the IP, while zone 3, below the centre air vents, was a new feature. This housed the warning and information systems, including the bank of six warning lamps for oil, coolant, low fuel, low washer fluid, brake pads, and seatbelts. An analogue and digital clock were also fitted. In addition, there was a 'graphic module' depicting the car in plan view to show whether doors are closed, and a low temperature 'snowflake' ice warning on top Ghia models. There was an optional trip computer, too – all very high-tech for 1982. Finally, zone 4 housed the radio/cassette, with spring-loaded cassette slots, plus a speaker balance joystick. Overhead there was an aircraft-style roof console with sunroof switches and two swivelling map lights.

Cabin materials were also a definite step up from those on the outgoing Cortina. This also reflected research conducted into female taste in upholstery and switchgear, via consumer clinics during development. New structured velour Sandford and Chatsworth fabrics were used, together with cut pile carpet, and a brushed nylon headliner. The parcel shelf was covered in a needlepunch felt, and housed an integrated first aid kit.

Creed saw the project through to production but was then seconded to Dearborn in 1982 to follow through with the interior program of the 1986 Ford Taurus and Mercury Sable. Although due to return in 1985, in a repeat of the situation with Colin Neale, he chose to switch to Chrysler instead, where he remained until his retirement in 2008. Likewise, Ray Everts was drafted back to Dearborn for the crucial Taurus/Sable project, and was replaced as Chief Designer of Ford Germany by le Quément.

Job One in Genk was June 1982, with the car launched in September, under the slogan: 'Man and Machine in Perfect Harmony.' Dagenham production was added in 1983.

Final production version of the Sierra in basic 1.6-litre form. Taking its lead from the surface treatment of the Porsche 928, it heralded a sea change by employing soft, organic forms, which contrasted with the sharp, origami treatment that was then the norm. The Sierra was unusually colour-sensitive, looking somewhat heavy in solid colours, as shown here.

The Sierra 'Boilerhouse Project' was hosted in October 1982 by art critic Stephen Bayley, aided by Martin Burgess. This was the first time a car design project had been presented at a public exhibition in the UK, and was a significant milestone for Ford Design. (Courtesy Martin Burgess)

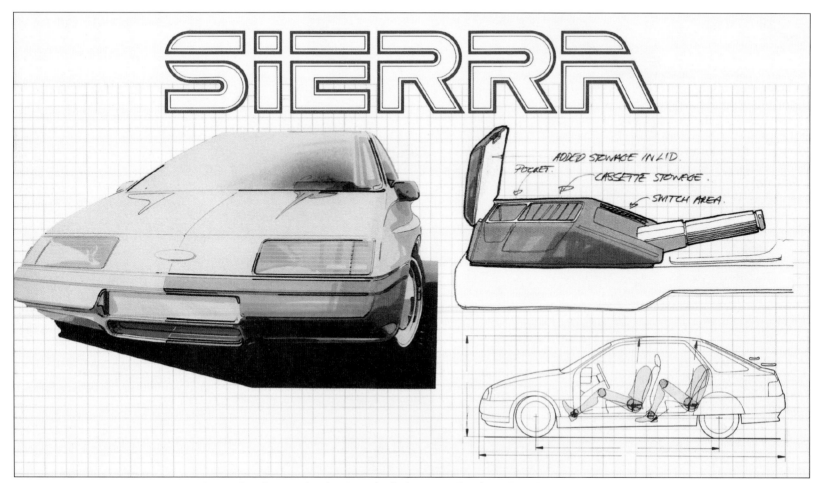

Promotional poster for the Sierra 'Boilerhouse Project,' entitled *The Car Program*.

Following the launch, there was some criticism of poor directional stability in crosswinds. But the biggest bone of contention was the car's looks. While Ford PR waxed long and lyrical about 'aero styling,' the Sierra soon acquired nicknames including 'jelly mould' and 'the salesman's spaceship,' a snide reference to the car's popularity with fleet buyers.

In October 1982, London's Victoria and Albert Museum 'Boilerhouse Project' hosted an exhibition about how the Sierra had been designed. Arranged by design critic Stephen Bayley, the exhibition was the first time an automotive design project had been presented at a public exhibition in the UK, complete with clay models and interior bucks. As such, it was a significant milestone for Ford Design, bringing automotive styling the recognition and credibility it deserved as a professional design activity in the 1980s.

However, it was not always easy being a designer at Ford. Recalling his time at Dunton, Burgess says "Working on models with the clay modellers was a baptism of fire. In Design, there were three distinct people functions: designers, clay modellers and design engineers – plus the (external to Design) function of product planners. There was a large degree of rivalry, and, I have to say, significant antagonism, particularly between the designers and the clay modellers and the designers and the design engineers.

"The idea seemed to be to always catch out, or to wrong foot, the designer. It could be quite spiteful, and the idea of working together for the common good was alien. I disliked it, but people who survived the Ford mill could take on the world. I came to learn that elsewhere in the industry, the brutal killing machine that was Ford was held in awe."

DE1 Scorpio

The replacement for the Granada, the DE1 Scorpio, arrived in March 1985. This design was the third big aero-influenced project carried out by the Merkenich studio, with Dunton responsible for the interior design. This time around there would be no estate version, the five-door hatchback layout being deemed a good compromise for this executive sector. At that time, the large executive hatchback was fully in vogue, with models such as the Rover SD1, Saab 9000, Fiat Croma and Renault 25 selling in good volumes. It is easy to forget, but the Granada was still a decent value-for-money contender in those days against a BMW 5 Series or Mercedes E-Class in the executive E-segment, with a good reputation as a company car in the key markets of the UK and Germany.

The Fiesta was face-lifted for 1982, becoming the Mk II. It gained a new nose and totally revised interior with two different IP variants.

The styling followed the 'Aeroback' style set by the Sierra, with a flush sloping nose and slim headlamps flanking a thin grille slot. As on the Sierra, doors were a one-piece pressing, but were of the clamshell style with no exposed gutter seam – a new design for Ford that was shared with the US Taurus. The large hatchback opened to reveal a huge trunk that could be enlarged by folding the split rear seat.

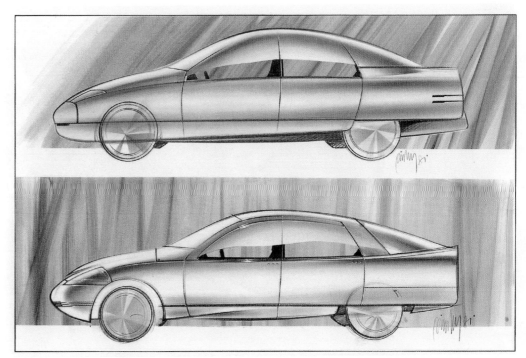

Aero sketches for DE1 Granada, by RCA graduate Pinky Lai.

Granada interior buck in Dunton. Under its compound curvature rear glass hatchback, the Granada boasted a large 439-litre trunk, although the track was considered rather narrow for the class.

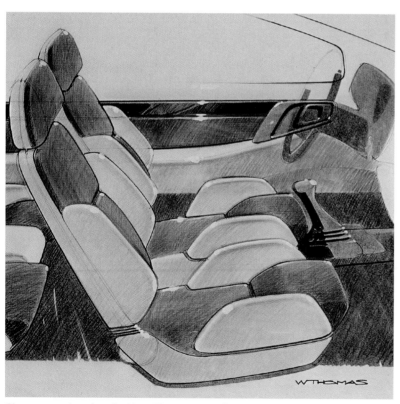

Sierra seat sketches by Wyn Thomas. Ford's interior sketching reached new levels of excellence with the latest generation of designers recruited to Dunton in the 1980s.

SVE and motorsport

Following the launch of the RS2000 and the closure of AVO in 1975, Ford had lacked a specialist vehicle unit. However, in February 1980 this was revived under the leadership of Rod Mansfield, former Engineering Manager at AVO. This new Special Vehicle Engineering unit, or SVE, comprised a small group of ten engineers based within Dunton, and was responsible for a string of exciting Fords during the 1980s.

In an interview with *Cars & Car Conversions* in June 1982, Mansfield said "People do desire more sporting, faster and jazzier versions of production cars, and although I guess the fuel crisis knocked it off for a while, you can't keep people down forever – they do want that sort of car. Certainly I think marketing, after the demise of AVO, had been desiring mainstream engineering to produce that sort of car. They would say something like, 'If only we had a top of the range Capri that we could sell, we'd sell more Capris.' That has been their requirement."

Thus, the first car from this group was the Capri 2.8 Injection, which was developed over nine months and initially sold only in left-hand drive form for Germany. This was followed with a right-hand drive version, then the Fiesta XR2 in 1981 and the Escort RS Turbo in 1985. The Dunton and Merkenich studios were fully involved in the styling additions for these cars, including clever use of decals and wheelarch extensions to give a strong, sporty image.

In addition to SVE, Ford had its motorsport division based at Boreham, responsible for building and developing the specialist rally and Group A saloon cars, and the two teams would work closely together, with SVE responsible for developing the road cars.

SVE was set up as a small department aside from the mainstream engineering group in order to develop the cars in a short space of time, although production would always take place within an existing Ford plant. "Everybody in Ford could understand it," continued Mansfield, "but it would result in a hell of a mess if you confused the mainstream programs with it. Therefore, obviously what you do is set up a separate department, which doesn't get involved with mainstream but does have full responsibility for carrying out these sorts of projects."

By 1991, Rod Mansfield had moved to Dearborn to extend the SVE setup in the US. SVE was later responsible for much of the Puma development in the 1990s, but by the late '90s SVE activities had been absorbed back into mainstream product development activity. Rather than being seen as a failure of SVE, it should be regarded as an example of how the efficient processes and methods developed by SVE could subsequently be adopted by the main program teams, becoming part of a more flexible product development workflow.

DE1 used an extended version of the Sierra platform and shared many basic components, including the front and rear suspension. Although the wheelbase was up by 150mm (6in) over the Sierra, the track remained similar, with only the front track being widened – by just 25mm (1in). Known as the Scorpio in Europe, the UK sales organisation insisted on carrying on with the Granada nameplate, due the difficult experience it had replacing the popular Cortina name with Sierra.

The interior design incorporated the very latest in terms of soft-feel materials and equipment. The IP continued the Ford house style with a wraparound black capping for the driver's binnacle. It was made using a process known as slush moulding, as used by

BMW and Honda, to give a high quality feel to the panel with a large-scale embossed grain. The 2760mm (108.7in) wheelbase offered an extremely spacious and comfortable rear cabin. Top versions had rear seats with an electric recline function and twin headphone jacks built in, features only recently available in flagship luxury cars such as the Mercedes S-Class. The design was handled by Martin Burgess, Alan Thorley and Paul Gebbett, the latter having rejoined Ford in 1982, having spent the previous nine years over at Vauxhall.

Throughout the 1980s, Ford had popularised the tilt/sliding glass sunroof with integrated louvered shutter, a feature that most other manufacturers had since copied. Finally, there was better awareness of decent vehicle security, with features such as central locking, high security Chubb door locks and radio aerials incorporated in the rear glass.

Scorpio was certainly the most impressive European Ford made to date and was recognised as such by the European press, gaining another Car of the Year award in 1986.

Motorsport's big gamble – RS200

By the early 1980s, Ford's motorsport activities in Europe were in disarray. With the introduction of the FWD Erika Escort it no longer had a competitive basis for a rally car, plus the whole rallying scene had been overturned by the arrival of the 4WD Audi Quattro. Following the setup of SVE and then the appointment of Stuart Turner to lead the Motorsport division in February 1983, there was a renewed commitment to developing a new generation of Rallye Sport Fords to bring excitement and competition wins back to the company. A new strategy was quickly rolled out to develop three Rallye Sport vehicles:

1. A Group A and N car for the clubman enthusiast. This was to be a turbocharged version of the Escort XR3 (the RS Turbo), followed by a derivative of the planned 4WD Escort.

2. A Group A saloon car racer, using a turbocharged 2.0-litre Cosworth engine to be based on the RWD Sierra (the Sierra RS Cosworth).

3. An international rally winner, a mid-engined specialist machine to be built under Group B rules, requiring 200 examples to be built for homologation.

Limited volume 'Evolution' models would also be brought out to ensure the cars could maintain their competitive edge.

The first two projects were engineered by SVE, with Merkenich handling the design input. For the last of these projects, Mike Moreton and Stuart Turner approached Dunton studio's new Chief Designer, Andy Jacobson, in March 1983 for support, and were rewarded with designer Tony Catignani, who was seconded to produce some preliminary sketch ideas for the first management review of the project.

The engineering design was put out for tender to four contending motorsport engineers, with Tony Southgate and John Wheeler being finally selected to develop the layout, which used the aborted Escort RS1700T Cosworth engine in a steel and aluminium honeycomb chassis. To avoid interfering with ongoing production programs in Merkenich and Dunton, it was agreed to use Ghia in Turin to develop the styling design, and Moreton visited Filippo Sapino in April 1983 to run through the brief with him. Thirty initial sketches were produced by Ghia and reviewed by Ford Motorsport later that summer. The only trouble was, it didn't like any of them …

"It was a great disappointment, so we talked to Andy Jacobson," says Moreton. "He seemed to understand what we wanted and offered to give us a theme sketch, using the Sierra screen as a key hard point." This relatively upright front screen had several advantages: it provided good visibility for rally drivers, would be easy to source worldwide in case of likely frequent replacements, gave a spacious cockpit that wouldn't get too stuffy and hot, and – last but not least – provided some family resemblance to the production cars.

Moreton collected the sketch from Jacobson's house in Boreham one weekend, and set off for Turin to tactfully see if Sapino might be persuaded to produce something like this. "Big mistake," continues Moreton. "He hit the ceiling as only an Italian can. 'These are only theme sketches, you guys don't understand them and you have the nerve to bring me a sketch done by this Andy Jacobson, which he rushed up over a weekend. I am sorry but you have to trust us or we will not do the job.'"

After 20 minutes and a few frantic phone calls to Dearborn, Sapino finally agreed to incorporate the Sierra screen in the design and discussions moved forward positively. By September, new sketches had been produced by Ghia for the second stage approval of $250,000 to produce a running prototype. Once granted, work proceeded rapidly at Ghia to produce a full-size clay of the design. This used round frogeye-style Carello headlamps, plus a bank of four distinctive Carellos mounted on a central block for rallies.

In addition to the screen, the doors were based on the Sierra too, suitably cut down and modified below the shoulder line to suit the new styling. Front and rear ends had large fully-hinged panels to allow easy access at rally service points. The clay model was approved in December 1983 at Ghia and shipped to the UK so that body moulds could be taken.

For the interior Dunton was again involved. Designers John Hartnell and Ian Callum were dispatched to Boreham to produce a wood and clay mock-up of the instrument panel, which was symmetrical for RHD and LHD and designed to be easily adapted for rally modifications.

Initial testing of prototype 001 in March 1984 found that the exterior design needed some fundamental modifications to make it work successfully. The rear engine compartment became far too hot, and wind tunnel testing showed that more downforce was needed to improve traction, especially at the rear. Hartnell and Callum redesigned the front air dam, the intercooler was mounted on the

RS200 prototype 001 in Dunton, with clay additions by Ian Callum and John Hartnell to increase downforce and improve cooling.

roof in a neat cowling, a big rear spoiler was added, and larger side ears were added for the rally cars to get air to the brakes. Far from detracting from the design, these changes added greatly to the character of the car and were incorporated from prototypes 002-006.

Subsequent development of the RS200 was somewhat convoluted. Manufacture of the remaining 194 cars for homologation was contracted out over a four month period from October 1985 to Reliant in Shenstone, Staffordshire, including production of the GRP body panels (or Kevlar on the rally cars). However, in spring 1986, FISA announced the cancellation of Group B from the end of that year, following a series of fatal accidents including Henri Toivonen and Sergio Cresto in their Lancia Delta S4. This meant the entire rationale for the RS200 was swept away overnight and Ford needed to rapidly refocus its efforts on marketing the remaining 148 cars to private customers. The Shenstone assembly was wound down in May 1986, and Aston Martin Tickford were then contracted to refine and rebuild the cars to fully saleable condition at £52,950, a difficult remit that took up to July 1989 to complete.

It had been a good decade for Bahnsen. By the early 1980s he was recognised as Ford's design figurehead, and had established a clear look for Ford in Europe across its car, van and truck ranges, with numerous design awards along the way. Likewise, Ford had achieved market leadership in the UK in cars and commercial vehicles, not to mention its superb tractor range. It was all looking so good, what could possibly go wrong?

RS200 model being inspected by Uwe Bahnsen and Andy Jacobson. John Hartnell stands right.

Uwe Bahnsen at his happiest, leaning on his most radical project. This was taken soon after the Sierra launch in 1982.

Chapter

6

The peak years

Although in its first full year on sale the Sierra held second place in the British sales charts, by 1984 it had dropped to fifth, well behind the Vauxhall Cavalier. By the end of the year the atmosphere at Ford was pretty torrid and the experience brought a very conservative mood back to Ford, with scapegoats being sought throughout the company.

Commenting on the Sierra, design critic Stephen Bayley wrote: "Not since the Edsel has a mass-market car been so controversial. Now that Sierras have passed out of even the provincial minicab trade, it's necessary to explain the mass-hysteria this car caused. It was bold, striking, contrarian, sophisticated and offered a complacent public a taste of what creativity could offer. Bahnsen said: 'I like people to think that cars are more than basic transport.' Unfortunately, people thought exactly that, but not in the way Bahnsen intended. People thought that the Sierra offered the unwelcome extra of cringing personal embarrassment."

Bahnsen ousted, conservativism rules

By now, Ford was committed to Bahnsen's DE1 Scorpio, too, and already the doomsayers were circling. By the early 1980s le Quément was back as head of the Merkenich studio. As Bahnsen's long-time protégé, le Quément was seen as being groomed to replace him as VP of Design, but the poor reception and sales performance of the Sierra, especially in the vital UK market, saw le Quément falling out of favour. With Bahnsen looking increasingly sidelined, and seeing their ambitions thwarted at Ford, in June 1985, le Quément decided to jump ship to VW, while fellow designer Harm Lagaay moved to BMW Technik, and subsequently to Porsche in 1989 as Chief Designer.

Under increasing pressure, Bahnsen took early retirement from Ford in 1986, going on to become head at the Art Center College of Design in Vevey, Switzerland, which he successfully ran between 1986 and 1995.

Bob Lutz had been the other main protagonist behind the Sierra, but had returned to the USA in charge of Ford International Operations in 1982, thus managing to avoid the flack once the car went on sale. As the heat turned up, however, he realised he was unlikely to be offered the top job by the Ford family and was lured over to Chrysler by his old patron Lee Iacocca in 1986 as Executive Vice President, also persuading designer Trevor Creed to join him to head up interiors. The car industry is a small world indeed ...

As first evidence of the reactionary approach running through the corridors at Warley, the Orion was developed to fill the gap left by Cortina/Taunus. Known as 'Project Apollo,' this was a straightforward three-box version of the Escort that was hastily developed during 1982 and launched in July 1983. The conservative fleet market in the UK was still wary of hatchbacks and there was a short-lived trend for booted versions of C-segment models at the time. Examples included the VW Jetta, Vauxhall Astra, Talbot Solara, Austin Montego, and Volvo 360.

Patrick le Quément led the Cargo truck project at Dunton. He left Ford for VW in 1985, subsequently becoming Renault's Director of Design in 1989.

Uwe Bahnsen and Andy Jacobson. Jacobson took over as VP of Design in 1986.

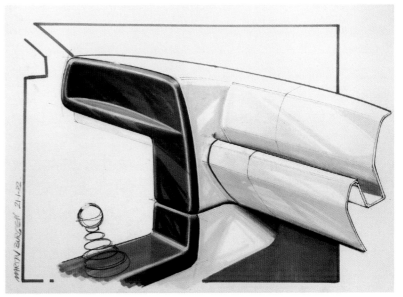

1986 Escort interior sketch by Martin Burgess. The program was initially managed by Ron Saunders, with John Hartnell as the 'Grade 9' supervisor. The final design was rather different from this early sketch, but the black capping theme was a mainstay of Ford interiors throughout the 1980s. (Courtesy Martin Burgess)

Two years later there was a face-lift for the Erika Escort, known within Ford as 'Erika-86.' This updated the styling of the previous Escort model with a large grey plastic bumper moulding giving a smooth style nose and the sawtooth rear tail lamps at the rear being smoothed over. The revised Dunton-designed interior built on much of the Fiesta Mk II face-lift work carried out in 1983, with use of a polypropylene plastic IP featuring a silkier touch than the older plastics. The new IP was inspired by the DE1 Scorpio, with use of softer forms throughout than the older Erika design but using a one-piece moulding. As on the DE1, the passenger side was scooped away and contained a deep storage pouch, while the driver's binnacle swept rearwards and was capped with a black plastic surround containing the secondary switches. The slider-type heater controls were redesigned as rotary controls, and moved down to the centre console area and Chubb-type high-security door locks were specified.

Next up was the Sierra Sapphire saloon, developed at some considerable cost of £228 million. Launched in February 1987 it sold well, not least because it included the Sierra styling revisions introduced at the same time. These included a proper grille aperture, less grey plastic and far nicer alloy wheels. Most importantly, the side windows were revised in two ways. Firstly, the upper edges were extended into the door frame pressing by 25mm. Secondly the radius on all corners was reduced, tightening the whole side view of the car and giving the impression of much larger windows. In some ways it was a repeat of the TC3 Mk V Cortina greenhouse exercise.

Ford Design in the UK – 70 years of success

The Sierra went on to capture much of the success of Cortina but it took until the Mondeo in the 1990s for Ford to wrest back the market from GM's Cavalier/Ascona for that success to be truly regained.

Following the departure of the successful management team of Bahnsen, le Quément and Creed, the design studios in Europe were once again led by a series of American design managers. First up was Andy Jacobson, who had been Dunton's Chief Designer since 1983, replacing Bahnsen as VP of Design in 1986. Like many Americans from Dearborn (and indeed Bahnsen himself), he found it easier to be based in the UK, close to London and FoE headquarters in Warley, and with better flight connections to the US and Europe than Cologne.

The Sierra was due for a face-lift in 1988, to tide it over until the Mondeo. This clay IP model for a revised 'Sierra X,' dating from April 1986, picks up many period interior themes being used on the Escort and DE1 Scorpio. The interior project did not finally go ahead. (Courtesy Martin Burgess)

Dunton studio in the early 1980s. Large plan chests and drawing boards were still very much in evidence in this pre-digital era.

Initial VE6 sketches by Neil Birtley, from 1981. (Courtesy Neil Birtley)

The VE6 Transit

While the car side was suffering numerous rifts and politics, the commercial vehicles team members based at Dunton had their heads down, and continued to be busy for much of the early 1980s on the replacement for the Transit van. By 1985, two million Transits had been sold, with Ford having more than 30 per cent of the European light commercial vehicle market. Despite having had a decent face-lift in 1978, by the early '80s it was showing its age.

As mentioned in the previous chapter, there had been an earlier project for a new Transit van back in 1974 – the Triton project. As part of that work, Ford had commissioned Heuliez in France to provide an alternative proposal, which turned out to be rather mundane and was rejected, although the design resurfaced some years later as the Renault Master! However, the idea that the front of a van should be a simple wedge was gaining currency, and this theme became the dominant one for the styling direction of the new project, codenamed VE6. It was a £400 million program, including £100 million in Southampton plant upgrades to include robotised welding lines – the first such installation in a Ford plant.

The VE6 design was led by Graham Symonds, with Neil Birtley being one of the main designers for the exterior and Mark Finney on interior. The overall aim was for a more efficient Transit, fit for the 1980s, with a strong emphasis on improved fuel economy, achieved through low drag and lighter weight, yet with a bigger and stronger body. This could be accomplished using new CAD design methods for body engineering and advances in technologies and materials to give fewer rust traps in the body and lower overall maintenance costs. Work started around 1981 with a series of full-size clay models being produced. As on the Cargo truck, there was a desire to give the VE6 a recognisable Ford look, including a three-plane front end, housing a wide slatted black grille with large rectangular headlamps and flanking orange turn signals. A lot of time was spent in the wind tunnel to

VE6 sketch. Aero priorities led to the investigation of rear wheel spats. (Courtesy Neil Birtley)

refine the design, with a final 0.37 Cd figure achieved, giving an 8 per cent improved fuel consumption.

One major objective was an improved driving position. The seats were moved forward and mounted higher up to give a more comfortable steering wheel angle and better vision over the plunging bonnet. Following the latest ergonomic practice, the design team began by laying out the cab first, then fixing the key lines of the interior and exterior design once the package had been established.

The new cab was wider, allowing more relaxed three-abreast seating and less wheelarch intrusion than the old model. The one-piece IP was made from polypropylene, and was one of the largest of its type made for the automotive industry, with a transverse metal reinforcing strut to reduce rattles. The style mirrored that of the recent 'Erika-86' and Fiesta models, with sliding heater controls and

a black-capped binnacle moulding, this being much deeper than on the cars. Extensive customer research revealed the need for lots more storage spaces, too, and easier access into the cab for short, multi-drop deliveries. Seats incorporated blown polypropylene headrests too, echoing the design of the Erika Escort.

Although the cab was all-new, much of the rear underbody was carried over from the outgoing van. The rear axle on the SWB was pushed rearwards 123mm (4.8in) to allow for a sliding side door width of 1028mm (40.5in), enough for loading a 1.2m by 0.8m wooden Euro-pallet sideways through the aperture. SWB models gained independent MacPherson strut suspension for improved ride and handling using 14in wheels as before. The LWB model with dual rear wheels used a carry-over rear floorpan and axles from the old model, and stayed with a solid I-beam front axle arrangement for now.

Transit VE6 sign-off model in Dunton showroom, December 1982.

VE6 clays in the commercial vehicle studio, circa 1982.

Helped by the use of CAD analysis tools, the bodyshell was just 415kg, which gave improved performance, also helped by the availability of a new five-speed transmission, based on the Sierra and Granada gearbox. The engine line-up now comprised a 1.6-litre, 2.0-litre and 3.0-litre V6 petrol, plus a 2.5-litre DI diesel. To provide more versatility, a new LWB derivative with single rear wheels was developed for transporting light but high cube loads. In addition, an extended wheelbase (EWB) dual rear wheels chassis cab version with a 3472mm (136.7in) wheelbase was available through SVO, giving payloads from 908kg to 2212kg on the chassis cabs.

As before, a wide range of standard body options and specifications was offered. This included 13- and 17-seater Crewbuses using longitudinal slatted wooden benches, low and high roof options for the SWB van, and a double crew cab option for the LWB chassis cab.

Since 1963, Ford's team of dedicated engineers, finance and purchasing specialists had steadily developed the SVO setup to offer an outstanding range of unique vehicles, options and equipment. Working closely with specialist body builders and suppliers, SVO was now able to offer a range from ambulance and PSV conversions, 4x4s, and parcel delivery bodies to police vans. Over 20 per cent of production from Southampton now had some SVO content.

However, with the imminent sell-off of the trucks division and the Langley plant to Iveco, SVO had to relocate back to Dunton soon after the VE6 was launched in January 1986. This effectively marked the end of the UK Ford truck engineering operation, with the Transit team absorbed back into Dunton main engineering offices, and staffing at truck product planning at Trafford House in Basildon being drastically reduced.

Disposing of trucks and tractors

In 1983, Ford was approached by the UK government to engage in talks to merge the commercial vehicle business with Leyland trucks, which led to discussions about whether Ford might buy the whole of the government's share in British Leyland. In the end, Ford decided to sell the trucks division to Fiat-Iveco in 1986, forming Iveco Ford Truck Ltd, or IFT. Production of the Cargo and Transcontinental trucks continued at Langley.

Since the 1960s, Ford had also achieved market leadership in tractors, although all design work was centred in America rather than the UK. In 1975, the 1000-Series was redesigned as the 600-, and shortly after, the 700-Series, which featured new styling and a greater level of cab comfort. The top-spec 'Q cab' reduced noise levels to 82db. With the 1980s came the 10-Series which debuted in 1981. This comprised 10 models ranging from 41hp (2910 model) to 110hp (8210 model).

Ford purchased New Holland tractors in 1985, but was soon looking for a way out of the tractor business entirely. In 1991, the Basildon plant of Ford-New Holland was sold to Fiat-Iveco as part of the sell-off of the whole commercial vehicles business. The deal required that Fiat stop using the Ford name on tractors, and from 1999 Fiat removed all Ford identification from their blue tractors, rebranding them 'New Holland.'

Celebrating 20 years of Dunton

In October 1986, Dunton Research and Engineering Centre celebrated its 20th anniversary. In the past two decades it had grown considerably and was now home to 3500 staff, with over 33,000sq m of workshops and test facilities. The high speed test track running past the design centre had been completed in 1973, and other special skid pans and handling tracks had been added, although the main development proving ground was in Lommel, Belgium. Construction on a new £10 million Electrical and Electronics Operations Technical Centre had started in 1986. Data and communication links had been established from 1978, with Dunton and Merkenich able to access Ford's Cyber 176 computer mainframe in the US by satellite. Now, the engineers were able log onto Ford's Cray, Multics and DEC VX machines in Dearborn too.

In 1981, the design centre block had been extended by 1200sq m (12,900sq ft) when the feasibility section was extended out into the viewing yard, although at 6870sq m (74,000sq ft) the yard was still large enough for long-range viewings. The showroom now had three turntables for design presentations, fax and slide presentation facilities had been introduced and the video conferencing suite arrived in 1984 – the first such facility in Europe.

CAD comprised mainly computer analysis in the early days, used for body engineering, stress testing, and chassis design. The first few CAD workstations for Ford Design had arrived in 1985, to support the advanced exterior studio.

Dunton aerial view, 1987. The design block is the nearest building, with the reception entrance to the right. By 1987, the studio had expanded into the viewing yard – compare to the photo on page 76. The looped test track was added in 1973.

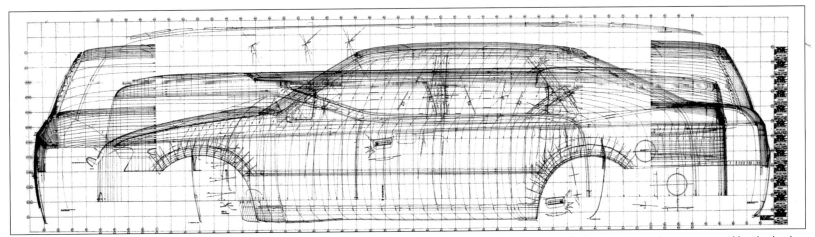

Gerber plotters were used to generate full size linesdraft plots, such as this of the DE1 Granada. These overlaying cross-sections were used by the body engineers to develop the final press tooling for the body.

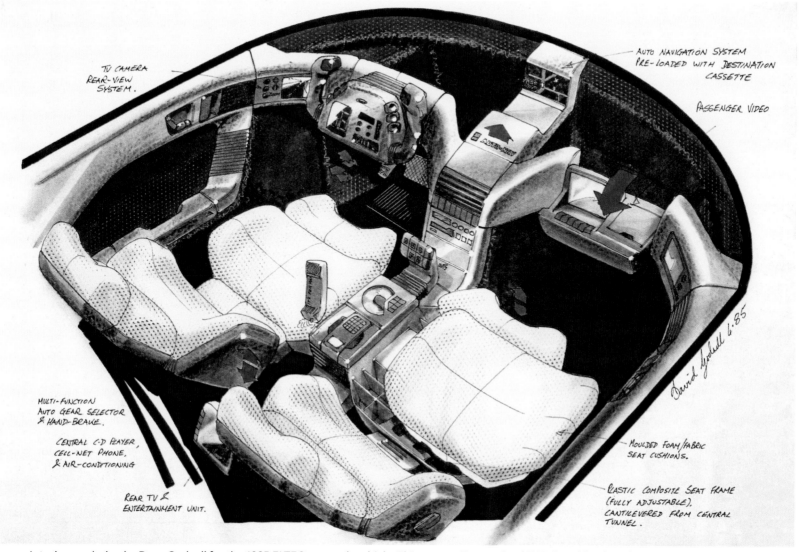

TV CAMERA REAR-VIEW SYSTEM.

AUTO NAVIGATION SYSTEM PRE-LOADED WITH DESTINATION CASSETTE

PASSENGER VIDEO

MULTI-FUNCTION AUTO GEAR SELECTOR & HAND-BRAKE.

CENTRAL C-D PLAYER, CELL-NET PHONE, & AIR-CONDITIONING

REAR TV & ENTERTAINMENT UNIT.

MOULDED FOAM/FABRIC SEAT CUSHIONS.

PLASTIC COMPOSITE SEAT FRAME (FULLY ADJUSTABLE). CANTILEVERED FROM CENTRAL TUNNEL.

Interior rendering by Dave Godsell for the 1985 ELTEC research vehicle. This was an Escort-sized FWD hatchback with a special low-drag body. Microprocessors controlled the aluminium 1.3-litre engine, CVT gearbox, air springs and dampers, and ABS brakes.

The studios had also been upgraded, now comprising three main studios, covering car interiors, advanced exteriors, commercial vehicles, colour and trim, plus special value programs – namely, for special editions or support for SVE. The first computerised scan bridges arrived in 1979, followed by motorised scan/mill bridges in 1985.

When asked about how cars would look in future, Andy Jacobson said "I would say a drag coefficient of 0.25 is a very aggressive number for a mass-produced car – in pure body aerodynamics it's very difficult to achieve. It means spending a lot of money on special airflow devices like ducted cooling and shielding, sealing off gaps and perhaps running on special narrow tyres."

Ford had expanded the design staff continuously throughout the 1980s. New designers included Graham Thorpe, Ian Callum, Jim Kelly, and Dave Godsell. As well as collaborating with the RCA in London, Ford had also begun to recruit graduate designers from the new Transportation Design course at Coventry Polytechnic (now Coventry University). The first young graduate recruited from the Coventry course was Anthony Grade in 1980, then Steve Aris and Simon Spearman-Oxx in 1987, followed by designers David Woodhouse, Neil Simpson, Paul Gibson, Martin Frost, Stuart Cooper and Phil Simmons. Moving the other way was Neil Birtley, who moved to Coventry University as a tutor in 1986, staying until his retirement in 2008, and Ron Saunders who became a tutor at Coventry and subsequently, from 2002, the RCA.

Dunton studio at its zenith

In the mid-1980s, Dunton design studio had expanded headcount to nearly 300 staff. This well-oiled machine had the capability to produce multiple full-size exterior and interior clay models, interior package bucks, plus fully-detailed exterior and interior GRP models for product committee reviews and customer clinics. It could also produce running prototypes, such as the Eltec concept of 1986.

Design teams were organised into three groups, comprising a total of 52 designers. The 22-strong interiors team was headed by Ron Bradshaw, with commercial vehicles managed by John Fallis. Colour and trim was led by Eric Archer, with 15 specialist designers to handle all Ford Europe paint colours, interior fabrics, plastics development and colour and grain mastering. A small team also handled special editions projects and body graphics, including badges and emblems.

The clay modellers were managed by Gerry Brown, Jack Bish and John Cradduck with modellers split into 26 experienced lead modellers and 44 staff and younger modellers divided into exterior and interior teams. In addition, there was a separate hard modelling group of 50 who undertook all GRP mouldings, wooden armatures and detailed hard plastic models such as air vents or heater control panels. Vic Smith headed up the experimental trim shop, with 13 trimmers on board.

Next, there was design engineering, managed by Geoff Howard and John Weaver. Within that group of 65 there was a feasibility team that would develop the initial package drawings with engineering, and release detailed design solutions for engineers to productionise. Two other teams looked after regulations, homologation, supplier approvals and master model sign-offs. Another design quality group (surveillance) team of older, experienced designers ensured that parts released for production complied with acceptable standards within Ford. Charlie Thompson and John Pritchard were part of this team.

Final detail preparation of an interior 'half buck' in Dunton's workshops. (Courtesy Martin Burgess)

A demonstration of the immense resources that were used at Dunton in the 1980s. This shows the interior team involved in producing no less than 11 interior bucks for the CDW27 program. (Courtesy Martin Burgess)

Finally there was a support group of 30 staff for design project timing, timesheets and front office administration, including the design studio car fleet. This group included a team of nine shifters and stores people.

Merkenich studio had a similar structure within design, comprising 21 designers, 60 clay modellers, 40 wood and metal fabricators, 28 design engineers, plus 12 ancillary staff. However, it was around half the size overall, and did not routinely handle interiors or colour and trim. Compared to the combative atmosphere in the early days of Ford of Europe, designers from UK and Germany were now encouraged to do six-weekly swaps to build skills and spread team spirit across the two studios.

"It's worth emphasising how exhaustive the concept stages were at that time," recalls Martin Burgess. "Several designers were tasked with presenting proposals in sketch form and then in clay model form, for every single interior element."

"I can well remember the line-up of steering wheel proposals where most of the designers in the studio had produced one model – and some more than one. The steering wheel concept clay proposals for the Toni program amounted to 12 models. These days there would probably be just a few sketches by one individual, resulting in one clay model of, for instance, a steering wheel – but I think that the exhaustive competitive approach did have merit."

Pragmatism rules: Fiesta Mk III, Escort Mk IV

This was the juncture when an all-new worldwide program designation system was devised. This new Mk III Fiesta program was called BE13. The 'B' represented the vehicle segment (B car) and the 'E' represented the global region – Europe – and the 13 showed that this was the thirteenth program to adopt the new designation system. In fact, the very first program to use this designation system was the Granada/Scorpio – the DE1 ('D' segment/'E' for Europe/'1' for the global first).

The Fiesta BE13 was designed during 1985-'87. The original Bobcat had sold over five million by this point, achieving everything that had been expected of it, but after 12 years it was clearly due a major revamp. The BE13 was to be based on a new platform ditching the old car's rear beam axle for a semi-independent torsion beam arrangement, and addressed the principal weakness of the previous generation – the lack of a five-door version. This was tackled with an increase in wheelbase of 158mm (6.2in) that allowed the new Fiesta to compete head-on with the bench mark Peugeot 205, a car proving phenomenally successful for Peugeot in the 1980s. The BE13 program cost £550 million, with the new car unveiled at the end of 1988, officially going on sale in February 1989 with prices from £5199 for the Fiesta Popular 1.0-litre.

As usual, the exterior was done in Merkenich, with the interior as a Dunton project. As on the outgoing Fiesta and latest Escort, the IP was a large one-piece polypropylene moulding styled very much in the vein of the Escort, with four air vents, a proper lidded glovebox and generous dash top storage areas. This time around the interior team of Tom Scott, Martin Burgess and Anthony Grade came up with a single design for the Fiesta that was common to all variants rather than a separate low-grade and higher-grade IP as before. The seats used a new foam in situ process with fabric bonded to the foam and stitch seams moulded in, a technique that was also applied for the later CE14 Escort.

The BE13 Fiesta was launched in 1988. Shown here in three-door form is the 'S' version.

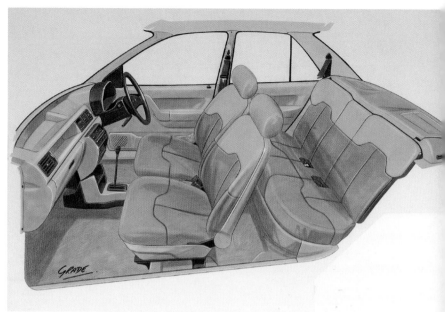

BE13 interior rendering by Tony Grade. The IP was a large one-piece polypropylene moulding. (Courtesy David Ginn)

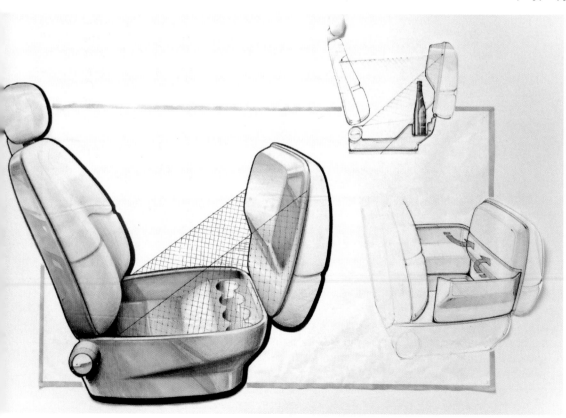

Fiesta seat sketch by Martin Burgess, showing a neat storage layout that was not pursued for production. The 'plastic seat' was a key part of the Red Book costings for the BE13. (Courtesy Martin Burgess)

Dunton also developed a new derivative of the Fiesta, the Courier van. This was a 'high-cube' style van based on the BE13 chassis, launched in 1991. Ford had offered a simple panel van version of the original Fiesta but this was a more serious project to offer a much-needed addition to the light van range. Renault had offered the R5 Express high-cube van in 1986 to replace the old R4 Fourgon van, and it had proved a big success. This high-cube format was quickly copied by GM with the Corsa, and Fiat with its Uno-based vans, whereas Ford had missed out on this expanding market for small B-Segment vans, particularly in southern European markets, where the ability to carry a 1.2m by 0.8m wooden Euro-pallet was a key selling point.

With the wheelbase extended by 255mm (10in) over the BE13 Fiesta, the Courier van offered a tall, boxy cargo compartment with a useful payload of 515kg. To achieve the flat load floor, the engineers found the Fiesta rear suspension turrets were too tall, so, thinking quickly, they negotiated to use the rear floor pressing and flat torsion bar suspension from the R5 Express, supplied from Renault. If you can't beat them, join them!

As usual, the interior was designed in Dunton, pretty much in parallel with the BE13 project, and the CE14 Escort cabin shared the overall theme and much of the switchgear of the smaller car. One example of the more orthodox design approach was the deletion of the innovative stubby indicator stalks used on the Erika-86 that were dropped for more conventional items designed for the Fiesta. Likewise, the independent rear suspension was deleted in favour of a Fiesta-like torsion-beam setup.

Having been so dominant in the light commercial field in the 1970s with the Escort van, Ford had taken its eye off the ball somewhat during the mid-'80s and lost market share to both Renault and Vauxhall. However, the Fiesta Courier and CE14 Escort vans would soon redress that weakness. The CE14 van was a full Dunton project run by Pete Ballard, although much of the work was outsourced to consultancy MGA in Coventry during 1987-'88. As before, this used the short front doors from the four-door Escort to allow maximum loadbed length. To increase the load capacity a stepped roofline was used with a gentle transition rather than the brutalist, utilitarian approach taken on the Fiesta Courier. The issue of the transition of the hatchback door shoulder running rearwards into the van rear was solved by sweeping the line up immediately after the door. Although this was a more cost-effective solution than the previous generation it did mean it lost much of its unique character with the deletion of the extra side window.

The stepped roof design of the CE14 van was partly to combat the Bedford Astravan/Opel Kadett Combo that GM had introduced in 1986 and was built in the UK, at Ellesmere Port. In addition to the normal Astravan, a high-cube van known as the Astramax was offered and, like the Renault Express, this was a gap that Ford needed to plug in its light van offering. Rather than develop two distinct versions, the new CE14 van was an attempt to bridge the market with a single new model. The 2598mm wheelbase – extended by 73mm (2.9in) over the Escort estate – could offer a payload of up to 640kg (12.5cwt), a useful increase over the outgoing van.

Almost simultaneous with the BE13 Fiesta was the CE14 Escort project, begun in 1986. Despite using a largely carry-over platform it was still a £1 billion investment for Ford. As with the new Fiesta, more rear seat space was required to remain competitive, hence the wheelbase was extended by 125mm (5in). Although the Erika had been a decent package in 1980 and around 150mm bigger than the Golf Mk I, the 1982 Golf Mk II had caught up, boasting a slightly longer wheelbase, hence the need for a better package for the CE14.

There was a deliberate policy not to innovate with this car – the Sierra showed that advanced-looking Fords were hard to sell – and that meant making more of the same. One part of the development process that reached new heights around this time was the extensive use of design clinics to get customer feedback at every turn. This almost guaranteed a conservative design outcome, since customers will inevitably rate highly an evolutionary design that provides some comforting familiarity to them over a more radical concept, even if by the time the car is launched events may well have moved their design taste forwards. Hence the German-designed exterior carried on the general 'bustleback' volumes of the outgoing Mk III Erika with a six-light greenhouse and slightly softer forms, as introduced on the face-lifted Erika-86 and BE13 Fiesta.

Within weeks of going on sale in August 1990, Ford realised the press reaction to the new Escort Mk IV was lacklustre and pressed ahead with an emergency face-lift, pulling it forward to September

Rendering of the Escort CE14 van by Steve Harper. The project was outsourced to consultancy MGA in Coventry, the first of several such outsource programs. (Courtesy Steve Harper)

1992, barely two years after the original car's launch. It was not so much the styling that was under fire – more the suspension settings and unrefined engines – but Ford product planners realised they would need visual changes on the car to accompany the engineering improvements if they were to make any headway with wooing customers back to the Escort. Stronger competition now included the VW Golf Mk III and GM Astra Mk III, while Rover's Honda-engineered 214/216 series was selling strongly, aping the 'bustleback' look pioneered by the Escort. Spearman-Oxx had previously been at Rover and was able to assess the situation clearly: "The previous Erika Escort was good, but then Rover took one step forward and Ford took one step back and suddenly Rover were leaps ahead of us. It got very analytical with CE14, the philosophy of not over-delivering was rife."

As well as a revised grille and tail lamps, the upgrades included the introduction of the new DOHC Zetec petrol engines and an RS2000 range-topper. However, the noisy Endura diesel engine remained, although detail engineering changes did improve its refinement. This was an interim face-lift, with more far-reaching changes being introduced for the 1995 mid-life overhaul.

Fresh Management at Dunton, outsourcing arrives

Andy Jacobson continued as head of the Dunton team until he returned to the US to take over the truck design studio in 1989. He was succeeded by the quiet, but very genial, Jim Arnold, then on his final secondment before retirement.

"Jim reminded me of the actor Walter Matthau," recalls Spearman-Oxx. "He'd lean back in his chair, look like he was thinking deeply but was actually peering at a row of photos of staff and names hidden under his desk. 'So ... er ... er ... oh, Simon! ... how's it going?' He could be quite comical."

At the same time, Fritz Mayhew took over running the Merkenich side. Mayhew had previously worked in Europe on several occasions and was conversant with the German setup. The Dunton studio management was handled by the duo of Dave Turner and Ray Everts. They were close associates who had worked together on the Taurus/Sable project in Dearborn. As was the norm, they enjoyed the front executive offices at Dunton, together with Arnold.

According to Spearman-Oxx, Turner had an interesting approach, loving the conceptual slant to design. "His arrival would be preceded by his coffee cup held aloft, proclaiming 'Are we looking at today or

New developments in fabrics and materials

The 1980s saw an increasing use of patterned fabrics in Ford interiors. Whereas the first brushed nylon fabrics introduced in the early 1970s followed the convention of a single plain colour, new jacquard weaving methods allowed the use of multiple colours and more intricate patterns for automotive fabrics during the next decade. These initially tended to be flat woven styles eg 'Monaco' striped cloth on the Fiesta XR2, or 'Murray' cloth on the '86 Fiesta Finesse. Later on, brushed velour-styles were introduced for top models such as the polka dot 'Olivia' velour on Escort Ghia, 'Daytona' velour on XR3i and 'Savoy' on Sierra Ghia, with plain crushed velour fabric being used on seat bolsters and headrests.

The number of interior colourways and fabrics also increased, meaning the colour and trim team needed to expand to handle the growing workload. By 1986 the Fiesta sported three interior colourways, with four available for Escort and no less than five for Sierra and Granada. More interior plastics were colour-keyed to match, leading to further complexity in interior parts and inventory. Meanwhile, the Capri stayed with just one interior colour – grey.

On the Sierra, every trim grade had a dedicated fabric style – seven different fabrics in various colourways, 15 in total. Even the Fiesta had 11 different fabrics over the three colourways. The Sierra introduced brushed nylon headlinings for the first time in a European Ford, the material also starting to be used in small areas on door panels. For the flagship Scorpio Executive, American-style ruched leather was re-introduced for the first time on a UK Ford since the Mark IV Zodiac.

Finally, steering wheels were now soft-feel 'blown PU', replacing the older, hard phenolic plastic items of the previous decade.

Dunton showroom, 1987.

Ford senior design executives at a Dunton model viewing, circa 1989. (Left to right) Jim Arnold, FoE Design VP; John Doughty, Chief Designer; Andy Jacobsen, previous FoE Design VP; Jack Telnack, Global Design VP, Fritz Mayhew, incoming FoE Design VP; Manfred Lampe, Design Program Manager CDW27.

Telnack gets the top job

In June 1987, President of Design Don Kopke duly retired at the age of 60, and was replaced by Jack Telnack, who remained in this top post for the next decade. Born in 1937, Telnack grew up in Dearborn and was steeped in the culture of Ford from an early age. After studying at the Art Center he joined Ford in 1958, initially in the Lincoln-Mercury studio. He rose steadily through the ranks, including an early stint running Ford's studio down in Melbourne in 1966. Telnack replaced Joe Oros as VP of Design in Europe from 1973-'76, keeping an office in Dunton, so was well-versed in European design taste as the downsizing trend in American cars returned in the late 1970s. Telnack's other interest was sailing and powerboats, keeping a couple of boats up on the Great Lakes and in Florida. This gave him a good understanding of fluid dynamics, which he applied to promoting aerodynamics in car design, particularly the Sierra and Taurus.

tomorrow?' or 'I've heard Mitsubishi are seeing how ugly they can make a car – isn't that great!' It was part of the exercise of challenging the obvious solutions as a designer, to loosen up people's thinking." Another of his mantras was 'Challenge it, don't just make it look nice. Hate yer mother,' – ie do the opposite of the thing you're supposed to love. "The front of the BE19 Fiesta was typical," continues Spearman-Oxx. "Often, we'd get to the end of a project and whatever was there

[in the clay] – well, that was it. Sometimes the design process became a game of consequences: we can change another bit today. Change the bumper, change the door. At the end of the day we might as well have changed everything and started again!"

With the bulk of design resources being directed into the main programs during the late 1980s, some minor projects were outsourced for expediency. The DE1 Granada face-lift was entrusted to the UK designers, Merkenich being too busy to handle it.

The notchback saloon version of the DE1 was due to be done in-house at Dunton, but, for some reason, in 1988 the model was outsourced to AC Autokraft, not long after the Ford takeover.

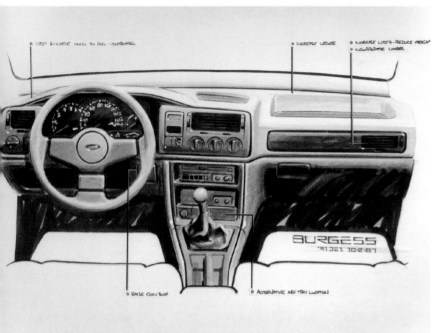

Revised DE1 IP sketched by Martin Burgess. The idea was to use the CE14 Escort theme, but upgraded for the Granada/Scorpio. (Courtesy Martin Burgess)

The notchback used a six-light cabin treatment, with the rear overhang some 75mm (3in) longer, and with far less tuck-in than on the hatchback to give a 50mm (2in) wider trunk opening. Simon Spearman-Oxx takes up the story: "They took a hatchback DE1 and some panel beaters to produce a steel prototype. The rear appliqué panel and tail lamps were moved back in space, and they filled in the gaps. It was shown to management as a quick exercise to get approval to start a proper clay modelling program, but was approved as it stood, and it seems no further modelling work was ever carried out!"

The styling for the 1992 face-lift of the DE1 was updated to share some cues with the forthcoming CDW27 Mondeo design, particularly the grille and headlamps. A new IP was designed, abandoning the sweeping style of the original for a more orthodox linear design using rectangular air vents and rotary heater controls. At the same time, an estate version was announced. This DE1 estate project had also been outsourced, this time to Worthing-based consultancy IAD and, as with the AC project, was overseen by Jim Hirons. Developed during 1990-'91 as a low-investment project, it used the rear tail lamps carried over from the Sierra estate that rather diluted its character, making it more anonymous than it deserved. It was a brave attempt by Ford to regain the big estate car market it had dominated with the former Granada estates, but seven years' absence had seen that market irredeemably lost to the Vauxhall Omega and Volvo estates.

The revised DE1 Granada was launched at the Brussels Motor Show in 1990. Seen here is the final interior design. Timbalex printed wood was used extensively on Ford interiors in the early 1990s, especially for Ghia variants.

Ford goes shopping – and acquires three premium brands

Discussions in 1983 about merging the commercial vehicle business with Leyland trucks apparently changed Ford's view on BL, which they found in some aspects of industrial relations and productivity to be ahead of Ford. There was also Land Rover, which held particular interest for Ford, being profitable and not overlapping with any existing Ford models.

BL was required to provide Ford with detailed financial information for these discussions, which was leaked to the press, and a political storm ensued with the Thatcher government. At that point the discussions between BL and the American company ceased. However, there was an underlying wish by Ford to shift its perception in the UK back to where it been in the 1960s, as a go-getting company producing interesting cars with low-volume producers like Lotus, or engaged in motorsport with companies such as Cosworth. Plus, there was a desire to move into more premium and niche markets where profits might be greater, as proved by BMW.

The first move was to buy Aston Martin in October 1987. Ford VP Walter Hayes was brought out of retirement to be its Chairman and to develop a new strategy for Aston Martin as a viable low volume manufacturer that Ford could support. So far, so good.

Four weeks later, Ford bought a controlling interest in AC Cars, a tiny sports car maker based at Brooklands, Surrey. This move came from a project to show a Ford-based AC concept, styled by Ghia, which had been shown on the Ford stand at the London Motor Show a year previously. The plan was to develop the 5-litre Ford V8-powered AC Ace into a production car, but, by 1990, the deal had unraveled and the two parties decided to end the deal.

The next step was to acquire Jaguar, which had been privatised from BL in 1984 and was openly up for sale. Despite lengthy negotiations with GM, in the end it was Ford who won the deal. By 2 November 1989, Ford announced it had slowly acquired a 77 per cent share, and offered to buy the remainder outright. The UK government relinquished its 'golden share' almost immediately, and the deal went through at £8.50 per share, which valued the company at £1.6 billion. Jaguar was now part of Ford, the start of an 18-year ownership, albeit one that would never prove as profitable as originally hoped.

From Jaguar's side, the level of funding provided by Ford was a very positive change compared to the interminable delays and postponement that was the bane of the company throughout the 1980s. From Ford's point of view, the addition of Jaguar meant a lot of engineering support had to be urgently provided, especially from Dunton, and a whole raft of engineers were soon making the long weekly commute up the M1 to Coventry.

Ford arrived with very fixed views on Jaguar it seems. The design ethos came directly from Jack Telnack, who was passionate about Jaguar and loved the heritage, believing that was what Ford had bought. But, as the decade progressed, the reality was that it led to somewhat caricatured proposals with Jaguar elements simply laid on graphically, where the design had to be instantly recognisable as a clichéd Jaguar for senior Ford executives to evaluate.

As a result of the ongoing turmoil at Jaguar, Manfred Lampe was installed as Chief Designer at Jaguar in 1990 to replace Geoff Lawson. In return, Lawson was offered the post of Chief Designer at Dunton, but, after strong appeals to William Clay Ford, he refused to move and demanded to stay on to lead the Coventry studio in an awkward partnership with Lampe.

In 1999, Ford created Premier Automotive Group, an organisation that included Jaguar, Aston Martin, Lincoln and Mercury with the idea that the premier marques could share parts and engineering expertise to reduce costs and speed up model programs.

Brilliantly exciting: Escort Cosworth

Dunton also handled number of projects for Ford Motorsport. While the Sierra RS500 was done in Merkenich, the 'Transit RS Tug' and trailer for the works RS200 proved a nice compensation project for the UK design team. Another exciting project came its way in 1989.

In September 1988, Motorsport boss Stuart Turner had an initial executive meeting to show his plans for the ACE14 project – the Escort Cosworth 4x4. By March 1989 this was put for approval. SVE would take care of the engineering, while Karmann would help develop the body engineering and production, with Job One scheduled for October 1991, and a plan for 5000 cars built and motorsport homologation obtained by mid-1992.

The concept behind the ACE14 was a brilliant piece of thinking by Motorsport engineer John Wheeler. The aim was to create a compact new rally weapon using Sierra Cosworth 4x4 running gear with a north/south engine layout and mount it in a clever amalgam of Sierra underbody and floor mated to CE14 Escort sills and upper bodyshell. The 2525mm wheelbase of the forthcoming CE14 would be extended by 25mm (1in) to more closely match the Sierra 4x4 floor and running gear. The 40mm (3.5in) difference in body width was accommodated by shaving 20mm per side from the floor, bulkhead and associated underbody pressings and welding them to the existing Escort sills and bodyside pressings with a handful of new pressings required to complete the assembly. The small difference in wheelbase compared to the standard Escort did not matter for the front and rear fenders, since these would anyway be modified to accommodate the wider tracks. It was a very neat solution.

With the design departments at Merkenich and Dunton overloaded with work on the CE14 and the new CDW27 project

Jaguar X-type.

Transit RS Tug team in Dunton.

(Mondeo), MGA in Coventry was approached to help out with design work. Ford had been impressed with the smooth progress achieved on its recent work for the CE14 van, and were happy to outsource this more prestigious project to the company, whose design studio was led by ex-Ford designer Peter Horbury.

Initially, an aero model was developed there. MGA designer Steve Harper was delegated to lead on the project: "A steel mock-up rolling chassis had been hand built by Karmann and this was delivered to MGA," he recalls. "Together with my team of modellers we created the design for new bumpers, fenders, bonnet features and undertrays in modelling foam and aluminum sheeting, ready for the first wind tunnel testing.

"This was duly tested in the Merkenich wind tunnel in July 1989 where Gert Hohenester and his team saw it and felt that they should have their creative input on such an exciting project, which was seen to be outside their control. But – thankfully – John Wheeler and SVE fought to keep it as a UK Motorsport project." Further refinement of the design was developed on a second clay model that was done

The initial Escort RS Cosworth model being prepared at MGA for aero testing, July 1989. The clay model in the background was a second model used to develop the final surfaces. (Courtesy Steve Harper)

Finished red prototype of the RS Cosworth, ready for the dealer launch in January 1990. (Courtesy Steve Harper)

in the MGA studio. In the middle of the year, Ian Callum and Neil Simpson were brought in by Dave Turner to oversee the whole project, finish the details including the huge rear 'batwing' and ensure it could be fully approved by October 1989.

Just before Christmas it was decided to show the RS Cosworth to add some glamour to the dealer launch of the new CE14 Escort, just as had been done with the Escort RS2000 back in 1974. The prototype model was hurriedly completed in five weeks ready for the event in January 1990.

The Escort RS Cosworth was the last Ford project completed by Callum. Like Peter Horbury, Callum was tempted away from Ford in spring 1990 to head up a new design studio for TWR, later joined by Simpson and several modellers, including Sean O'Malley and Andy Miles. Although he did not realise it at the time, it was not to be his last involvement with Ford, however.

This 'Cab Forward' sports car by Ian Callum was done as an extensive design exercise for an Escort-based coupé in the early 1980s. Cab Forward packaging was very fashionable at Ford at the time, and was exploited for the CDW27 Mondeo. (Courtesy Martin Burgess)

Full-size tape rendering of an Escort-based coupé done on a Mazda 323 basis by Martin Burgess. Lead-based (and toxic) Flow-Master inks, which are banned today, were used to produce these large renderings. (Courtesy Martin Burgess)

The $6 billion CDW27 Mondeo

The biggest project that occupied Dunton in the late 1980s was CDW27, started in 1986. This was Ford's first true world car since the Model T, a vast $6 billion project that would not only replace the Sierra in Europe but also the Tempo/Topaz in the US. To ensure that the requirements for the European and US markets could be accommodated, the pre-program work was carried out in Dearborn. Engineering responsibility and production design work transferred to Europe in 1987, when Richard Parry-Jones became program manager for CDW27.

Leading the design side for this project was Manfred Lampe, a long-time Ford Dearborn designer and keen Ferrari enthusiast. Indeed, Lampe edited the Ferrari Club of America's in-house magazine, *Prancing Horse*, for over 15 years and owned a number of classic models, including a 512 S Berlinetta used in the film *Le Mans*. Lampe had been second in command of Ghia Design Studio in 1984, but was seconded to manage the CDW27 project from late 1986, based in Merkenich.

Dunton's responsibility was for the complete interior development of both the European Mondeo and the US versions, with Interior Design Manager John Hartnell heading the project. The design team comprised Mark Adams, Steve Aris, Martin Burgess, Ian Callum, Paul Campbell, Brian Osman, Cliff Pickering, Alan Thorley and Harry Uden.

There were two major stages to the CDW27 interior design concept development. "The protocol was internal studio competitive designs, with each of us working on a clay model IP proposal," recalls Burgess. "Once again John Hartnell felt under great program time pressure so he encouraged us not to dwell on protracted sketching, but to get quickly into the clay."

Talking to *Automotive Interiors International* magazine in 1993, John Hartnell said "Initially we did three IPs, one for Europe and two for North America. There were different themes for each one. Then we did a further three panels and took them out to market research.

"I thought that my first design was quite handsome and it did reasonably well at the clinics," continues Burgess. "However, John Hartnell attended the US clinics and also the Ford studio in

Phase 1 CDW27 Mondeo IP proposal from spring 1988. This proposal for the US Ford Contour was by Ian Callum, and is being worked on here by Geoff Heywood. At this stage, the Contour was destined to have a bench seat, hence the truncated centre console. (Courtesy Martin Burgess)

Harry Uden, Ian Callum and Mark Adams discuss a further CDW27 interior buck. (Courtesy Martin Burgess)

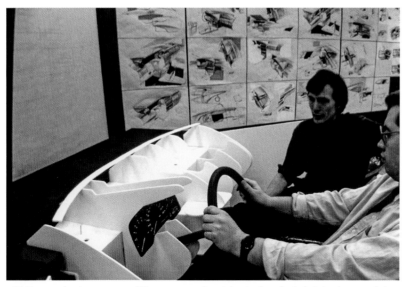

At times, designers used Foamcore sheet to make sketch interior models, one way of avoiding union rules on no clay modelling by designers. Here, Alan Thorley and Steve Aris evaluate a quick three-dimensional mock-up. (Courtesy Martin Burgess)

Dearborn and he was taken aback. His exposure to the trends in the Dearborn studio brought him to the realisation that we had to 'up our game.' John telephoned me at Dunton from the US to say we had to start again. The constant search – particularly in Ford in the US – for a design 'breakthrough' had yielded such results that John recognised that our offerings, tidy as they were, did not represent the sort of modernity now required."

So began the second phase of CDW27 IP concepts in summer 1988, which were done at an even faster pace. "We were all working evenings and weekends, and it bore fruit with significantly more modern – and simply better – design work being presented at the second stage of clinics."

Adams remained with the CDW27 project, and subsequently managed the cabin for the US versions of the Mondeo – the Ford Contour and Mercury Mystique – while the final European IP was the work of Martin Burgess.

Adams admitted they used the clinics to get feedback on the main theme and ambience rather than details. "We deliberately did some with big binnacles, and so on. We tried to polarise the earlier designs so we got feedback on larger-scale concerns, as opposed to minor criticisms about the style and placement of knobs, etc."

An alternative model by Alan Thorley, which continues the orthodox Ford interior themes from the Escort and Fiesta. (Courtesy Martin Burgess)

The CDW27 was an international car, but it was delivered as three distinct models: the European Ford Mondeo, US Ford Contour, and the Mercury Mystique. This is an early Mercury Mystique proposal. The final Mystique IP was the work of Brian Osman. (Courtesy Martin Burgess)

The Mondeo IP was the first design in which the unit was built up off-line, and then bolted in as a complete assembly on a steel cross tube, including the steering column, wiring loom, heater box and instrument cluster. This allowed the unit to be pre-tested prior to fitting, avoiding costly refits and rectifications once it was installed. Feasibility engineer John Percy (centre) demonstrates the idea. (Courtesy Martin Burgess)

At first there was an American interior and a European interior design but as the program developed these became very similar in their layout. "The Euro-Japanese look if you like was the basic requirement," says Burgess. "We were conscious of how successful the Honda Accord was in America. At the time, it was the top seller and very well regarded by customers, and we thought if that Euro-Japanese approach was acceptable, then we could do the same." For the American versions, the knee bolster and large airbag requirements forced the whole IP further into the passenger compartment, although the steering wheel position remained the same. In addition, the recessed tray on the passenger side had to be deleted for American versions to accommodate the airbag door.

The CDW27 project was an early example in Ford of simultaneous engineering, where the feasibility and engineering is carried out in parallel to the styling development – a standard practice today. It also meant that the entire interior could be approved by the product committee in one session rather than being signed-off sequentially, as each area such as IP, console and seats were finalised. Unlike the Erika Escort, strenuous efforts were undertaken to avoid 'double-engineering' the car, only creating differences between the European and US versions of the car where strictly necessary.

Final clinic model for the E4 design proposal – the European Mondeo. (Courtesy Martin Burgess)

Clay models for seats were trimmed using real fabric materials, to simulate a finished seat for design viewings. (Courtesy Martin Burgess)

One exterior model was also produced at Dunton by young RCA graduate Mark Adams, and was used for the initial customer clinics in 1987. It is seen here in the yard. Behind it is the latest Sierra Sapphire four-door. (Courtesy Martin Burgess)

Mark Adams tapes up the rear of his Mondeo model. CDW27 design work was largely completed by 1990, with the launch in January 1993. The Mondeo was widely admired at the time, and garnered another COTY award for Ford in 1994. (Courtesy Martin Burgess)

The reaction to conservatism: radical makes a comeback

The CE14 Escort and face-lifted DE1 Granada were the final projects of the 'conservative' design phase that had ruled at Ford in Europe since 1985. Around this time there was a call by the media for more innovative design in cars. In July 1990, *CAR* magazine ran an eight-page article questioning why all cars looked the same:

"The range of cars sold by Britain's Big Three – Ford, Vauxhall and Rover – has never looked more similar. This is particularly true of the nose treatment: the face of a car ... But are stylists – and the managing directors who tether them – so devoid of flair that they all have to follow the leader? Clone car design is stifling interest in motoring,"' it stated. The debate was widespread, leading to various car design chiefs – including Patrick le Quément, now Chief Designer at Renault – to claim they were looking to promote strong design identities for their brands.

Ford decided to react to this sentiment by using the oval grille as a key recognition feature across the range, both in Europe and the US. In due course it was added to the '95 Escort, and, in bolder form, to the Mondeo update in 1996. Future Fords, the thinking went, would have a strong family identity, like BMWs, with an emphasis on individuality and straightforward pleasure of ownership. Fritz Mayhew explained Ford's new philosophy: "We're now getting high-personality front- and rear-end design themes highlighting grilles, badges and lamps," he reported to *CAR* magazine. "Lamps are going to be the new jewellery of the nineties, driven by new technology. We'll also see the re-emergence of chrome but used in a bold, simple way."

However, the most radical example of this new approach was reserved for the DE1 Scorpio face-lift for 1994. Knowing that Ford would be abandoning this market and the car would not be replaced,

Euro car clones cover
of *CAR* magazine, 1990.
(Courtesy *CAR*)

The ultimate reaction to the 'Euro Clones' debate was the 1994 Scorpio. Few cars have polarised opinions as much as this one!

Mayhew, Everts and Turner decided to adopt a deliberate 'grand finale' design strategy, a final throw of the dice for the car to go out with a flourish. The problem was, the car quickly became a topic of ridicule when first shown in October 1994.

"There's no getting away from it: this car is ugly,'" pronounced *CAR* magazine. "You don't often find yourself staring at a brand-new car in sheer, flabbergasted disbelief, but that's the reaction that most decently clued-up people experience when they set eyes on the new Scorpio."

James May, writing in *The Independent* agreed. "Most criticism has been levelled at the car's boss-eyed, gawping expression ... The problem is that the core of the car – the cabin area – has remained essentially unchanged, so the old car's high waistline and slab sides stay. This gives the impression that the new, rounded nose has simply been stuck on, which it has. The car's most unfortunate aspect is its rear, where the single strip of lights has sunk to the bottom of the boot like cherries in a failed fruit cake. It looks too American.'

Dave Turner tried to defend the design: "The restyle is radical to signal the changes under the skin, and to give the car individuality." Did he find it beautiful? "Yes. Categorically," he replied to *CAR*. According to Spearman-Oxx, the Scorpio redesign had started with some quick digital sketches, to see how different the car could be made as a quick demonstration for journalists to counteract the former accusation that all cars looked alike. "Dave saw this as his 'Harley Earl dream machine' ie a blank canvas that could be experimented with," he says. "Gert Hohenester did the back end,

with a slim tail lamp like the Porsche 911. It was like a Buick showcar of the time, a very polarising design."

The need to package airbags at this point meant yet another new IP for the Scorpio. Designed at Dunton, it followed the theme developed for the Mondeo, with a softly-sculpted, arc-shaped binnacle and large edge radii. This latest Scorpio sported a further example of a new type of plastic wood process, developed by the supplier company Timbalex. This used a photographic wood print film suspended in a bath of water, with the component to be decorated being brought up beneath the film, which then drapes itself around the shape. It was a popular process used throughout the 1990s on a number of Ford Ghia models, including the Mondeo and Escort. Together with the ruched leather also introduced around this time, it wasn't however perceived as particularly sophisticated by many European customers, being seen as too transatlantic. Sadly, as with the TC Cortina interior, it dated fast.

By summer 1998, the Scorpio was quietly dropped from production in Cologne – a sad end to what had been a fine lineage of large Fords in Europe. In the late 1970s the Mk II Granada had been a very credible alternative to a BMW 5-series or Rover SD1 but the image of the Scorpio had dropped a long way since then.

Ford's policy was that the new S-type Jaguar was likely a better bet to recapture Ford's share of the executive market, which did indeed prove to be the case. In any event, under the forthcoming Ford 2000 program, it was hard to see how a new RWD Granada project could ever have made it off the ground in Europe.

Chapter

7

New Edge, new politics

"Due for launch this summer, the Puma takes the Ford Fiesta platform, sends it down the gym and gives it a muscular, seductive little set of sweeping curves and sharp lines. If the Ford range was the Spice Girls, and if the Mondeo is Mumsy Spice, then the Puma is Scary Spice. Just as pop groups can now be designed and manufactured from scratch in no time at all, so can cars." So said the magazine *Design Week*, in May 1997.

Following the brief flirtation with radical design under Dave Turner, the next few years led to a rich era for Ford styling. In the mid-1990s, Ford had discovered a bold new design language that was to rejuvenate the product line-up and return the company to marketplace prominence that soon eclipsed the embarrassment of the Scorpio. Design chief Fritz Mayhew was now pushing for a thoroughly new direction, which finally emerged as 'New Edge' design.

At this stage, Ford Design went through a period where the personalities of design management were not promoted nor made public as much as in the past when Bahnsen and le Quément held sway. In fact, Mayhew took over the top job from Jim Arnold as VP of Design in September 1993, while Turner returned to Dearborn to lead on the 'modern heritage look' Thunderbird that emerged in 1999.

The arrival of digital design and New Edge

Back in 1987, Claude Lobo had become Chief Designer of Advanced Program Definition and Computer Aided Design for Ford of Europe, and was leading a group to experiment with new computer graphics for computer aided styling (CAS). In 1984, Japanese knitting machine manufacturer Shima Seiki had developed the SDS-310 Shimatronic Design System. This was an early computer graphics software not unlike the Quantel Paintbox that, crucially, used a touch-tablet and pressure-sensitive pen, rather than a mouse. Ford adopted the Shima Seiki system wholeheartedly in the late-1980s, and introduced it in most of the design studios, including Dunton and Merkenich.

Like the Quantel Paintbox, the Shima Seiki was a breakthrough in design. Commonplace in most design software today, the pen used with the Shima Seiki system was a world first, and offered designers a new level of control. By the late 1990s it had fallen out of favour, and designers would use readily-available Adobe Photoshop and Illustrator software to produce 2D renderings.

The design studios also used Conceptual Design Rendering Software (CDRS) to produce 3D digital models of their designs and young designers were encouraged to experiment with the new software. Three such designers were Coventry University graduates Chris Svensson, Chris Hamilton and Pierre Webster, who all shared a house together as students. Svensson first arrived on a Dunton internship in 1991, and was also sponsored by Ford to the RCA.

Svensson confirms how New Edge came about: "I am seen in the design community as one of the instigators of New Edge design, but Mayhew was the real push here." The story goes that as he and his

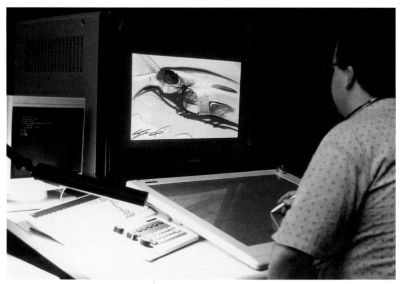

Designer Steve Sykes using the Shima Seiki design system.

The 1995 Ford GT90 was the first manifestation of 'New Edge' design. Using a Jaguar XJ220 aluminium honeycomb monocoque with carbon fibre panels, it featured a 5.9-litre V12 mated to an XJ220 gearbox.

After working in Dearborn, Chris Svensson returned to Dunton in 1997, becoming Design Manager for the studio from 2006 to 2009.

wife shared a lunch in a London restaurant in early 1994, Mayhew was suddenly distracted by the bottle of Evian water their waiter had placed before them. The jagged mountains etched along the top of the bottle reminded him of the recent edgy design sketches done by Svensson and colleagues in the German studio. Mayhew brought the Evian bottle to Dunton that afternoon, and it became one of the influences of the 'Edgy' design theme of the Ford Ka. Mayhew later coined the term 'New Edge' for this look, which builds a design from intersecting arcs and creases with lightly twisting surfaces, rather than depending on soft, flowing curves. "At the RCA we were into this product design look of how you break up the masses with self-coloured parts versus glossy parts, which Fritz really liked," confirms Svensson.

During that spring, Lobo was appointed Director of the Advanced Design Studio in Dearborn, and took the New Edge look (and Svensson) with him to use on a new clutch of concept vehicles. The Ford GT90 in 1995 was the first car to feature New Edge styling in its earliest form, using sharp creases and flat sides. Later concepts included the Ford Indigo, Synergy 2010, and the Mercury MC4.

The following year, the Ford Ka became the first production vehicle using this design language, followed by the face-lifted Mondeo in 1996, the Puma in 1997, and the Focus and Cougar in 1998.

Ford 2000 plan

Ford's senior management was instigating big changes, too. In November 1993, Alex Trotman became the first foreign-born Chairman and CEO of the company. In April 1994, Trotman announced that the company was to become a single global entity by merging North American, European and International operations together into a single organisation. This was to be the biggest shake-up for the company since FoE was created in 1967, and would be effective from 1 January 1995. Trotman had risen through the ranks from joining Ford of Britain in 1955 to become Chairman of Ford of Europe by 1984 – a powerful endorsement of his shrewd abilities as a manager.

This 'Ford 2000' plan called for dramatic cost reductions to be obtained by re-engineering and globalising both organisations and processes. As part of these changes, the phrase 'product development' replaced 'engineering' as the main term for the development process through to production. There were to be benefits in manufacturing and purchasing through a reduced number of suppliers. The goals of Ford 2000 were:
- Cut management ranks by 15 per cent.
- Create five vehicle centres (VCs) to design small cars, large cars, luxury cars, personal trucks, and commercial trucks.
- Merge Ford operations in Europe and North America.
- Coordinate product plans with Mazda.

Ford had gained several non-Ford designs in Latin America, plus a number of Mazda-designed models. Now it had Jaguar and Aston Martin to contend with, so this all seemed a logical step at the time. The European design studios had traditionally reported through International Operations to Dearborn since the late 1940s, but that was about to change.

Jacques 'Jac' Nasser, an energetic Australian, was promoted by Trotman to push Ford 2000 through. He had been made Chairman of the board of Ford of Europe, was Vice President of Ford Motor Company in 1993, and then group Vice President of Product Development in 1994. By 1996, Nasser headed Ford Automotive Operations.

One of boldest moves was to change Ford's traditional role as a manufacturer of its own components to being a shrewd buyer of them from outside suppliers. Many of its disparate parts-making businesses were spun off into the entirely separate Visteon supplier company. Visteon and its workforce then had to compete for Ford contracts. Meanwhile, relentless cost pressure was applied to Ford's existing suppliers. Nicknamed 'Jac the Knife,' Nasser became known for getting results with his sharp cost-cutting efforts with Ford's component supplier base.

Trotman's other action was to centralise Ford's design and engineering activities under a single new organisation, Ford Automotive Operations (FAO) that would take care of global product development. From now on, Europe would be responsible for developing all small- and medium-size FWD vehicles, while North America would concentrate on larger FWD cars, large RWD cars, together with light trucks and sport-utility vehicles (SUVs). Commercial truck development would be centred in Dearborn, too.

In fact, Design had already begun to operate on a more global basis. In 1993 Jack Telnack was put in charge of all seven of Ford's design studios worldwide, more than a year before Trotman's Ford 2000 worldwide reorganisation. "We were thinking and operating on a global basis before Ford 2000, experimenting with electronic design and satellite-linked studios," said Telnack. "Maybe it's right that design was on the leading edge of that, because we're supposed to be aware of technology and the latest development techniques."

Back in Europe, Claude Lobo had returned to take over from Mayhew in 1996, becoming Director of Design for Small and Medium Car Vehicle Center (SVC) – effectively the old Ford of Europe VP position, in charge of both Dunton and Merkenich studios.

Ford had already started down this road of global platform sharing from 1992, and examples at that stage included:
- 1992 CDW27 – European Mondeo, US Ford Mystique, Mercury Cougar, 2001 Jaguar X-type.
- 1993 Nissan Terrano II / Ford Maverick, made in Spain.
- 1994 Ford Probe, Mazda 626, Mazda MX6.

However, this program would be accelerated from now on, with the following models being developed as shared platforms:
- BE13 platform – the Ford Ka and Puma were to be developed off the old Fiesta platform, including a Mazda2 version of the Fiesta, manufactured in Dagenham.
- 1995 VX62: Ford Galaxy, VW Sharan and SEAT Alhambra. This MPV used a modified Mondeo CDW27 platform. Begun in 1988, this proved a very protracted seven-year program with partner Volkswagen.
- 1998 DEW98 – large RWD platform shared by Lincoln, Ford Thunderbird and the Jaguar S-type. Failure of the last Scorpio convinced Ford not to invest in another large saloon in Europe, a wise decision given that the mainstream executive market was contracting so fast.
- 1998 C170 Focus. A major global platform, also used for the Transit Connect van.
- 2004 C1 platform shared with the Focus C-Max, Focus Mk II hatchback, Kuga, Volvo S40/V50 and Mazda3. It was also used for the Mazda Premacy/Mazda5, the second generation 2006 Volvo C70 and the C30.

With the announcement of the Ford 2000 strategy, questions were being raised as to whether Dunton was really needed, and what its role was under the new SVC strategy. Under this new setup, design and engineering activity would be centred in Germany, while commercial vehicle development would gravitate to the US. At Dunton, a new Cold Development centre was opened in 1994, but apart from that the headcount reductions were soon starting to bite. Aside from minor Transit face-lift work, there wasn't much on the commercial vehicle horizon either. Things were looking bleak.

Salvation soon arrived from a couple of unexpected quarters. As part of the cost reduction plan, Ford's smaller sites around Essex were shut down and these groups were instructed to relocate to

Sir Alex Trotman opened the new link office block in December 1997. The ground floor corner entrance now forms the main reception area for the Dunton site.

risky – design. This presented a dilemma. The stakes were high, and there would be casualties by the end of the decade.

Ford of Europe also saw changes, with the main headquarters moving from Warley in the UK to Cologne. The shift began when Jim Donaldson became President of Ford of Europe in 1998, but speeded up during the next few years as more German staff were recruited.

In making the move, Ford was performing a delicate operation, moving European headquarters out of the UK market where it still dominated into one where it was much weaker. However, the reasoning seemed to be that if Ford could succeed in Germany, it could succeed anywhere. Ford was a distant third to VW and Opel in Germany, and the company believed it had to increase market share there in order to return European operations to profitability. The move was mostly complete by 2000, and resulted in the transfer of about 150 jobs, most of those being the staffs of Vice Presidents who now operated out of Germany.

Dunton, which suddenly found itself in need of more space, not less. Therefore a new central office block and reception area was built that linked the single-storey design block with the main engineering offices next door, and was opened in December 1997 by the now knighted Sir Alex Trotman himself. As an ex-Dunton product planner he undoubtedly had a soft spot for the site that, for now, helped to keep it within Ford's plans.

On the design studio front, the new remit for developing several models simultaneously meant the studios in Germany and England were forced to abandon the exterior/interior split that had existed since 1971, and to allocate model programs wherever there was capacity and resources. Merkenich was tasked with developing more variants from the CDW27 Mondeo platform such as the Cougar coupé, plus co-ordinating the global C170 new Escort program that would become the Focus.

At the same time, there was an urgent need to develop the next Fiesta and create more niche spin-offs from the B-platform, so those projects were redirected to the UK. Suddenly, Dunton design studio was busy doing exteriors again, including some initial Ka and Puma models. On the other hand, development of Motorsport RS and ST models now shifted to Germany, rather than being the preserve of the SVE group at Dunton, but overall the outcome for the UK studio was looking very positive.

Gradually, there was a shift to develop models in Germany, with England still taking care of the Transit and commercial vans. However, Ford found itself with two slightly conflicting agendas here: a pragmatic Ford 2000 regime, and a desire for quite daring – even

Small car programs in Dunton: Ford Ka and Puma

As described, one objective of Ford 2000 was to see more spin-off models using the same basic platform, something Ford had been good at in the past with the Corsair and Capri, for instance. Now, the attention turned to seeing what could done to extend the usage of the Fiesta platform, which would see it going in two quite different directions.

The first was to see how a new A-segment car might be developed. Up to then, the A-segment market was dominated by outdated models that had long since paid for their tooling such as the BMC Mini, Fiat 126, Renault 4 and Skoda Favorit, together with a few small Japanese models from Daihatsu and Suzuki. Within Ford, much the same arguments were used as for the initial Bobcat project – there was no profit in such cars. However, in 1991 Fiat launched the new Type 170 Cinquecento that revived the segment, selling 200,000 in the first year and producing strong growth in southern European markets such as Spain and Italy. This was followed up by the Renault Twingo in 1992, a highly-innovative small car package, designed under the leadership of Patrick le Quément.

Around 1992, Ford therefore decided it should enter the segment in order to expand market share, to get a stronger foothold in those growing southern European markets and to challenge Fiat. It was to prove a sound judgement: the A-segment market in Europe grew to over one million units by the late 1990s, with the Ford Ka selling at a healthy 140,000 units per year.

Studies for the design direction of this new baby Ford were under way during 1993. Ford decided to use the existing BE13 Fiesta platform with a complete reskin and the generous wheelbase would endow it with a strong, solid stance to become its characteristic feature. Costs were kept low on this project BE146 by simplifying the number of parts from 3000 to about 1200 to reduce the build time and to offer just a single powertrain option – the simple pushrod 1.3-litre 'Kent' engine, now called Endura-E. In addition, production in Valencia was based around the latest thinking in manufacturing, a supplier park, where parts are made very close to the assembly plant and supplied on a just-in-time basis to minimise costs.

Ka concept model shown in 1994 was designed by Craig Metros and displayed a softer, cuter version of the styling than the final design, using round 'frogeye' headlamps and a very rounded rear window. In 1996 Ghia also produced the Saetta cabrio concept shown as a fun take on the Ka just prior to the production launch.

Chris Svensson's ideas for the BE146 Ford Ka evolved into a highly charismatic design, which used New Edge form language in a more sophisticated way than had been shown with previous studies, such as the GT90. This prototype shows the bumpers still under development.

Pierre Webster discusses the Ford Ka IP clay model with lead modeller Eddie White. The Ka interior design continued the bold look of the exterior, using sweeping curves and circular air vents.

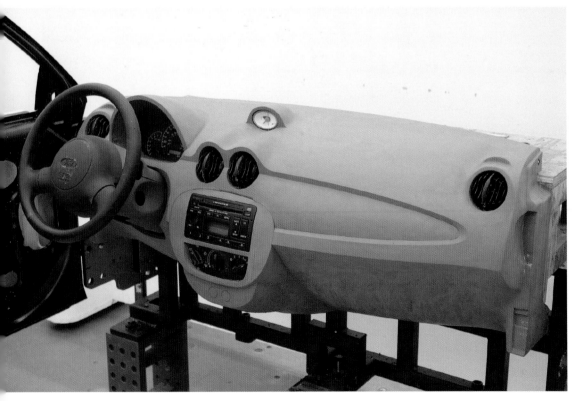

Despite being a young graduate, Chris Svensson became the lead designer for the exterior, which was based loosely on a model he had shown at the RCA: "The main theme at the start was done by American designer Craig Metros," he explains. "It had a high level of feasibility to it, but after a design review my design was chosen as having more future to it, more radical. Therefore Craig's theme was chosen as a show teaser to show the world we were working on a sub-B car." According to Svensson, the subsequent pink show car shown in Geneva in 1994 was done as a conventional sketch and clay program, rather than a digital model. "In fact, we didn't have the plate space to work on it, so it was done on the plate for the wind tunnel area in Merkenich."

Designers Mark Adams and Pierre Webster spent 18 months on the BE146 interior. Adams had joined from the RCA in 1986, while Webster arrived at Ford in 1991, fresh from his Coventry University studies. Design Manager Ray Everts installed Webster into the colour and trim studio in Dunton, as work was beginning on the new Escort project – eventually to become the Focus. Webster was asked to reinterpret his initial sketches towards this new BE146 project, as they were deemed too radical for the larger car. The subsequent interior with sweeping curves and round air vents was a youthful, bold design that suited the character of the new model perfectly.

The second direction was to look at a new compact coupé. Since the demise of the Capri in 1986, Ford lacked a presence in the European coupé market, which had been abandoned to Japanese makers. As a stopgap, Ford introduced the US-built Probe into European markets in 1994, but ultimately wanted a smaller model it could manufacture and sell in higher volume throughout Europe, one based on the Fiesta platform.

Once again, it was GM that provided the spur to Ford. Having launched the Vectra-based Calibra coupé in 1990, Opel followed

Alternative theme for the Ka instrument panel.

up in 1994 with the Tigra, based on the small Corsa platform. Rumours of the Tigra development around 1993 helped Ford planners to push for the Puma project to go ahead, believing it would create a new market and expand demand for compact sports coupés in Europe, something that had only previously been the domain of the Honda CRX and Nissan Sunny ZX.

Design work for this project SE161 began late in 1993, with Svensson again being the lead designer on this project, under the direction of Manager Chris Clements. The exterior was designed in Cologne as a fast exercise using CDRS software. By January 1994, the final design choice was ready to be milled out as a full-size clay model. By mid-March, the clay was complete, with a full interior and ready for review by the product committee, who approved it for production. It had taken just 135 days to reach this point from issuing the first brief to the designers – a remarkable result for the time.

At this point the project was shipped to Ian Callum's TWR facility near Oxford, and refined using conventional clay development methods and skilled modellers to get the light lines of the complex rounded surfaces to flow correctly. A Porsche-like 'whaletail' spoiler was also added to improve the air separation and stability at the rear. "For the first mock-up model we actually used tail lights from the Toyota Supra, the only true round lamps available at the time" says Svensson.

Another problem was that the headlamp position was in direct conflict with the underlying structure. "The slim mouth and big eyes were critical for that car. We wanted that graphic but there was sheet metal under there," he continues. In the end the lamp graphic was 'cheated' using blacked-out areas to lower the lamp reflector to the same position as the BE13.

The interior, meanwhile, was a wholly Dunton project. The Puma kept the same cowl point and basic IP as the Fiesta, although it gained a new centre console and door linings. Likewise, the seats were based on Fiesta frames but utilised new foams.

The Puma used a carry-over IP from the latest BE91 Fiesta, shown here. The Puma revisions to the doors and console were a joint exercise by Pierre Webster and Simon Bury. The increased level of detail design in Ford interiors was part of the latest 'surprise and delight' mantra, to maximise customer appeal.

Pressing the New Edge panels did not make Manufacturing's lives any easier. The sharp angles and tight radii that defined New Edge were not easy to form – especially when using stiff, ding-resistant steels that had become commonplace by the 1990s. However, when interviewed by industry magazine *Ward's Auto World*, John Fleming, Chief Engineer of stampings and structures at Ford's Vehicle Operations at the time, gave New Edge the thumbs up: "We tend to take it as a challenge. We all like cars, and when a new design looks good, there's a real desire to go out and do it," he said. Others in Ford felt New Edge design could save production time, the turned-up edges themselves ostensibly making the panels a bit easier to align, since flushness of surface was not so visually critical.

Meanwhile, the Fiesta itself was heavily revised under the BE91 codename to become the Mark IV model. The main improvement was the use of all-aluminium 16-valve Zetec SE engines in 1.25- and 1.4-litre variants, and revised chassis settings to give vastly-improved ride and roadholding. A new 85mm (3.5in) longer front end was added to suit the new engines, and to meet latest crash regulations. This sported the latest Ford oval grille panel, which on top level Ghia models was designed in a chrome lens finish to extend the lamp theme across the entire front end – a typical Dave Turner addition. The rear tailgate pressing and lamps were revised in the style of the Ka, and a new IP was designed with more rounded forms, shared with the Puma. Launched in September 1995, it succeeded in reviving Fiesta sales to become Britain's best-selling car from 1996 to 1998.

The BE91 Fiesta sported a longer front end to meet the latest safety regulations. The Ghia version shown here featured a Dave Turner-inspired chrome lens finish to the grille.

This 1996 Mondeo face-lift was CD162. It took the oval theme to new extremes, with the entire grille echoing the shape of the blue Ford logo.

Following on from the 'muchness' phrase used for the Sierra interior program, Ford coined a further new slogan in 1996. This was dubbed 'surprise and delight' – "When the interior has been designed with human ergonomics in mind, it creates a 'surprise and delight' factor that greatly contributes to the customer's overall comfort and satisfaction with the product," said Richard Parry-Jones – now Vice President of Production Programming. "Even on small cars like the new Fiesta, our customers demand ever more attention to interior design detail, and they're looking for features and comforts that at one time could only be found in much larger, more expensive cars."

CE99 and C170 Focus

When it came to replacing the Escort, Ford reverted to revolutionary form, combining Mondeo style dynamic excellence with New Edge styling. The result was unequivocal: the original Focus was the UK's best-selling car for every year it was in production. This was to be the boldest new program in Europe since the original 'Bobcat' Fiesta. At the time the first Focus was being conceived, Ford began to

reassess its approach to rigid cost control. European Chief Executive Jac Nasser held controversial long-term views about the company's future, and also understood the self-harming potential of products such as the current CE14 Escort, and was keen to promote a new generation of engineers and designers.

Ford's engineers were in near revolt about the cost-cutting that had been rife on the CE14 and BE13 Fiesta. 'Never again' was the battle cry at Merkenich and Dunton, and by not rejecting their demands Nasser helped create the design and engineering hot-house that cultivated the Focus. Although he was ruthless with suppliers, he fully understood the need for quality in design and excellent engineering for the cars themselves.

Once again, rising star engineer Richard Parry-Jones was the man behind the Focus product development. He had begun his 'dynamic craftsmanship' mission in 1993, but it reached new heights with this latest project, codenamed C170. "The original Focus program demonstrated the value of being bold and taking some risks," he said, "such as in strikingly original design, innovative packaging and unique suspension design – but it also showed the importance of fanatical attention to every detail."

The first designs for the Escort replacement were actually started in 1991, with models being prepared in both Dunton and Merkenich studios under the codename CE99. "It struggled to coalesce and it bumbled along for years making little sense and getting nowhere fast," recalls Martin Burgess. In the end, the designers decided they had seen enough of the organic radical look and came up with statements such as 'no more loopy bits' and 'death to ellipses' to clarify their next intentions.

Once the Ford 2000 strategy had been announced, the project was brought under tighter control and soon became a global initiative, to be developed in SVC, with Chris Clements initially leading the program, which was now known as C170. "Fresh, breakthrough design was still the order of the day and Dunton was on a roll: we were making leaps and bounds in design," continues Burgess. As the project developed, Australian John Doughty was appointed Design Program Manager, based in Merkenich.

A four-door version of the CE99 project in the yard at Dunton, done by Simon Spearman-Oxx. In the background is a two-door coupé proposal for CE99, by Martin Burgess. (Courtesy Martin Burgess)

CE99 clay model proposal from this somewhat baroque era. In the background, Mark Adams gives the model a passing glance. 'We wanted more cab forward proportions, only possible with a higher cowl to get over the HVAC. That's when we moved to C170, the original Focus' explains Spearman-Oxx.

The reverse side of the same clay model, finished in Di-Noc film. The 'sad face' was fortunately not pursued!

In Europe, North and South America, and South Africa, the C170 Focus would replace the various versions of the Ford Escort, Ford Laser and Mercury Tracer sold in those markets. In Asia and Australasia, it replaced the Ford Laser. This led to some difficult compromises. Whereas the European engineers wanted the car to offer class-leading dynamics and refinement to out-compete the Golf and Astra, in the US the Focus would be a price-sensitive entry-level car, competing with Korean and Japanese imports where chassis refinement was not so critical.

The interior was developed in Dunton, with the key sketch coming from Burgess. It continued the arc-shapes originally introduced in the Mondeo, and developed with the Fiesta and Ka. "My rough instrument panel sketch for the C170 was liked by the interior studio Manager Mark Adams and Chris Clements, and I was quickly co-opted to work with them in the C170 studio."

The big difference for the C170 was in the package, with a much higher seating position – or H-point – which was some 80mm (3.25in) above that of the Escort. This reflected the trend at the time for C-segment hatchbacks to move to a taller layout, halfway to a MPV, something that the Honda Civic, Fiat Stilo and Peugeot 307 all sought to emulate.

Following US criticism of the latest Taurus and Sable, there

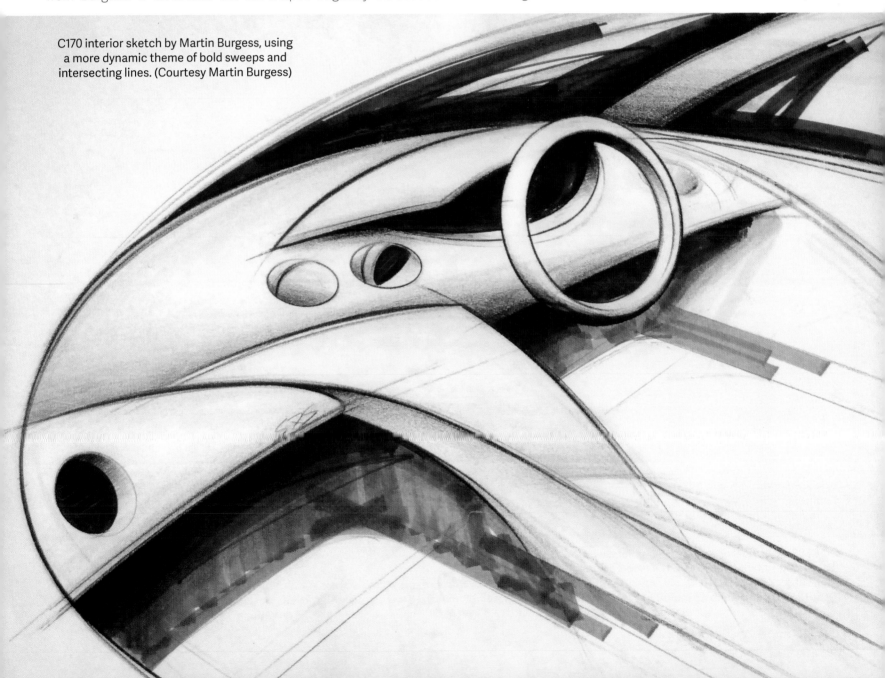

C170 interior sketch by Martin Burgess, using a more dynamic theme of bold sweeps and intersecting lines. (Courtesy Martin Burgess)

CE99 interior proposal carried on the oval shapes and round pods used in the Ka.

A C170 Focus interior clay model, painted and dressed for a market research clinic. Burgess: "We went to market research clinics with high hopes, and my theme was confirmed by the respondents as the strong favourite." (Courtesy Martin Burgess)

were severe misgivings about the radical C170 styling in 1996, particularly the C-pillar and rear lamp treatment. Was this going to alienate customers, or lead to a repeat of the Sierra fiasco? It was a huge gamble. Models were hastily reworked and presented in a more toned-down form, just as the styling was about to be signed off but the design team fought hard to retain the original theme, firmly believing that the car would resonate strongly once seen and subsequently driven by the public. After much wrangling, it was given the green light and was signed off in January 1996, giving just 24 months to Job One.

The Focus was launched at the Geneva Motor Show in 1998, going on sale that autumn. The Focus range included three-door and five-door hatchbacks, a five-door estate, and a four-door sedan that was targeted at the US and Asian markets. The Focus represented a high point of New Edge design, with a strong design character that proved hugely popular with customers. The decision to keep the daring styling was rewarded with another COTY award in 1999. This was exactly the accolade that the design team needed to regain credibility, although by that point things had moved forward for Design, and the team behind the Focus was no longer in place.

Rationality returns: The arrival of J Mays and Mondeo Mk II

Over 2.5 million Mondeos had been sold in Europe since the 1993 launch. However, sales were declining from 380,000 in 1994 to 232,000 in 1999 as the D-sector market contracted and the replacement model needed repositioning if it was to reverse this trend. More positively, one third of Mondeo sales were in the UK, where it had regained much of the ground lost by the Sierra and become a standard choice as a company car, much like the Cortina in the 1970s.

The new CD132 Mondeo had clear aims: it would be roomier, repositioned half a class higher, and packed with eye-catching equipment to counter the move towards premium marques by larger-car customers. The GM Vectra and VW Passat were the main rivals, with the Passat a clear bench mark for interior space. The car would need to grow accordingly, with a longer front overhang for crash structure and a 50mm (2in) increase in wheelbase to 2754mm to provide more rear cabin space. The trunk aim was for 500 litres, the biggest in class. In the event, the interior was nearly as big as the old Scorpio.

This was the first Ford created without a

The Focus was awarded Car of the Year in 1999. Besides courageous and fresh looks, the car was praised for its wide range of body styles, equipment, build quality and roadholding that was the new reference in its category, thanks to multi-link rear suspension.

Racing Puma and Focus RS

The Racing Puma came about from the race and rally programs carried out on the Puma from 1997 by the Ford Rally specialist team at Boreham. Shown in concept form as the Puma RS at the 1999 Geneva Motor Show, the production version was developed throughout 1999 using a tuned 1.7-litre Zetec-SE 153bhp engine, 75mm wider front track and 90mm wider rear tracks, plus uprated springs and dampers. Chris Clements was the main designer involved, and developed the concept into a very subtle design with new rear fenders, wider aluminium front fenders, new bumpers with integrated front splitter and tasty 17in Speedline Corse Turini alloy rims.

The interior gained Sparco racing seats were trimmed in blue Alcantara suede, which was also used on the steering wheel, door linings, rear seats and rear cabin. Production of this specialist vehicle was outsourced to Tickford in Daventry, with initial plans to produce 1000 units, all finished in Racing Blue pearl and destined for the UK market.

Despite this, it was not a success. At £22,750 it was seen as not only too expensive, but with insufficient power compared to the standard car at £15,000. In the end, just 350 were produced, with many ending up on the Ford management car scheme as a way to shift the stock.

The Racing Puma was followed up by the Focus RS. Following the arrival of Martin Leach in late 1999, Ford was keen to reinvigorate the Motorsport line-up of ST, RS and RS Cosworth models that had added such glamour to the Blue Oval during the 1980s.

The Focus RS came about through the dogged determination of chassis engineer Neil Briggs and designer Dave Hilton. They 'hijacked' Leach on an early visit to Dunton, and launched into a 20-minute pitch to him for their idea for a 200bhp WRC Focus for the road. After 15 minutes he stopped them, said he'd heard quite enough ... It was a great idea, just get on with it!

The program was approved in April 2000. It was developed through Ford Racing, with Tickford responsible for the engineering. The design model was done off-site by Hilton at GMD in Coventry, with the model being trucked down for all reviews in Dunton. It was launched at the British Motor Show in October 2000, going on sale in autumn 2002 at £19,995.

The design followed the template of the Racing Puma with 50mm (2in) extended front and rear fenders in steel covering the 18in x 8in OZ wheels, a deep air dam for the intercooler and cooling ducts for the Brembo brakes. The cabin included blue-faced RS instruments, Sparco blue and black leather seats, plus aluminium and carbon fibre details.

To manufacture it at an acceptable cost, unlike the Racing Puma it was built off-line in Saarlouis, with a run of 4500 cars. Hilton recalls how Leach dealt with a potential crisis at the plant just prior to the launch: "Saarlouis said it's too wide for the paint booth and wanted the car to be narrower. What! This news surprised me. I'd seen the booth, it seemed big enough. What they really meant was that there was a structural pole in a bend on the way into the paint shop. Leach told them to 'just cut the goddam pole!'"

The Racing Puma was a purely Dunton exercise, led by Chris Clements.

The Focus RS was modelled in Coventry at GMD. Seen here with early clay additions, the air duct in front of the rear wheel was later dropped. Bonnet vents were also tried but – perversely – they increased underbonnet temperatures. (Courtesy Dave Hilton)

The Focus RS used a 215bhp, 2.0-litre Duratec engine with Garret turbocharger and Quaife torque-biasing differential. Eschewing the flamboyant Escort Cosworth rear spoiler, the small amount of rear lift on the Focus RS was reduced with a discreet rear bib spoiler.

paper engineering drawing. Dunton and Merkenich employed their latest C3P CAD system, which was reckoned by Chief Engineer Paul Mascarenas to have eliminated a whole level of prototype build, and carved 13 months out of the three-year program. Design work started in spring 1997, with Manfred Lampe and Gert Hohenester responsible for the initial exterior model, under the direction of Claude Lobo. Parry-Jones – now VP of worldwide product development – was also closely involved with development of the car.

The 2001 Mondeo Mk II was roomier, better equipped, and more elegant than the outgoing model. Mays: "We tried to wrap the tail lamps around to visually shorten the rear overhang. Those lamps eat up a good 200mm around the side of the car."

The Scorpio debacle had irked Jac Nasser and he was about to have his revenge. Prior to this time, Ford Design management was always promoted from within and never, ever, recruited externally. It was therefore a shock when J Mays was hired in October 1997 by Nasser from design consultancy SHR to take over from Jack Telnack, who decided to take early retirement after a 40-year Ford career.

43-year-old Mays had grown up in Maysville, Oklahoma. His father owned a large cattle ranch, but also operated a go-cart track where J and his brothers spent many summer weekends. After studying at Art Center in Pasdena, Mays joined Audi in 1980, where he worked on the B3 Audi 80, launched in 1986. After a brief excursion to BMW, he rejoined Audi, where he was responsible for the AVUS concept, Audi TT and VW Concept 1, and stayed in Germany until 1995.

"Jac Nasser actually leap-frogged Jack Telnack and canvassed all of the Ford designers worldwide on what direction we thought design should take and which competitor we most admired in design terms," explains Burgess. "Largely, the answer which came back to both questions was ... Audi. So when Jac Nasser was considering a replacement for Telnack he already had the 'Audi' thought in his mind."

"I have been brought in to make some changes and I fully intend to do that," Mays told *Ward's Auto World* in an interview at the time of his appointment.

Not wishing to hang around under the new boss, Fritz Mayhew decided to take early retirement too at the end of 1997. "I was very much a part of Jack's team. We worked closely together, there was a natural connection," commented Mayhew. "I feel close to Jack personally and professionally. His retiring certainly had an influence on my decision to leave." Mayhew retired to resume a career as an accomplished watercolour landscape artist, going on to exhibit widely in Detroit and Florida.

On his first visit to Merkenich, Mays was apparently appalled by the new Mondeo models when he first saw them, and took his concerns to Nasser. He believed the New Edge proposals – while stylistically interesting – lacked the quality and elegance necessary to compete against the Passat, Audi A4 and Alfa Romeo 156. Mays wanted to reskin it immediately. Nasser agreed, but Parry-Jones insisted he took no more than three months to avoid wrecking the CD132 program timing.

Thus, in early 1998 Mays moved to Cologne and effectively redesigned it himself. By this stage the Mondeo program had already been running for six months, and it was essential to keep all the established hard points and basic proportions. In the event, the centre line didn't change, with the bonnet, windscreen, roof and trunk profiles all remaining the same "We went from a six-light to a four-light DLO and changed the design language to be more in line with Focus. We gave it more of an upscale look, with a more vertical front end," explained Mays to *Autocar* magazine.

This was clearly a difficult time for Lampe and Hohenester and both also elected to take early retirement that spring. To compound

J Mays replaced Jack Telnack as VP of Design in 1997. His passion for cars began at an early age, sketching them from five-years-old. His first car was a Datsun 240Z, soon followed by a 1955 Chevy Bel Air coupé, although both were later traded in for a Jaguar XJ12 – an early sign of ambition!

Chris Bird joined Ford in 1998 as Director of Design. From this time, the office for Design leadership in Europe moved from Dunton, and resources shifted increasingly to Merkenich.

the new mood sweeping through the studio, in September 1998 Mays poached an old colleague from Audi, Chris Bird, to help him push through his ideas. By December, European Design Chief Claude Lobo decided to resign, too, and in January 1999 Bird replaced him as Director of Design for SVC. Lobo was 55-years-old, and had been with Ford for 32 years. It was the final passing of the old Merkenich team who had worked there since Bahnsen's time.

"J laid down the building blocks and I implemented them," commented Bird to *Autocar*. "We kept Lampe's proportions. Within that we completely reskinned the car, giving it a tauter, more elegant and classier appearance. The result overall retains suggestions of Ford New Edge but is far more refined than the first proposal. Timeless rather than trendy."

Over in Dunton, the interior was progressing, too. The aim was to give the design the precision and quality of an Audi with perhaps slightly less German austerity. Soft-feel quality was designed throughout the cabin, and the longer wheelbase meant all the door apertures were bigger. Ergonomics were more considered too. As a way of simulating the declining mobility of older people, the designers and package engineers donned 'third age suits' to check the package, while controls needed to pass the 'glove test' so they could be operated with ease in cold countries such as Scandinavia.

The cabin employed the latest safety features too, including two-stage front airbags, front side airbags, and curtain airbags in the cantrails. Equipment levels were raised, with electric windows and air-conditioning on every model, and fitment of a 6 CD in-dash autochanger. There was more rationality applied, too. The four IP air vents were an identical shape, which saved time and money. On the previous Mondeo all four were totally different ... "The fact that we've gone more geometric on these interiors creates order and harmony that maybe wasn't there on past products," said Mays unapologetically.

When the CD132 Mondeo was announced in September 2000, the car was seen by the press as something of a test for the capabilities of the new Ford team in Europe, namely FoE President Nick Scheele, Engineering Chief Martin Leach, and Design Chief Chris Bird. Mays explained the resulting design to *Autocar* journalist Gavin Conway: "We were aiming to take the design direction that started with Focus. We have tried to take some of the visual clues of the Focus and apply them in a more upscale way." Conway suggested some Teutonic influence, but it was denied. "If there's anything that has a little of VW influence it is that sense of solidity. That is a property that is not the preserve of the Germans, it is just a way of doing a vehicle to give it a more milled look."

A new Transit

One big casualty of Ford 2000 was the Transit. Since 1986, the commercial truck engineering group in Europe had been decimated, with most engineers either having left or moved to Iveco. The only thing left was the Transit. To recap a little, the VE6 Transit had gained a face-lift in October 1991 – the VE64. Although it was a £300 million program, the exterior styling changes were negligible, comprising a new horizontal grille and rounded top corners to the headlamps. However, underneath, the Transit was heavily revised, with the rear floorpan totally re-engineered behind the cab to meet the latest rear crash regulations. This new floorpan for the LWB versions allowed for single rear wheels to be used, meaning the width of the loading floor between the rear wheelarches was increased by 365mm (14.4in) and thus a Euro-pallet could be accommodated over the axle for the first time. Not only that, but the rear axle was shifted rearwards by 550mm (21.6in), together with flat-topped rear wheelarches for better weight distribution and more practicality. Elsewhere, the body was upgraded and strengthened, with independent front suspension and 15in wheels being used across the whole range.

Next up was the VE83 update that came in September 1994. Exterior-wise, this was distinguished by the use of the corporate 'Smiley Face' front grille and larger door mirrors for the Transit. Although at first glance the exterior changes were minor, this time the cabin was heavily redesigned, with an emphasis on car-like quality, safety and comfort. The seat frames were strengthened, with the centre front seat and rear seats for the 15- and 17-seat minibus versions gaining full three-point seatbelts to meet latest safety requirements. Likewise, the IP was totally redesigned to accommodate optional twin airbags, and the styling picked up on themes from the recent Mondeo saloon, with multiple oval shapes used as motifs. NVH levels were much improved, too, through use of better door seals and tighter shutlines, while security took a step up, with higher quality door locks and alarms being fitted, reflecting the increased values of toolkits and cargos now being carried.

As part of the VE83 redesign, the Tourneo nameplate was introduced to denote the eight- or nine-seat minibus versions of the Transit with side windows. Since then, the Tourneo models have become ever-more luxurious and MPV-like, in order to fully compete with other van-based models, particularly the VW Caravelle and Mercedes Viano.

Once the VE83 was in production, that team too was dispersed, leaving very little in-house resource at Dunton for further Transit development. Once the new structure was announced by Trotman, it was clear that the replacement for the Transit would now be entirely designed in the US, even if the van had never been sold in that market.

In the early 1990s, work had begun on the next-generation Transit. The initial plan was for two projects: a smaller FWD van coded VE104 with a lower load floor, and a larger VE129 project, effectively a reworked Transit VE83. Nasser rejected this two-model proposal, so a revised VE160 concept program was started. Graham Symonds was put in charge of its design at Dunton, with engineering being outsourced to engineering consultancy firm Hawtal Whiting, in Basildon.

Now, of course, the Ford 2000 global strategy in 1994 recommended that all commercial vehicle product development should be centred in Dearborn, where CAE techniques and expertise were far stronger than in Europe. Hence, from early 1995 the Dunton-based Transit team was relocated to the US, with around 35-40 staff moving at first, including Symonds.

Hawtal Whiting hoped to retain involvement in the program, but by summer 1995 it was let go, despite having a major engineering operation in Detroit. A completely new start was made on Transit, with Dave Grandinett as Chief Program Engineer. Although Transit had proved a huge success, with a 39 per cent share of the UK van market and sold in over 60 countries, it was still not a global vehicle. The overall aim for this all-new generation was to design a versatile van that would be 'Best in Class' in terms of load dimensions, handling, dynamics, running costs and security, to span the one-tonne and two-tonne van market.

The big debate on this VE184 program was over the drivetrain layout. A RWD layout with dual rear wheels was definitely preferable for the heavier chassis cab versions, including pickups and tippers, and would allow easy adaptation as a 4WD version, too. Meanwhile FWD could allow a simple dead rear axle, giving a 100mm (4in) lower rear load floor – a huge advantage for the panel vans. How to reconcile the two layouts? This proved extremely challenging, given

The 1994 VE83 Mk V Transit introduced the 'smiley grille' and new IP, together with the 2.0-litre DOHC 8-valve engine, as used in the Ford Scorpio.

that the FWD layout was with a transverse east-west engine with an end-on transaxle, while the RWD layout used a conventional in-line engine, gearbox, and propshaft.

After much deliberation, it was decided to engineer both versions within this huge program, and to design a chassis and front structure that could accommodate both layouts – an industry first. To meet the aims of a truly versatile vehicle, three wheelbases would be offered of 2933mm, 3300 and 3750mm, with four possible lengths and three different roof heights. To cap it, there would be an all-new range of Duratorq diesel engines that could be fitted either north-south or east-west in the engine bay – no mean feat.

Regarding other commercial vehicle activities at this time, Ford started to homologate some of its global models for sale in Europe, including the UK. The Ford Explorer was imported from the US from 2000, and offered for sale to compete against full-size Jeep and Toyota 4x4s, but it struggled to gain a foothold in the market. More successful was the second-generation Maverick that was based on the US Ford Escape, sold from 2001-'06, with switchable 2WD/4WD and a towing capacity of 1700kg (3747lb) that proved popular for towing large caravans. Sharing many parts with the Mazda Tribute, it was assembled in Saarlouis for sale in Europe, from parts imported from the US and Japan.

VE184 Mk VI Transit arrived in January 2000, produced in Genk and Southampton. VE184 was RWD with an in-line 2.4-litre Duratorq diesel engine and gearbox. The VE185 was the FWD version, with a transverse engine layout and 100mm (4in) lower rear floor that followed around a year later. The 2.4-litre Duratorq could not be made to fit in this configuration, so a 2.0-litre Duratorq engine was developed.

Finally, the Ranger pickup was sold in Europe from 2005, including a useful double king cab version, all produced in Thailand. From 2011, the latest T6 Ranger range was offered in Europe too, with a rugged 1269kg payload and 3500kg towing capacity.

More politics, more disruption

In 1999, Trotman retired a year ahead of schedule. His departure, however, was slightly dimmed by a disagreement over who should succeed him. In the end, William Clay 'Bill' Ford Jr, great-grandson of the company's founder, prevailed upon the board to split Trotman's role so that he – Bill Ford – became Chairman, and Jac Nasser was appointed Chief Executive. The decision was announced in October 1998.

Nasser was a man who was not known for patience. To stem heavy losses in Europe and South America, Nasser quickly reversed large parts of Ford 2000, and, in particular, restored decision-making power to Ford's regional organisations, a move that was certainly appreciated by European managers. One of the first decisions he made was to bring the VE184 Transit project back to the UK in summer 1999, along with nearly 400 jobs, revitalising the atmosphere at Dunton for commercial vehicle development.

Thus, by December 1999, Martin Leach was Head of Product Development in Europe and was reporting to Nick Scheele as Ford of Europe Chairman, rather than to Parry-Jones in Dearborn. "Ford still designs global vehicles and powertrains, and it maintains a global purchasing operation. But sales and marketing must remain local," said Scheele. "What's left today of Ford 2000 is what I thought it should be in the first place. What we discovered about Ford 2000 was that you can't run a corporation as big and complex as Ford from Dearborn."

Talking to *CAR* magazine in 2000, Parry-Jones also commented that the Focus program was a good example of how Ford could reduce costs yet maintain product excellence: "The Focus is an efficient low-cost product. We got together with suppliers early, we shared all the targets and then not only did the design, which was the old way of working, but also the sourcing footprint, logistics system, inventory, tooling costs – everything to minimise the costs of the vehicle."

In 1999, Ford made a healthy profit of almost $6 billion (£3.6 billion) but the majority of those profits came from US trucks and 4x4s, such as the F150 and Explorer SUV. Things then changed rapidly. By 2000, things were looking bleak, with a scandal over deadly accidents involving the Explorer vehicles and the defective Firestone tyres with which they were fitted, resulting in a $3 billion (£1.8 billion) recall. With Ford losses continuing to mount, Jac Nasser was increasingly under the spotlight, and was falling foul of the Ford family, not helped by the fact that he had been the main protagonist for expansion into expensive ventures such as PAG and Jaguar's involvement in Formula 1 racing.

The Firestone recall was a hugely costly dispute between the two companies that led to Congressional hearings to establish who was at fault – not something the Ford family relished at all. The $580 million (£350 million) loss in just the third quarter of 2001 was the final straw: after barely three years in the job, Chairman Bill Ford fired Nasser in October 2001, just weeks after the new Fiesta launch.

In the wake of Nasser's departure, the entire PAG organisation came under pressure, and soon projects at Jaguar, Aston Martin, Lincoln, and Volvo were curtailed. With his patron now off the scene, PAG boss Wolfgang Reitzle also decided to call it a day, and departed soon after in early 2002. In the final analysis, Nasser was a brilliant leader with ideas well ahead of his time but he tried to do too much too quickly and alienated managers, dealers, suppliers and ultimately the Ford family – which still held 40 per cent of the voting rights in Ford company shares.

J Mays and Ingeni studio

In 2001, J Mays commissioned a new 'design and creativity studio' in London's Soho district, as an urban think tank for Ford's European brands. "The company with the best people wins," he said to *CAR* magazine. "And getting the best people is about location. We've got one of the best in London and one of the nicest buildings. This will attract designers who wouldn't normally consider the auto industry."

Designed by architect Richard Rogers, the 3020sq m (32,431sq ft) Ingeni building in Broadwick Street was designed to have a rotating team of 30 designers over six floors working on new models for Ford's eight brands, as well as on non-auto products such as sunglasses, watches, furniture, guitars and bullet-proof briefcases. It was operational from summer 2001, initially headed by Henrik Fisker, later by Gerry McGovern. However, it proved short-lived, being shut down by December 2003 in a desperate bid to cut costs in the wake of the Firestone tyres scandal that cost Nasser his post.

Ford did not immediately get rid of the £15M ($25M) building, however. It retained part of the upper floors as PAG's European headquarters and Mays's main office, along with the basement restaurant and Bean-Stalk, a graphics business 70 per cent owned by Ford. It was finally sold in 2010.

"We were making our numbers, but Ingeni doesn't fit into Bill Ford's back-to-basics company philosophy," said Mays in 2003. "I can understand the brands being unhappy funding Ingeni. It was inevitable under the circumstances."

In many ways, it was a missed opportunity that Ingeni wasn't developed as a central London studio for Ford. Nissan's studio in Paddington, set up at the same time, showed that a central London location can prove highly attractive to lure top designers.

Ingeni studio in Berwick St became the headquarters of J Mays in London. It was also the base for the entire PAG operation, headed by Wolfgang Reitzle.

Chapter

8

Downsizing at Dunton – but a variety of new projects

After the turmoil at the end of the Nasser era, a calmer stability in Ford was established. Martin Leach had been appointed VP of Product Development in Europe in January 2000, having previously been CEO at Mazda. With the Focus and new Mondeo successfully launched in Europe, Ford Design could turn its attention to a raft of new projects for the new millennium, although, by the end of that decade, the scene at Dunton would be rather different.

Chief Designer Chris Bird was 42-years-old when he arrived at Ford in 1998. In fact, it was not the first time he had worked for Ford, having begun his career as an interior designer in Dunton design studio, after his graduation from the RCA in 1981. He then went to work for Audi AG in Ingolstadt, Germany, in 1986, becoming Chief Designer at Audi in 1995, responsible for many production exterior designs, including the A4, A6, A8, TT and AL2 concept.

With the old guard now gone, and with J Mays' full support, Bird strengthened the senior team. In summer 2000, Bird hired Nikolaus Vidakovic – then at Hyundai, but previously an old colleague from VW Group – to head up Interiors.

Having lived in Germany for most of his working career, Bird decided to be based firmly in Cologne, meaning that the focus of attention was now increasingly the Merkenich studio rather than

Nikolaus Vidakovic was brought in as Chief Designer for interiors in summer 2000, having previously worked with Chris Bird at VW Group.

In 1999, the Fiesta received a final minor face-lift aimed at giving the car a New Edge look, with a Puma-inspired face, new bumpers and wheel designs, it was colloquially known as Mark V in the UK. Seen here is the clay model with Di-Noc finish in the yard at Dunton. The design was handled by Martin Burgess, Paul Coucill, and Pete Ballard.

skills in metalwork. "They could bash out a metal inside-outside model – a 'runner' even – in a way impossible elsewhere," recalls Martin Burgess.

Exterior design returns to Dunton – the B-car program

After 11 years in production, the Fiesta was due for a major redesign that would be launched in September 2001. Under the Ford 2000 strategy, this was part of a trio of B-cars that would replace the Fiesta three- and five-door and introduce the taller Fusion model.

With Merkenich fully loaded with the Mondeo and Focus projects, it was decided to give Dunton the complete program to handle and thus introduced a major program of exterior design that had not been seen since the early 1970s.

The old model's weakness was the cramped cabin, although its great strength was its excellent dynamics, vastly improved by subtle steering and subframe revisions introduced for the BE91 revamp. This B-car program would use a totally new architecture, known as B2E, which was much stiffer and designed to last two generations, with variants of it utilised by Mazda for the Mazda3 and Demio models, plus the low-volume Ford StreetKa roadster. Although the platform was new, the steering and suspension setup was carried over, with engineers from the Puma project working on chassis and suspension and briefed by Martin Leach to make it as thrilling to drive as the new Focus.

During development, the Peugeot 206 was the bench mark, but then the Skoda Fabia arrived and was seen as the best package to beat. In the end, the wheelbase was increased by 41mm to 2487mm to give 60mm more rear knee-room, with the front track pushed out by 48mm at the front and 71mm at the rear to give the largest footprint in its class.

As with the Focus, what was really different this time was the height. This was increased by 97mm, with the seating H-point up by 45mm to give better vision for smaller drivers. It was part of the overall trend in smaller cars to offer a much better package within a given overall length, thus reversing the trend for ever-lower rooflines that had dominated car design since the 1940s.

The first investigations for this major project were led by Chris Clements, who went to Dearborn for the pre-program work on this trio of B-cars, together with designer Stuart Cooper. "Both were back and forth across the Atlantic regularly in the course of this

Dunton. The previous union agreement whereby 60 per cent of the design and development work would be allocated to the UK was revisited around this time and work was increasingly shifted to Germany, with the headcount at Dunton reducing drastically from the previous numbers employed in the 1980s.

Under Vidakovic, the Interiors team was strengthened, with most interior work for future Focus and Mondeo projects now undertaken in Germany, leaving Dunton to look after the Fiesta and commercial vehicles. The Colour and Materials group at Dunton was also steadily downsized around this time, with a new group in Germany being established for the larger workload that the Focus and Mondeo programs would require.

It was not only Dunton that saw cuts. With money now tight throughout Ford, an announcement was made in March 2001 to close the Ghia studio in Turin, with Filippo Sapino set to retire after 32 years with Ford. The 48 staff employed were redistributed within Ford, with just five designers remaining for a further year to work on digital projects until the building lease expired. Designer Claudio Messale moved into the Merkenich studio as Chief Designer for the C-Max and Focus Mk II. Colour and materials designer Sally Erikson moved to Dunton, while Dave Wilkie stayed on in Turin for a while to develop the Ford StreetKa with Pininfarina. It was a sad end to what had been a fabulous studio for Ford in Europe, one that had unique process, and several of us contributed exterior concept designs including myself and Dave Wilkie," comments Burgess. Following the philosophy of Mays and his VW team, the aim was for a competent, mid-European design look that was rational and fundamentally simple.

By 1999, the program was moving into production stage, and Mark Adams took over as project manager for the Fiesta, codenamed B256 for the five-door. With 14in wheels being used again, Adams insisted that studio models were shown with these standard wheel sizes, rather than more flattering 15in or 16in items until the basic proportions were resolved. "The whole car has really benefited," he asserted to *Autocar*. "It means the styling will look good even to the buyer of the cheapest model. The days when base models could be allowed to look inadequate are long past."

The sixth generation Fiesta introduced a six-light body style for the first time, emphasising the car's spacious interior package. "We tried to avoid the MPV look, like that seen on small Hondas," commented J Mays. Length was increased by 89mm over the old model, to 3917mm.

The three-door version came one year later than the five-door. Following Japanese practice, and to give more differentiation, it had a more raked C-pillar with the roof sloping more strongly towards the rear, and shorter tail lamps. Shown here is the finished clay model of the B257.

The exterior design followed the Focus, with a swooping roofline profile, high-set rear lamps and bulging wheelarches to give it a good stance and accommodate the wider tracks. Overall, it was more orthodox than the Focus, particularly at the rear where the vee-shaped rear window of the larger car was replaced with a rectangular item. The front corners of the car were pulled back sharply to reduce the effect of the overhang and bold rectangular headlamps were mounted either side of the slim arc-shaped grille to give a confident snub-nosed look.

"The Fiesta's design is simpler, but deliberately there's a lot of Focus in it," commented Chris Bird to *Autocar*. "The big lamps give the Fiesta a really friendly face." Adams concurred: "It's all quite deliberate. The big lights give the car a fresh, optimistic look and radically change an observer's view of the car's scale."

The car was launched in five-door form at the Frankfurt Motor Show in September 2001, with production starting at Cologne in summer 2002. At the same show, a number of key competitors were also launched including the Honda Jazz, Citroën C3 and latest VW

Polo, meaning the new car would face stiffer competition from day one.

The three-door version was designed at the same time in Dunton under the B257 codename but the launch was delayed by a full year. With the three-door Fiesta, the idea was to give it a coupé-like profile this time to appeal to a younger audience and to give a more sporting stance for the subsequent ST versions. Up to that point the three- or five-door versions of the Fiesta, Escort and Focus all shared the exact same roof profile and silhouette, whereas some Japanese rivals such as the Honda Civic or Mazda 323 allowed the three-door to have a quite different character, and Ford was keen to try out this strategy.

The third member of this program was the Fusion. This was fully developed by Chris Clements's team as a baby SUV under the 'Urban Activity Vehicle' or UAV tag. The nearest equivalent at the time was the Honda HRV, on sale from 1999, a high-rider UAV that did not pretend to be a baby off-roader in the guise of a small Suzuki but rather something more style-orientated, with most sales being of the 2WD version rather than the 4WD option.

For the Fusion, codenamed B226, the product planning and design teams used extensive focus group consultation, with feedback being used to inform the design. Three design proposals were shown as 2D images for initial focus groups, and modified following their comments. Three full-size clays were then developed and re-presented for further feedback, with a final design proposal being signed-off as a see-through GRP model.

Interiors for both models were all done in Dunton, too, resulting in a wide number of clay models designed by Paul Campbell's team. Designers included Martin Burgess, John Hancock and Cliff Jones, although they found the conflicting direction and constraints from the focus groups difficult to handle, and the resulting production designs were fairly uninspiring.

In the end, the intended strategy behind the Fiesta and Fusion was rather undermined,

The Fusion was shown in concept form at the Frankfurt Show in 2001. It used Hella bi-Xenon headlamps and a small, 1.1-litre, three-cylinder turbocharged DISI engine to showcase the innovative technology that Ford was developing at the time.

Originally launched in 2002 under the tagline 'Tough, Urban, Cool,' the Ford Fusion struggled to gain sales in a market that was becoming full of alternative compact lifestyle vehicles.

The Fiesta interior abandoned the swooping forms employed on the outgoing model and introduced a more sober cabin. For the first time the IP could be split with a lighter colour used for the lower areas, adding to the feeling of space.

because the styling differentiation was too subtle. Although the three-door Fiesta was different from the five-door, there was not sufficient change to project a stronger image, and many people failed to notice the modifications. Likewise, the Fusion looked very similar from rear three-quarter view to the five-door Fiesta and the lack of a specific 'tough' character and no 4WD option rather limited its appeal as a baby lifestyle vehicle.

Writing about the Fusion in 2010, Clements commented "It is possible that, with hindsight, the dependence on market consultation could be seen to have moved the design towards the status quo at the time the process was undertaken, which inhibited risk-taking. If one of the more dramatic concept designs which were on offer had been selected, then a more striking design could have resulted."

A new type of Transit: the Connect

On the commercial vehicles side, the Transit Connect was the next project for Dunton, being done almost concurrently with the Fiesta and Fusion from around 1998. Initial planning and pre-program design had been carried out in Dearborn under the commercial vehicles group, but the final stages of detail design and development were handled by Dunton.

With the rise of the artisan owner, the van market in Europe was changing. In the 1980s, the high-cube van market emerged, where light vans were designed to accommodate a Euro-pallet to become more practical. By the mid-'90s the light van market was shifting yet again, this time becoming rather more sophisticated with higher demands for style, comfort, and safety – so-called multivans.

Ford planners realised they needed a different kind of light van, not simply a van-derived version spun off the new Fiesta

The Fusion interior mirrored the geometric theme of the Fiesta and used common parts including the steering wheel, instrument pack, centre stack, air vents and switchgear.

platform but something bigger, which could out-compete new French rivals such as the Citroën Berlingo and Renault Kangoo multivans. The decision was taken to base it on the global C170 Focus platform, with an increase in wheelbase, slightly wider tracks and a simplified rear suspension using a dead axle and leaf springs. Just like the larger Transit namesake, this new Transit Connect, codename V227, was planned with two wheelbase options, both sizes resulting in a longer van than the French models. The SWB version with 2664mm wheelbase (some 66mm longer than the Escort van) was offered in T200 guise with 683kg payload or T220 with 843kg payload. If more payload and space was required, then the LWB T230 model with a higher payload of up to 902kg was available, for a premium of around £1000. This not only had a 250mm longer wheelbase and slightly longer rear overhang, but had a higher roofline, with a height of 1981mm.

Launched just a few months after the Fusion in February 2002, the Transit Connect was initially assumed by many observers to be simply a van derivative of it, not least because it shared the styling theme and square headlamp motif of the Fusion. Of course, it was considerably different, being engineered and constructed as a proper commercial vehicle, with reinforcing of the bodyshell using high-strength steels and double-skinned bodysides. As an example of its capability, the SWB Connect van could even accommodate two Euro-pallets loaded through the rear doors.

Included in the project was the Tourneo Connect. The Tourneo nameplate had been used on the passenger version of the larger Transit and the Tourneo Connect was designed as a multivan vehicle with side windows and separately removable 60/40 split rear seats – something neither of its main competitors featured. It also boasted the option of twin sliding side load doors as well as twin rear doors or a tailgate.

In short, there was nothing quite like this on the market at the time. What the Transit Connect offered was loadspace capacities not far off that of the original Transit van combined with a low load floor and a car-like cabin and driving position. Indeed, not since the original 1965 Redcap Transit project had Ford designers and engineers tackled a van project with such dedication. It was a great example that when Ford sets out to do something with conviction, it usually comes up with an outright winner.

The Escort van and the Fiesta Courier had been assembled at Halewood and Dagenham respectively, but both plants were due to cease Ford car production (Halewood was to be handed over to Jaguar, whilst Dagenham was to become an engine plant

The Ford Connect was built at Kocaeli in Turkey, part of the Ford-Otosan venture that had assembled Transits since the 1960s.

Ford Connect Tourneo, seen here in LWB form with the higher roof.

only) so a new production facility was needed. Thus, the decision was taken to build the Transit Connect at an all-new production facility at Kocaeli, Turkey that was part of the Ford-Otosan venture, which had assembled Transits since the 1960s.

From New Edge to Kinetic Design: the arrival of Martin Smith

Initially, Mays had been publicly supportive of Mayhew's New Edge design look. In 1998 he said to *Ward's Auto World* "By Edge design I mean a precise, technical design language. It doesn't need to cancel out other looks and it might evolve into something we don't define as Edge, but the priority will be on precision and a technical look. We

can't use it across the board between brands but it will be applied to one brand [Ford].

"We will define a form vocabulary that defines each brand. It's a mistake to send mixed messages to the customers. It will take a decade to do it, but we'll be creating internal competitors." Mays was certainly right about the timescale – it took until the close of the decade to fully bring a new look to all the Ford models, not to mention the PAG brands of Jaguar, Volvo, Lincoln and Land Rover.

May's opinion then changed. Talking to *Autocar* in September 2001, Mays said "I don't talk about New Edge, I prefer the term Ford DNA. The family look stretches from Ka to Galaxy." When asked whether he was happy with 'Ford DNA' he was blunt with his answer: "If you came to a Ford motor show stand three years ago it was a mess. We had a pot-pourri of inconsistent designs. Today there's a much stronger identity."

Realising he needed to strengthen his European design capability, in 2004 Mays decided to bring in Martin Smith from Opel to become Executive Design Director Europe. Smith had been a fellow colleague from Audi days, but had departed in 1998 to become Opel's Design Director. Like Bird, Smith had also started his design career at Dunton, being an early intern student from the RCA in 1972.

"I was sponsored by Ford, and lucky because I didn't have an art school training but an engineering background," recalls Smith. "I'd no idea how to sketch, or how to hold a Magic Marker even. When it came to the summer vacation there was an American VP of design – Ken Nelson – who didn't want students in the studio. I was devastated and wrote a strong letter to him, which didn't go down well with HR ... I was put in the drawing office for about six weeks, where people like Ron Saunders and Trevor Creed would come over and set me projects." With no offer from Ford upon graduation, not surprisingly Smith took up an offer to join Porsche in 1973, the start of his career in Germany.

With both Bird and Smith based in Merkenich, Dunton's future as a studio once again looked shaky, with threats of possible closure. As the B-car program wound down there had been a period of downsizing in the studio, with around 20 designers leaving Ford from 2001 onwards. Mark Adams joined Opel, Matt Weaver went to Nissan, Stuart Cooper and Niki Smart to GM, while others transferred overseas to Dearborn, including John Hartnell, who sadly died there soon afterwards. Likewise, there was a general drift away for the skilled modellers and engineers, many of whom started to work for engineering consultancies around Europe on a contract basis.

To fill the gap, Dunton found time to get involved in a variety of side projects. Mays was keen to see more concepts produced by Ford, and so the studio was engaged in producing the Fiesta RallyeConcept and the Visos showcar, and one year later supported the cars for the *Thunderbirds* film (see sidebar, page 178).

Martin Smith arrived in 2004 as SVP of Design, having previously been with Opel and Audi.

Ford Fiesta RallyeConcept RS

Ever keen to find new projects to satisfy his motorsport passion, in 2002, Chief Designer Chris Clements led the design for a concept based on the latest three-door Fiesta. Following the style set by Hilton's Focus RS, it was unveiled at the Birmingham Motor Show in October that year, with engineering by the RallyeSport team and targeted towards the Super 1600 rally series. Tracks were pushed out around 100mm each side on 18in 15-spoke magnesium wheels. Fitted with an uprated 200bhp 1.6-litre Duratec engine and six-speed Hewland sequential gearbox, it was a dramatic exaggeration of the basic Fiesta theme, with a huge trapezium-shaped mesh lower grille and slotted side intakes ahead of the front wheels. Even though the interior was dominated by the integrated roll cage and rally seats, this was no crude motorsport special, but rather a full-on design exercise that sported computer-generated blue and purple body graphics on the silver body – very different from the simple RS stripes employed in the 1970s.

The Fiesta RallyeConcept was built in 2002 as a way of demonstrating Dunton's capabilities at a time when the studio seemed under threat of closure.

The trio of Fiesta RS concepts developed in Dunton are shown with the production Fiesta ST. The blue car was a production RS proposal, not pursued, while the silver and white Rallye RS cars were more extreme iterations, with wider tracks.

Ford Visos concept

The Visos concept of 2003 was the first true showcar produced by Dunton for some years. Taking the Capri as a reference point, it aimed to showcase the latest thinking in aerodynamic aids and LCD screen technologies for the interior.

"From the outset of the project we wanted to create a vehicle that incorporated clean, elegant lines and dramatic proportions that conveyed its purpose and character," said Chris Hamilton at the Frankfurt Show launch. "Using Active Surfacing, we were able to hide the aerodynamic aids normally associated with high-performance cars and only call on them when required. This retains the purity of Visos' purposeful exterior shape without compromising its performance potential."

The Capri references included two intake vents on the rear fender and the C-curl DLO motif, while the body surfacing was very plain, featuring a wide shoulder that broadened towards the rear. This was accentuated by angled, horseshoe-shaped rear lights with a third brakelight mounted in the rear hatch. This light also accommodated additional cameras for rear visibility.

The idea was the greenhouse could give an appearance similar to a futuristic aircraft cockpit. The windscreen, roof and rear screen blended into one, incorporating at the rear a deployable aerodynamic spoiler, and in the roof a pair of retractable panels that allowed easy access to the rear seats.

"We partnered with Sony to incorporate state-of-the-art electronics technology into Visos," said designer Paul Campbell. Ford also worked with Biganimal Design in London to explore new ways to display and interact with information on the LCD screens. The result was systems that were deemed intuitive to use, yet allowed full control over all aspects of the car – from in-car entertainment to the GPS navigation and the climate control system.

Reflecting on the car today, Chris Svensson says "Visos was a bit of a nightmare, there were so many inputs! It started life as the next-generation Capri but got watered down more and more. It ended up as an amalgam of other department's wants and needs. It lost its personality."

Visos concept. Simple surfacing was enlivened by 20in wheels that filled out the lightly flared wheel arches.

FAB 1 – Dunton to the (International) Rescue

It all began in January 2003, when film company Working Title approached Ford with the opportunity of working in a collaborative role as design and technical consultants on the new *Thunderbirds* film. Dunton was given responsibility for the main design execution of Lady Penelope's FAB 1, with Chris Svensson leading the project, working closely with the filmmakers and visual effects specialists. It was an offer he was keen to accept.

"Being involved in a film like this is unusual and exciting for automotive designers," said Svensson at the time, "especially for my generation who remember watching *Thunderbirds* as kids. However, some of our younger designers didn't have a clue what it was all about to begin with, so we got hold of some videos to educate them. There was a total enthusiasm from everybody to take part and that came across in the amount of work and ideas that were put forward – not just vehicles, but furniture and product design as well."

The core team comprised Svensson as Project Director, who worked on the initial theme selection and detail execution. Not surprisingly, Ford decided to use the latest Thunderbird as the 'image' car for FAB 1. Daniel Paulin did the exterior, and Tony Hunter, on assignment from Land Rover, worked on the interior. Hunter was chosen as he had previously worked on a special edition Defender for the film *Tomb Raider* in 2001.

A number of variations on the Ford Thunderbird theme were reviewed internally before the designers took the sketches to Pinewood studios for discussion with the film makers, who were more than enthusiastic with the caricatured 28in wheels for the six-wheeled monster.

"We wanted to make the car much lower and sleeker," says Svensson, "but that wasn't possible because they'd already done a lot of development work. The basic architecture was fixed so our job was to design the front, back and the interior, as well as all of the detail execution."

The Dunton studio designed the huge 23-foot long car in CAD, which was then built down at Pinewood studios as a simple GRP mock-up model, the whole process taking around three months. In addition to FAB 1, Ford also supplied a pink SportKa and several other vehicles to appear in the film. All the vehicles were shown on the Ford stand at the British Motor Show in 2004 as part of the film's promotion.

Speaking about it more recently, Svensson admits had it not been taken in the correct light-hearted spirit it could have killed his career ...!

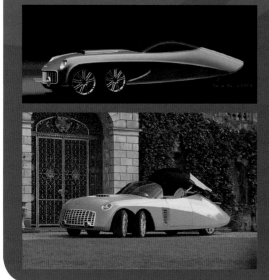

Sketch for FAB1, by Daniel Paulin.

The finished Thunderbirds FAB1 car for the 2003 *Thunderbirds* film.

At the beginning of 2006, Chief Designer Chris Clements took early retirement. A solid and practical designer who loved motorsport, he was finding the uncertain future difficult and turned his focus towards working with masters students at Coventry University and the RCA on industry projects. He also collaborated on several books and later wrote for the Design Council about the automotive design process. At the same time as Clements retired, so too did many of the talented cohort of designers that joined in the 1980s: Simon Bury, Andrew McColm, Martin Burgess, Brian Osman, Alan Thorley and John Beck.

Filling this void was Chris Svensson, who returned from Dearborn to take over as the Senior Manager of Dunton studio from 2006-'09. During this period, the studio was chiefly engaged in designing the Mk VII Fiesta, covered later in the chapter. "After Martin Smith arrived, he didn't want to do pre-programs out of Dunton, so the work moved more to commercial vehicles," says Svensson. "I became Chief of Commercial Vehicles, both exterior and interior. Some commercial interiors had been done in Merkenich, but now they were all done in the UK again."

From September 2003 Lewis Booth replaced Martin Leach as President of Ford of Europe, becoming Chairman and CEO in 2004. Like Leach, he had previously been CEO at Mazda.

Recalling his arrival, Smith comments that "J had offered Chris the job to run Ford in Germany, and Chris with J's encouragement had pursued these Germanic styles. Competent cars, with a rational mid-European design philosophy. Lewis Booth comes along, doesn't like it, there's a bit of conflict with J – 'This is too boring,' he said. Lewis wanted drop-dead gorgeous cars that he could stroke – he's a real enthusiast. 'Get someone in to design something I can stroke,' he said. After I came in their relationship improved no end, and J got the freedom to do what he subsequently did."

Smith started at Ford on 1 Aug 2004. "On the second day Lewis and J showed me the new Mondeo, they'd been struggling with it. It'd been pulled and manipulated by all sorts of people," recalls Smith. Agreeing that they should start again, Smith was given carte blanche, and assembled a team together, designing a new model in Merkenich. "It was finished by November, we got it all signed off and approved by Christmas. In four months we completely did the car again."

In that period Smith also sketched out a design strategy, things he thought were key to establishing a new Ford identity. "The designs at the time were professional, but had no spark to them. I did a storyboard showing what the key elements could be. A form language that was more muscular, tauter, more refined, with bolder graphics, a new front identity with a trapezoid grille and bold wheelarches as on the Focus. I showed it to J, and he agreed. 'But show that to Lewis,' he advised. Well, we showed this PowerPoint on brands and what aspirational brands aligned with Ford in terms of products, what colours were associated with Ford, and some ideas applied to the new Mondeo. Lewis wasn't so impressed, he thought

Lewis Booth was chairman and CEO for Ford of Europe from 2004-'08. He was also Chairman of PAG before the disposal of the various companies from 2007-'11.

it all a bit airy-fairy. 'Stop showing these pictures of posh bloody handbags and just do some cars!' he said."

According to Smith, the new CD345 Mondeo embodied all these elements. "I then persuaded J and Lewis that to launch this new strategy we needed a spectacular showcar – which became the Iosis. We took all those themes, exaggerated them and enhanced them, and produced it at the same time as Mondeo as a signal of where this new design direction was going."

Smith confirms that there was no name at that point. "We started in New Year 2005 on the Iosis as a promotional vehicle for the new design language, which people would recognise afterwards that the Mondeo embodied all of these elements." The Iosis was shown to the media at Canary Wharf in London in August, just before the Frankfurt Show launch. "PR were well involved, but we still needed a name. Someone came up with the term 'Kinetic Design' and once Kinetic Design had been coined it stuck – it expressed everything we wanted to say. 'Energy in Motion' was another tagline we considered, suggesting it looks like it's moving when it's standing still – Lewis loved that one, too."

The CD345 Mondeo was rapidly designed in the autumn of 2004 and launched in 2007. Sizewise, it was actually bigger than the old Scorpio, but with sales far reduced from the heady days when the Mondeo would sell over 300,000 examples per year.

The Focus Mk II and C-Max

The second generation Focus was planned for launch in 2004, with work starting in 2001. Rather than a reskin of the old car, the Focus Mk II, codenamed C307, used a new platform called C1 shared with the Focus C-Max, Kuga, Volvo S40/V50 and Mazda3. The C1 platform was engineered in Merkenich, as the 'C Technologies Program,' said to be one of the largest platform-sharing programs in history at that time. Among all of the cars, the floorpan pressing itself was different, but the front and rear subframes, suspension, steering, brakes, safety and electrical components were shared, in total around 60 per cent of the total components. Part of the motivation behind this new platform was to allow for the higher payload and weights that the heavier C-Max and Kuga spin-offs would demand, something the C170 platform could never accommodate.

In fact, Ford was caught off-guard in two ways with the original Focus. First, the lack of a compact MPV derivative as pioneered by Renault with the Scénic and Citroën with the Picasso was a missed opportunity, and one that took until 2003 to correct with the launch of the C-Max. The 1996 Scénic compact MPV had been a spectacular success for Renault as part of the Mégane line-up, and every maker was looking to move into that market, including VW with the Touran and GM with the Zafira. A number of studies and models were carried out to design a MPV based on the C170 platform, particularly a package that could offer a clever fold-away third row seating like the Zafira, but it was to no avail. The window of opportunity was rapidly passing, and the planners refocused their attention on a C-Max based on the forthcoming C1 platform.

Although the Mk I Focus had a higher H-point than the Escort, the new C214 C-Max would offer a true MPV seating position, and five adaptable seats in a one-box body, with a vast 1672-litre trunk capacity. Although the wheelbase was harmonised with the new C307 Focus at 2640mm, the floorpan used a double skin to give a higher flat floor in the cabin, with the roof a good 70mm higher than the Focus hatchback.

The second area where the original Focus was caught out was interior quality. The Focus Mk I was launched concurrently with the VW Golf Mk IV, a car that fundamentally altered the quality standards in that segment. The Focus, with its polypropylene IP and hard plastics used in the cabin, was never on a par with the Golf, although its chassis qualities and fine Zetec engines redressed the balance somewhat.

Thus, the C-Max and new C307 Focus would get significant interior quality upgrades, using some parts developed for the new Mondeo, such as the steering wheel, instruments and switchgear. The IP was made from far higher quality plastics than before, and the overall feeling of solidity increased markedly, in a deliberate attempt to emulate the standards set by the Golf.

The slush-moulded IP top pad was extended down to surround the centre stack, which used rotary heater controls on base versions and a push-button climate control panel for higher versions. As on the Mondeo, the four air vents were the same shape, and carried over the oval theme that had been a hallmark of the original Focus.

The C307 Focus and C214 C-Max were developed in Merkenich as global products with a full line-up of body variants and engines. The C-Max was given priority, as Ford was very late into this market by now.

The Focus was designed as a three-door and five-door hatch, plus the five-door estate. The four-door sedan version was previewed as a concept developed by Ford Australia at the Beijing Motor Show in mid-2004, and joined the range after the hatchbacks. Compared to the C170 predecessor, the new Focus had a 25mm (1in) increase in wheelbase, was 168mm (6.6in) longer and 8mm (0.3in) taller. The big difference was in width, where the new car was 138mm (5.4in) wider at 1840mm – some 30mm (1.3in) wider than the Mondeo.

The new Focus C-Max was previewed at the Paris Motor Show in 2002, and was on sale in 2003, two years ahead of the Focus Mk II. The C307 Focus was launched at the Paris Show in September 2004, complete with a concept version of the coupé cabriolet, dubbed 'Vignale.' This would eventually go into production with Pininfarina in Turin from 2006, replacing the StreetKa as their main production output for Ford.

The production C-Max MPV arrived in 2004, using the new C1 Focus platform.

The C307 Focus Mk II was a purely Merkenich project, including the interior. New technologies included a KeyFree system, solar-reflective windscreen and adaptive front lighting, Bluetooth hands-free phones and voice control for audio, telephone and climate control systems.

The three-door body was offered in sporting ST guise with a 2.5-litre Duratec engine with 222bhp and – seen here – in ultimate RS form from 2009 with 301bhp. The vibrant 'Ultimate Green' paint colour was one of three colours offered.

Developments in digital design

Digital design methods had improved substantially since the early CAD days, and were now used regularly to present design ideas. In 2004 Dunton installed a full-size virtual reality suite with an 8-metre by 3-metre 'Powerwall' that allowed designers and senior managers to view 3D life-size digital images of new model proposals.

"I've always held out that the optimal process is a mix of human skill and using CAD and digital tools to speed up the process, rather than to *be* the process," continues Smith. "So we always took a more classical approach of an eye-catching sketch, then doing more realistic sketches, and taking that relatively quickly into scanning them and transferring into 2D images in Photoshop. Thus, in the very early stages you can produce a convincing image to project onto an 8-metre screen and show to management as though it's a 3D model in the yard, yet it's just a 2D rendering."

Smith described to the author how he liked to go from 2D to 3D relatively quickly, at the same time taking early 3D data, and milling scale models to test out proportions and themes. "The modellers then manually refine them. A mix of skilled manual modeller and digital modeller. I always like to play out the two skills together. Then go quickly into full-size milled model, cleaned up by the modellers, put tapes on it, digitise again, refine in CAD and come back to the model. The change happens before your eyes. The problem with CAD is that you cannot see what is changing on screen, only at the end. It's often fantastic, but I prefer a modelling process that's out there on the studio floor, throwing tapes on, blacking out the windows, getting a feel for the whole thing. Once you've got that, the adjusting of lines is easy. Then you take a scan, refine in CAD, remill and look again. That's a good process."

One of the first projects to benefit from this leading edge technology was the Ford Transit face-lift (or MCA in Ford terms – Model Cycle Action). At this stage, the VE184/185 received a MCA to the body, including new front and rear lights, a new front end, and a new interior featuring the gearlever mounted high up on the IP. Known as V347 for front-wheel drive and V348 for rear-wheel drive, it was introduced in August 2006, and proved a high spot for the studio, providing a much-needed boost to morale. The new front end was particularly successful, giving the Transit a fresh look that many outsiders believed was a completely new vehicle. Besides the styling changes, the powertrains were revised with a new generation of 2.2-litre and 2.4-litre TDCi diesel engines offering more power and stage IV compliant emissions.

Seen here in SWB low-roof form, the Mk VII Transit V347/348 was a particularly successful face-lift of the earlier V184/185 design and introduced a new generation of 2.2-litre and 2.4-litre TDCi diesel engines. In many ways the new front end was a similar exercise to the old '78 Transit, providing the van with a powerful new lease of life.

The Transit was offered in limited edition SportVan form in 2007 as a way of strengthening the image of the Transit as part of Ford's line up. This successfully built on the Transit SuperVan image from the 1970s. Available in Performance Blue with white bonnet stripes, it featured 18in alloy wheels, a full body kit, and optional leather seats.

347/8 Transit
de door graphic change

Original carry-over door graphic

Revised door graphic & new logo position

The Transit door pressing was lightly revised to allow a new side glass graphic, although the window glass itself remained unchanged.

Interior mock-up of V347. The design followed the geometric, rational look that was fashionable on the cars at this point. The high-mounted gearshift allowed a walk-through cab for the first time.

One Ford arrives and PAG disappears

From 2007 Ford saw another reorientation in its operations. New global CEO Alan Mulally introduced a new 'One Ford' strategy that saw the company adopt a global product approach, designing and building cars for a single customer base, not divided by regional or national borders. Although at first sight this looked like a revamp of the Ford 2000 program, the big difference here was that regional R&D centres such as Dunton had more control of projects, and

could design them around global Ford regulations and manufacture, rather than everything being directed by Dearborn.

The new CD345 Mondeo being designed in Merkenich was based around a new midsize platform that had been introduced in 2006 for the S-Max and Galaxy models. Known as the EUCD platform (for 'European C-D class'), it was loosely based on Ford's compact Focus C1 platform, and shared many suspension, steering, braking, and electrical systems. The EUCD platform was also used for Volvo's S80, S60, V60 and V70 models, the Mazda6, plus the Land Rover Freelander LR2 and related Range Rover Evoque.

A further new model of the EUCD architecture was the Kuga, also designed in Merkenich. Seeing the rise of the compact sport-utility vehicle market, Ford decided it was essential to offer a new type of compact off-roader that was far more attractive to active families than the old Maverick and Fusion models had proved. In many ways, the Kuga compact SUV would take on the mantle of the Capri in the marketplace as the high-volume speciality derivative based on a mainstream platform, and – ironically – it appealed to the same target customer: successful, young, family men who wanted something a bit special that demonstrated they had not given up on an active, sporting life, but wanted to share it with their young children.

As Ford implemented its One Ford plan, it decided to divest itself of its luxury brands that made up Premier Automotive Group, beginning with Aston Martin in 2007. The following year Jaguar and Land Rover were sold to Tata, followed by the sale of Volvo Cars to Geely in 2010. The Mercury brand was also discontinued at that time, and Ford's 33 per cent stake in Mazda was sold off over the

Alan Mulally in the Dunton studio with the Iosis concept from 2005. Mulally was CEO from 2006-'14, and successfully steered the company through the difficult financial period of 2008-'10.

The Ford S-Max and Kuga were both examples of new model introductions that brought Ford into more fashionable market segments for the new decade. The CD340 S-Max was a joint development with the Galaxy program, and a large percentage of parts was shared across the two models.

The Ford Kuga was based on the EUCD platform with a shorter 2690mm wheelbase. Seen here is a Titanium version with 19in alloy rims. Both the S-Max and Kuga were Merkenich studio programs.

period 2008-'10 to stabilise its assets. Over the past two decades, Ford had spent $17 billion on building up PAG, but now, for the first time in many years, Ford management was able to focus entirely on its core products, utilising the Ford and Lincoln nameplates for all its markets around the world.

B-car part two: the 2008 Fiesta Mk VII

From 2005, Dunton design studio began to work on the next generation of Fiesta, the B299. Although only four years since the launch of the B256, Ford was keen not to be left behind again in this crucial small car segment, and needed to have a new model ready by 2008. This seventh generation Fiesta was developed under the GPDS (Global Product Development System), and continued with the existing global B-car platform, albeit updated so that it could be marketed in the US market, too – the first time since the original Fiesta had been sold there in the 1970s.

"I wasn't happy with first Fiesta sketches," admits Smith. "There were 20 different themes but no strategic vision behind them. I then showed the strategic presentation on Kinetic Design to the Dunton guys, said 'Look this is the master view, management are backing it, J is very much behind it, you've got to do the next Fiesta, a very important car. There's a wall full of sketches, but none of which have any brand identity or alignment with what we're trying to develop.'" One key addition to the senior team came with the arrival of Smith's right-hand man from Opel, Stefan Lamm, on 1 January 2005. "He saw the new Mondeo model, was surprised, he didn't expect we'd got that far along."

Smith then got Chris Svensson, Chris Hamilton, and other key players, and discussed with them the new Mondeo. "Take that and make it even funkier for Fiesta. Two weeks later I came back. The definitive sketch of what became Fiesta was on the wall, Chris [Hamilton] had done it. It had the dynamic wedge, the kick up at the rear, bold graphics etc."

Lamm also wanted to do an exterior model in Merkenich, so three themes were developed at 40 per cent scale until Easter that year. Marketing had also developed a new strategy for the Fiesta using focus groups and target customers resulting in the aim for a 'sprinty' car – something fun, young and trendy. The models were shown to Booth for comments but he was not entirely convinced, finding them too aggressive. However, the research results were unequivocal and Booth relented, admitting that the Fiesta needed a more sporty character to compete against the Polo and Clio. Smith and Lamm had also just completed the forthcoming Opel Corsa and had the benefit of knowing it would be a far more dynamic design than the current model.

The team employed tools and processes that were becoming common in the industry by this stage. Talking to *Car Design News*, Hamilton said: "[We went] straight onto a Wacom tablet and sketching in Photoshop. Once we've got things a little developed it's into an Alias model, throw it backwards and forwards between

Stefan Lamm arrived in January 2005 as Martin Smith's right-hand-man for exterior design.

engineering, develop it a bit more, mill it out, develop it by hand in clay."

"We ended up with pretty much three designs fairly quickly, then we went to two for a while, both going to full-size. And then it started to become clear from within design which was the preferred direction, so we were down to one model to push forwards."

Digital models of the sedan variant targeted at the US, India and China ran in parallel to the hatchback as well. "Once we got down to two [hatchback] proposals we did sedan derivatives in CAD. And

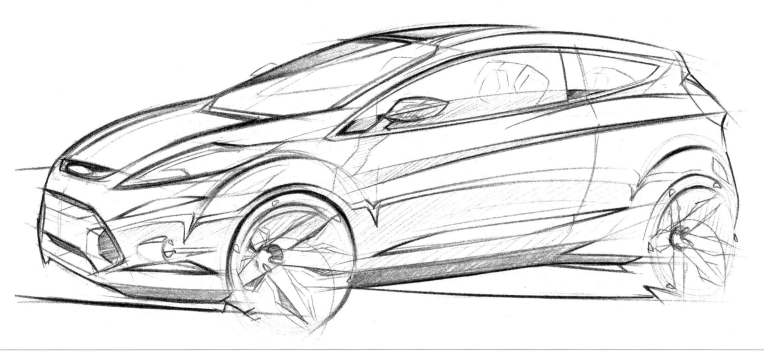

Sketch for B299 Fiesta by Stefam Lamm.

The seventh generation Fiesta was shown in concept form as the Ford Verve at the Frankfurt Motor Show, in September 2007. Rendering for the Verve showcar by Simon Collins.

once we got down to one main proposal, we took that to full-size clay in four-door also. The four-door was probably only one month behind the hatchback.

"We wanted the car to look sleeker so we pushed the A-pillar and the cowl forward, made the nose a bit smaller and the A-pillars faster; that all came from Design. So the initial first few months we were very clear about what we wanted to do and we fed that back to Engineering and then they told us what they can and cannot do."

This time around, the interior was developed by Vidakovic's group in Merkenich. The Kinetic Design theme included a wing-shaped IP, with a central area with mobile phone-type switches that fitted well with the 'sprinty' car aim, according to Smith.

The alternative full-size clay model from 2004 had a slightly different theme, with a kick-up at the front of the side window.

The preferred model undergoing final revisions. The clay model is covered with Di-Noc film to represent a paint finish.

The Fiesta B299, seen here in final five-door form. The new Fiesta was shown in production form at the Geneva Motor Show in March 2008, and marketed in Europe, Australia, and the US.

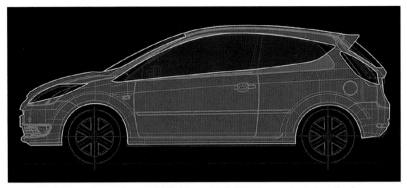

Package comparison of Mk VI and Mk VII Fiesta showing the key differences, mainly around the front end to meet pedestrian impact regulations. Despite the very different look, the two cars are the same length and height.

By 2012, the Fiesta had been face-lifted with a new front end, incorporating the latest corporate grille. The Fiesta remains Britain's best-selling car.

Group shot from 2008, showing the Dunton design team that worked on the new Fiesta. "Chris Hamilton led it, he was good at pushing engineering to do these swages, sharp angles and undercuts that they hadn't done before. An excellent result with the car," commented Martin Smith. (Courtesy *Car Design News*)

Stuart Robinson
Lead Alias modeller

John Rushmer
Alias - exterior detailing

Steve Moore
Alias - exterior

Chris Hamilton
Chief designer

Simon Spearman-Oxx
exterior detail design

Andy Wolton
exterior designer

Simon Collins
exterior designer

Emblems and logos have always formed a part of the design studio's remit, and demand a particular creativity from the designer to produce something fresh and original. The original Ka and Puma logos were memorable examples of excellent design, also this emblem for the Mk VII Fiesta.

Interior sketch for Mk VII Fiesta by Tiago Dias.

Interior of the production Mk VII Fiesta included a mobile phone-inspired entertainment system, and bold two-tone colour choices, such as this Soho Burgundy red colour.

Echoing this theme were the chunky rotary HVAC controls that sat at the base of the centre stack, styled to reflect the look and feel of high-end power shower controls. "Simple touches can radiate a feeling of quality," said Vidakovic at the launch. "These are critical touch points in the cabin, for both driver and passenger and creating a sensation of class through their styling and movement was essential."

This project saw Ford starting to use persona-based design techniques rather than rely solely on customer focus groups to understand customer taste. A design persona is a completely fictional character, created by the Marketing and Design departments, to which everyone involved in the development of the car can refer. The persona 'personifies' many of the lifestyle attributes that the car's target customer would have, and brings a human element to the dry statistical research drawn from polls and interviews. Based on psychological profiles, these characters are a more modern version of the 'theme boards' that designers once covered with snapshots and swatches of material to inspire a design. For the Fiesta, she was Antonella, a hedonistic, attractive 28-year-old woman who lives in Rome. Her life is focused on friends and fun, clubbing and parties. For the Kuga SUV, being developed in tandem in Merkenich, the persona was James.

To verify the design and the Fiesta customer, a concept of the winning Theme 1 three-door design was developed, later shown as the Verve. Smith: "We took cars to Italy and did focus groups with 27-28-year-old girls starting out professional life, who wanted a smart car. The Polo was seen as too dull, too expensive, but they all loved this aggressive design. It overwhelmingly won at research phase. We showed nail varnish colours too, it went down well. The numbers were very convincing, something like 85 per cent first choice."

The second generation Ka was the next project that used Kinetic Design themes. Codenamed B420, this was designed almost in parallel with the Fiesta, with some models done in Dunton as well as Merkenich. "We got the instruction to work with Fiat using the 500 platform," says Smith. "The execution was done in Cologne and Italy, with Claudio Messale playing a key role then with the Italian engineers. We managed to keep some of the cuteness of the original Ka, and took on a lot of Kinetic elements and rejigged them to create a new personality fitting to the target market: teenagers, college kids and older downsizers – quite a diverse group."

Ford Ka Mk II sketch by Paul Wraith.

Quarter-scale model of an early B420 Ka proposal, shown in typical studio 'work in progress' condition with modifications being added using tapes and clay.

The second-generation Ford Ka was introduced in 2008, based on Fiat 500 underpinnings. The Ka was designed alongside the Fiesta with substantial Dunton input to the design.

Like the Fiesta, the interior of the Ka was designed so that numerous colour and material variations could be configured.

Chapter 9

Dunton Design today

Under Alan Mulally's One Ford policy introduced in 2007, product development would now design and engineer the majority of Ford models for sale worldwide, with the Focus and Mondeo in particular being sold globally, not simply in Europe and Asia. Dunton would increasingly liaise with the other design centres across the globe, not just Merkenich and Dearborn, but also those in California, Brazil, Shanghai, and Melbourne.

It also meant closer liaison with the various manufacturing plants. That would now include Kocaeli, Turkey (Transit, Transit Courier), Craiova, Romania (B-Max), and Chennai (Ecosport) and Sanand (Ka+), both in India. Plus Silverton in South Africa (Ranger pickup).

Design Manager Paul Wraith takes up the story: "There was a real energy at that time, J Mays was on board, and the design organisation was moving rapidly away from those rounded, blobby design shapes into something much more formal. We were aiming to design more perceived quality into the car. A lot of pre-program work that had been done in the US was now moving back to Europe."

That included the B-car program, comprising the Fiesta, Ka, B-Max, and the latest Ecosport compact SUV, which all went through the initial pre-program start at Dunton and provided a lot of work for the studio in the period 2005-'08. Final production design for the Ka and B-Max was then developed in Merkenich, with the Ecosport being developed in Brazil. "We generated sketches for Ka, some clays, too," continues Wraith. "The ultimate design became more kinetic than our versions, which stayed closer to the original Ka. But the B-Max production car basically looks like what was handed over here."

According to Wraith, the B-Max was a complicated project, the assumption being that 'Fusion looks like a brick, so the new Fusion will do too.' "Then we added a sliding door on it and people quickly assumed it'll just look like a Connect," adds Wraith. "There was a lot of negativity initially as whether it'll work out. The kinematics of the door closure I worked out on CAD. Trying to get something that looks more like a passenger car was quite a challenge."

The Fiesta and B-Max projects were started at exactly the same time, but were launched some years apart. The Ford B-Max was launched at the Geneva Motor Show in 2012, and joined the C-Max, Grand C-Max, and S-Max Multi-Activity vehicle range.

Models such as the Ecosport, launched in 2012, typify the increasing importance of such speciality models in the line-up, offering the practicality and style prioritised by a growing number of family buyers. The Ecosport Titanium S edition was added in 2016.

Extending the Transit range

The other program that revived the studio at Dunton was more prosaic, but equally important to Ford of Europe. Once again, it was the faithful Transit that came at an opportune time to provide the studio with a slew of work from 2007 onwards.

As a One Ford vehicle, the new-generation Transit was designed by Ford of Europe and co-developed with Ford in the US. Launched at the 2012 Commercial Vehicle Show in Birmingham, this eighth generation of the Transit was the first to be officially sold in the United States and Canada, too. In a break from the previous generation of the Transit, there were to be two distinct body forms:

• Mid-size FWD only: now a distinct model, branded Transit Custom, codename V362. The aim was to compete with vehicles such as the Mercedes Vito/Viano, Renault Trafic, GM Vivaro and VW Transporter T5 with a more dedicated FWD van. In some ways, this was a rebirth of the old VE160 project – a less bulky van with a slightly lower seating position and height. As before, this was to be available in two wheelbases and two roof heights.

• Full-size FWD & RWD: a proper 'Two-Tonne' full-size derivative, to enable Transit to compete more effectively with the larger European vans such as the Mercedes Sprinter, Renault Master, GM Movano and VW T6. Codenamed V363, it also replaced the outgoing 40-year-old Econoline/E-Series in the North American market, with a payload capacity ranging from 900kg to 2280kg. The V363 series was launched in the UK in February 2014.

In essence, these eighth-generation Transits used the chassis and underpinnings of the outgoing V347/V348 series, but with a completely updated body and interior. The heart of the range was the Transit Custom that covered the payload capacity from 700-1400kg and load space of 6cu m to 8.3cu m. All Transit Custom models were FWD, with a low loading floor and rear dead axle mounted on leaf springs, and all used the 2.2-litre Duratorq TDCi diesel engine, mounted transversely with three outputs of 100, 125 and 150bhp, and fuel consumption reduced by 6 per cent over the older models. Although wheelbases were unchanged, the front overhang increased by 78mm to meet latest crash protection regulations, while the rear overhang was enlarged by 210mm to give class-leading cargo dimensions.

Transit Custom concept sheet, 2006. 'A bullet on the front with a box on the back.'

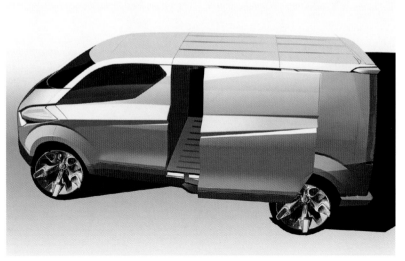

Early concept sketches for the Transit Custom program. Use of Photoshop allows designers to work directly over a drawing to turn it into a highly realistic image, without losing the dynamism of the original sketch.

Key sketch for the Transit Custom by Paul Wraith, Exterior Design Manager for the Transit Custom and Tourneo, Transit Connect, and Transit Courier programs. The V362 Custom program began in 2006.

Double-sided clay model of the V362.

"The Transit was a massive new program and it was decided to do it exclusively in Dunton," says Martin Smith. "We were too busy in Cologne to contribute to it at the early definition period, with Marketing." Seeing how Kinetic Design might be applied to commercial vehicles proved a tough exercise. "People were very sceptical about that," he continues. "The team in Dunton came up with great visualisations to explain the idea, a dynamic cab and very bold interior with tons of functionality and a basic box on the back. Paul Wraith and Chris Hamilton did brilliant sketches showing a bullet on the front with a box on the back, and people immediately got the idea for the design direction. I still think it's the best van on the road."

Transit Custom V362 was introduced in 2013 as the eighth generation of the original Transit One-Tonne van. It was awarded the International Van of the Year award in 2013.

Six different generations of Transit, spanning 48 years. Not shown here are the Mk III VE6 and Mk IV VE64.

Interior sketch for the Transit Custom, by Andy Collinson. Although not selected for the final Custom program, the theme went on to influence the smaller Transit Connect interior.

While Wraith led the Transit Custom project, Jordan Bennett was Design Manager for the Two-Tonne V363 Transit: "At the last count there were 27 different derivatives for the Two-Tonne versus the Custom," he says. "The manufacturing process was improved over the old Transit. It's a better-fitting jigsaw puzzle because this time around Design were more involved with the overall architecture – it's not just a styled engineering study. We've incorporated design thinking into all the panels, the way they go together. You can pick a line on the bodyside and track it anywhere now [over the variants]. It aids the manufacturing process too. The joins are all nicely worked out now whereas in the past they caused some problems."

The V363 program ran ten months later than the V362 Custom, with work starting in late 2007. The key objective was to be class leader for driver comfort and cargo capacity. This included a car-like cabin for the driver, with the best efficiency and maximum load capacity in the marketplace, plus best fuel economy for the engines.

The Two-Tonne employed the same Kinetic Design cues as the Custom. "I guess we'd instilled it in ourselves, it was such a design-led process," says Bennett. "It has form and sculpting you'd only associate with a car. It was quite difficult, you need to optimise the interior space so the envelope between the inside and outer surfaces is quite thin. It was a challenge to get any sculpting on the side."

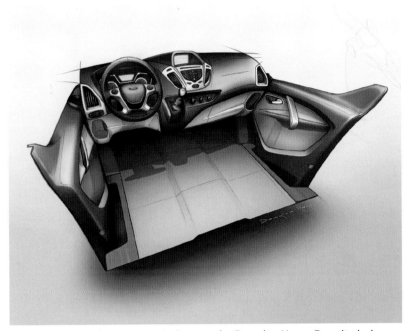

Interior sketch for the Transit Custom, by Douglas Hogg. Despite being a commercial vehicle, the Custom is typical of the current state of design, in that the interior is equally as expressive and sophisticated as those of the car program.

The V362/V363 generation of the Transit was the first to be officially sold in the United States and Canada. This diagram shows the range of the V363, which is offered in two wheelbases, three lengths, and two different roof heights. Load space capacities range from 6cu m to 15.1cu m. American Transit production began at the Kansas City assembly plant on 30 April 2014.

Clay model of the Two-Tonne. " By FC1 we'll usually go to full-size models," says Jordan Bennett. "Don't forget, even a 40 per cent scale model for a Two-Tonne Transit is still a big model! As big as a Fiesta …"

The interior featured a dual front passenger seat that flipped forward, accommodating a toolbox underneath. The centre seatback could also fold down to create a work table large enough to hold a laptop computer or tablet. Reflecting the growing sophistication of vans, the driver's seat now had an eight-way movement as standard, with a ten-way heated seat and armrest as an option.

Although the main IP moulding was unique to each model, the basic layout and many elements were shared, including the steering wheel, instrument pack, HVAC and centre Ford SYNC control panels. The gearshift in both was mounted high up on the IP, allowing a walk-through cab and three-abreast seating.

As on the outgoing V348, the Two-Tonne V363 Transit was available with the engine either mounted east-west and FWD, or mounted north-south, driving the rear wheels with 4WD as an option. However, this time all models used the 2.2-litre Duratorq diesel. For the North American market, certain attributes of the Econoline needed to be maintained, including barn doors at the rear and a low roof version unique to US versions. However, around 90 per cent of the engineering development was done in the UK, although US manufacturing was involved to ensure it could be built at the Kansas City assembly plant.

Transit Two-Tonne sketch by Jordan Bennett. "The side window has this 'shark fin' diagonal cut-off on the beltline. The previous Transit had it as a graphic, so we incorporated that into the Two-Tonne."

Production Two-Tonne Transit was launched in 2014 as a new model range to complement the Transit Custom. The front has wraparound headlamps and a powerful trapezoidal grille. 'This is a key feature for kinetic design' says Bennett. 'All the lines come from the grille and work their way out. It's a dynamic form.'

Completing the family: Transit Connect and Courier

When it came to planning the replacement commercial vehicle range for the 2010s, Dunton thought deeply about what was needed to achieve market leadership once again. This led to a radical rethink of the main Transit van strategy, and an expansion of the Transit Connect range to offer a comprehensive range of vehicles that could compete in every sector of the market from 500kg-2000kg payloads.

Launched in summer 2013, the new Transit Connect was based on the latest C platform, complete with its multilink rear suspension, replacing the dead beam axle of the previous generation Connect. Paul Wraith led the program, which offered two wheelbases of 2660mm or 3060mm as before, known as L1 and L2, and payload options from 625kg up to 1000kg. In total, three body styles were developed across the range, offering various seating arrangements to accommodate from two to seven people.

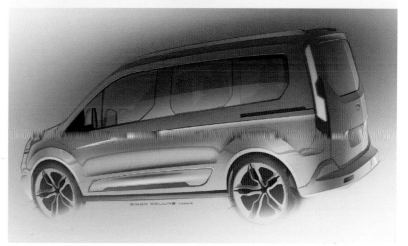

Photoshop rendering of the Connect Tourneo, by Simon Collins. Bennett: "We could just transplant the motifs direct from the cars, but the vans needed their own identity. I think we manage to achieve that when you look at the Courier, Connect, Custom and Two-Tonne, there's a common language."

Scale model of the Transit Connect.

Full-size clay development of the Connect Mk II showing the use of Kinetic Design cues in this smaller van package.

As well as two seats in the front row, the Double-Cab-in-Van version had an extra row of three foldable seats behind them, with flush-glazed side windows. A moveable mesh bulkhead safely separated the second row of seats from the loadspace. Meanwhile, the Kombi L2 had three side windows with flexible seating for the full seven passengers. Here, the second row seats moved forward and down into the footwell to fold flat, while the 50/50 split third row seats could also fold flat to create a large load area.

In addition, a five-seater Tourneo Connect passenger version was offered in both L1 and L2 lengths, with body-colour bumpers and slightly different rear door glazing, incorporating a wind-down side window. The engine line-up was also expanded to comprise a 1.0-litre 100bhp three-cylinder Ecoboost petrol engine, a 1.6-litre Ecoboost with 150bhp, or a 1.6-litre Duratorq diesel with various outputs from 75-115bhp.

The interior incorporated some clever new ideas. The van cab was available with an optional dual front passenger seat, so a centre third passenger could be carried for short distances. Both dual seat bases lifted up like Honda's 'magic seat' design to allow extra carrying capacity or a storage box and cubby for the driver. The lid of the instrument binnacle could be lifted to reveal a USB, AUX and 12V socket connector for aftermarket satnav devices or for charging mobile phones.

Since the Transit Connect had been launched in 2002, Ford had lacked a small light van in the 550-650kg class that could replace the old Fiesta Courier. This was redressed in 2014 with the launch of an all-new Transit Courier van, based on the latest Fiesta B platform. As with the Connect, a five-seater Kombi and plush Tourneo Courier passenger version were also offered, available with a trio of engines comprising the 1.0-litre three-cylinder 100bhp Ecoboost petrol or two Duratorq diesels of 1.5- or 1.6-litre capacity up to 95bhp.

As before, the 2.4cu m cargo area was designed to carry a single Euro-pallet, but this time it could be accessed through a

From a single model in 1965, the Transit van has grown into a full line-up of commercial van models. Seen here (left to right) is the Transit Courier, Transit Connect, Transit Custom, and full-size Transit Two-Tonne range from 2015. The Transit Connect is now built in Valencia, Spain.

The van range is complemented by a family of Transit Tourneo models, too. The Tourneo Courier and Connect are marketed as lifestyle multivans for young families, while the Tourneo Custom is aimed more at the business market of airport and hotel luxury shuttle buses.

sliding side door. The cabin had a number of neat solutions for toolboxes and cargo including a folding mesh bulkhead that allowed pipes of up to 2.6m to be carried within the van's compact 4157mm length. The upper IP was similar to the Fiesta, but extra wings on the side to meet up with the doors.

Finally, a simple panel van version of the B299 Fiesta three-door was continued, with a light payload of up to 500kg. With such a comprehensive line-up of five basic van models, available in multiple wheelbases and cab layouts, by 2015 Ford had regained market leadership in commercial vehicles in Europe, something it had not achieved since the 1980s.

Strategic planning and new mobility concepts

From 2007, the Ingeni studio in Soho was reinvigorated under J Mays with around half a dozen designers working on small mobility concepts, under Manager David Woodhouse. The remit also included strategic brand planning. "J was extremely talented at communicating a brand. He's brilliant and can tell a complicated story really well," comments Wraith. "We felt we needed to communicate what we did better, make sure we had flexibility to apply our Kinetic Design language over a range of products, to understand our customers better.

"We also need to allow the management outside of Design to believe in what we were doing. Engineers and accountants don't read sketches very well, nor believe in them, so you need to express yourself in a much more clear way. We therefore created a 'Blue Book,' a great tome for Design. It was important, so that for a period after that we were able to reconcile our proposals."

As a contrast to the Transit program, the Dunton team also became involved in several Ford Motorsport projects, including Malcolm Wilson's S2000 Fiesta and the Formula Ford Championship cars. "We turned one into a showcar with three-cylinder

Formula Ford Championship cars
being prepared in the studio.

Road-going Formula Ford Championship car in Dunton car park. *Top Gear* magazine drove it around London streets in December 2012: "It may be a mobile torture chamber in the rain, but this is a magnificent little machine."

EcoBoost engine with a power hike. Road registering a Formula Ford car with 180bhp and letting journalists drive it to McDonalds or Nürburgring was a great wheeze!" admits Wraith.

Another area that Dunton has become involved with is that of new mobility concepts for the 21st Century. This included Ford Smart Mobility experiments such as the GoDrive London car-share scheme. Like most car makers, Ford has an objective to become a leader in smart mobility, which includes car sharing, autonomous vehicles and car shuttles, and, with a lot of ongoing research based in London, it was natural for Dunton to embrace this area.

"The nature of that advanced work is different to producing regular cars," explains Wraith. "In place of a well-known circle of suppliers we're dealing with different partners. Not necessarily manufacturing partners, it might be city authorities or governments. The world is moving quickly towards electrification and disruptive brands are looking at this arena: Apple, Dyson etc."

Wraith goes on to explain that the design remit is not just about the physical entity but also the ecosystem and transport infrastructure, where it is no longer about the customers' whims and needs, but about legislative frameworks, and issues to do with pollution and city authorities. "There may be a collapse in the cost of 'last mile delivery' from around $5 to around $1.50, so how does that impact on the man in a van who needs to deliver goods or get his equipment into places to service them? In these critical environments how can we help them and contribute to that dialogue?"

Another outcome was an e-bike, as Wraith explains: "Our Palo Alto advanced research group set out an internal competition and out of 200 entries from Ford two of the top three were from Dunton. So in that area we're in a leadership position here. It's not unique to Dunton but we're good at it."

Dunton was also involved in the design of Malcolm Wilson's S2000 Fiesta.

Progress in digital design

Digital design software and methods have changed hugely since the 1990s, with all current automotive design graduates being familiar with Photoshop and Autodesk Alias software as part of their studies. Chris Svensson was one of the first in Ford who was using digital design software. "The RCA was purely traditional tools," he recalls. "Coming to Ford was the first time to use digital sketch tools and 3D surface build. Those Shimo Seiki machines were huge, massive. You had to go to the 'Shimo room' to use it ... now you can get an app on your iPad."

Svensson recalls that when he first came to the US in 1996 Ford was just beginning to look at early Alias software. "I had a system installed in my home in Birmingham as an Alias tester, an evaluator. I was a prolific CDRS user and they wanted me to test Alias. It was like $250,000 worth!

"It was an exciting time to be doing this rendering with computers, building your own CAD surfaces' he continues. 'Today we have Alias specialists for that, but back then designers just built their own models. You did it yourself. It was fantastic to sketch something and then build it, an amazing time."

Jordan Bennett explains the current setup: "We have a studio Alias modelling team. This is not A-class final surfacing, it's still sketching but in a digital form. Most designers can use basic Alias, so we'll sketch around the given package. Once that's confirmed we can use actual data to sketch over, build new data and mill out scale models. We continue to sketch and digitise and ping pong around until we get a solid 3D theme. We'll do this right up to FC4, which is a long way down the feasibility process."

Svensson sums up: "I look at what the guys sketch today and it's just phenomenal. I look back at the earlier stuff and it looks really primitive, a bit naive compared to what the guys turn out today. Pretty amazing really."

Digital image of the Transit Two–Tonne interior.

Update on Ford Design management

Together with the ongoing reorganisation in Ford under Mulally, Design also saw changes in its senior team. Ian Callum's younger brother Moray was promoted to Executive Director for Ford Americas Design in 2009, where he supported J Mays to integrate the design activities globally. Born in Dumfries, Moray had started with Chrysler after leaving the RCA in 1982, and subsequently joined Ghia in 1988. He came to prominence with the Via concept in 1989,

The electric bike project was one of the first results of collaboration on new mobility systems conducted by the design team.

and later designed the Ghia Lagonda Vignale, shown at Geneva Motor Show in 1993 with brother Ian's latest design from TWR – the Aston Martin DB7.

Moray remained at Ghia for a couple more years, then transferred to Dearborn, where he contributed to a broad range of Ford car and truck designs, including the 1998 Ford Super Duty pickup. He was appointed to lead Mazda's global design in 2001, and subsequently developed the 2003 Mazda 3, the MX-5, CX-7 and CX-9, and the 2008 Mazda 6, as well as a series of concept vehicles including the Washu, Ibuki, Kabura, and Senku.

After a 16-year tenure as Group VP Design, in November 2013 Mays decided to retire from Ford, and Moray Callum took over – the first time a non-American had held the top post. "A lot of credit goes to J in terms of us now being able to use any of the studios around the world to do any of our products," said Callum to *Car Design News*. "I think that's really good. You know the history. There were different studios designing different products for different countries, but now we really are a global design team." Since then, Mays has continued to live in the UK, and has become a visiting tutor at the RCA, thus continuing Ford's long-standing links with the college.

With a British designer as VP Design, it was fitting that an American designer – Joel Piaskowski – now took over the European design operations when Martin Smith took his retirement in July 2014. Piaskowski joined Ford in 2010 as its exterior design Director for the Americas, having previously been at GM and Hyundai.

"Ford of Europe is a much smaller scale than the mothership," says Piaskowski. "That has pluses and minuses. The pluses are it's more nimble, we can do things faster. The minuses are that you sometimes don't have all the resources that you have in Dearborn. But with the nimbleness you can compensate."

"It's an honour to hold this position, I don't underestimate the significance of it. I'm thankful for this opportunity, Moray is relying on me to run the European operation so I carry lot of weight on my shoulders. At the same time, design is fun. If you let this business get to you, you'll lose the vision of what we're contributing to the company. In many cases Ford of Europe has a big opportunity to contribute to the overall global scheme of Ford. We're working on a number of projects that will have that level of contribution, not just design but also from a Ford strategic standpoint. So still a very significant role in the global picture of Ford and Ford Design."

Compared to the past, the flow of designers is now a more international operation. Over in Dearborn, Callum is supported by fellow Brits Chris Svensson as Design Director Americas, and David Woodhouse, who heads up the Lincoln studio. Paul Wraith and wife Louise joined the team over there in 2016, too. Piaskowski concludes "I look at it as an opportunity to bring cultures together and internally [at Dunton and Merkenich] there are a number of cultures here anyway. You've got Eastern Europeans, Spanish, Italian, Turkish and Dutch designers, in addition to the Germans and British."

Moray Callum has been Vice President of Design since 2013.

Joel Piaskowski, Director of Design Ford of Europe since 2014.

Ford's current European structure, and the changing role of Dunton

When Dunton was first planned in 1964, its role was to design and engineer the Ford models for the UK market, with production based entirely in the UK. For the cars, this meant Dagenham and Halewood, for commercial vehicles it was Langley and Southampton, with tractors being produced in the new plant at Basildon.

By the time Dunton opened in October 1967, Ford of Europe had been created, and the remit had already changed. Now, Dunton would operate in tandem with Merkenich to cover the whole European market, with production across all production plants in Europe, including Cologne, Genk and Saarlouis. Into the 1970s, Valencia was added for the new Fiesta, and Ghia was established as a European advanced studio, although it always reported directly to Dearborn.

In 1971, it was decided to split the work of the two design centres on a 60/40 basis, with Dunton taking care of interiors, commercial vehicles, and colour and trim, while Merkenich focused chiefly on car exterior projects. This situation broadly existed throughout the 1970s and 1980s, until Ford 2000 was introduced in 1994, when a more global approach was adopted for the design centres and the work for Dunton and Merkenich was split depending on workload and available resources.

In 2000, Ford car production in Halewood stopped, ending over three decades of Ford Escort production, and the plant was transferred to Jaguar for assembly of the X-type. Two years later, production of the BE19 Fiesta was curtailed, and the PTA plant at Dagenham closed, marking the end of Ford passenger car production in the UK after some 90 years, although the press shop continued to stamp out body panels until mid-2013.

This was not the end for Dagenham, however, as by 2002 it had become a centre for diesel engine production, with a $500 million investment to produce the Duratorq and Lion V6 diesel engines, and Dagenham continues today as Ford's main plant for diesel engines in Europe. This is supported by the diesel engine development work conducted at Dunton, which has now become Ford's Center of Excellence for powertrain engineering and global lead centre for Commercial Vehicles. Dunton is also responsible as the global engineering lead for exhaust systems, powertrain mounting systems and powertrain controls, manual transmission, clutch and dual mass flywheel (DMF).

Meanwhile, Merkenich has become Ford's Center of Excellence for passenger cars (global B-/C-cars), product planning and design, and has become global lead centre for chassis and vehicle engineering, active safety, HMI (Human Machine Interface) and craftsmanship.

In addition, Merkenich has another annexe at Aachen in Germany, which is Ford's European Research & Innovation Center. This has global responsibility for advanced diesel engines, vehicle dynamics, driver assistance and active safety systems, and Connectivity, including car-to-x communication.

Aside from ending car production in the UK, Ford's plants across Europe have been drastically rationalised. In 2008, Ford acquired a majority stake in Automobile Craiova, Romania. This new plant initially took over production of the Ford Transit Connect, followed in 2012 by the new B-Max, together with manufacturing the small displacement 1.0-litre EcoBoost engine.

With the introduction of the V362/V363 Transit, European Transit production was shifted to Turkey, with the Southampton plant closing in 2013. Around 2.2 million Transits were produced in Southampton since production shifted there from Langley in 1972. Finally, from the end of 2014, the Genk plant was closed, with production of the Mondeo, S-Max and Galaxy all shifting to Valencia in Spain.

Dunton Design today

Today, the Dunton studio houses studios and workshops covering 4200sq m (45,000sq ft) plus a viewing yard, of 6870sq m (74,000sq ft). Back in 1967, Dunton had 28,762sq m of office space plus 33,000sq m of workshops. Each has now grown to over 60,000sq m.

Piaskowski explains the present setup: "Currently Dunton is exterior based and commercial vehicles. That doesn't mean it'll be that way forever though. We're looking at other projects for it. Dunton has done everything over time – cradle to grave – to now commercial vehicles. At Merkenich we're working with exterior, interior, and colour and materials. Dunton also has its own colour and materials facility, and they're supporting not only commercial vehicles, but also paint development. We're upgrading our facilities at Merkenich, getting more technology into the place, to better respond. We've got a lot of programs on our plate right now."

The work handled by Dunton studio also encompasses pre-program work, which includes market research and the basic proportions of the vehicle. "It covers the product definition within a given constraint or platform," explains Jordan Bennett. "The height, or base of the A-pillar can change, the wheelbase too a bit. It's the tuning before the product feasibility process."

Current studio manpower is around 40, with 10-15 designers, a similar number of digital modellers, plus the colour and materials team. In addition there remains a whole team for prototype build and studio engineering, many of whom are contract staff.

Design Technical Operations (DTO) is the current term for studio engineering. "The feasibility engineers are creative and flexible. They collect information from all the other areas here, exchange it with us and we work together to achieve the best result," says Bennett.

"I'm based in Merkenich but I'm in Dunton once a month," continues Piaskowski. "We also have reviews over [web conferencing platform] WebEx, sometimes they'll bring work over to Merkenich."

Bennett agrees: "There's no shipping of models to North America but occasionally we'll ship stuff over to Merkenich. The majority of Two-Tonne models are too big to ship, although the Connect and Custom are just okay. It's rare though, we prefer viewings here."

Colour and materials team. (Left to right) Louise Wraith, Julie Francis and Emma Lungdren.

Ford now has five stages of feasibility, FC1 to FC5, with most viewings and sign-offs done in Dunton. "We have various gateways, but physical properties are all viewed here," explains Bennett.

Dunton studio, with the usual mix of scale and full-size clays, plus interior half bucks.

Colour and materials development today

Colour and materials designer Julie Francis has been at Dunton for 13 years now, having previously studied textiles at the RCA. The colour and materials team is small compared with the teams at Dunton in the past, currently comprising four designers, with work focusing on the commercial vehicles (CV) range plus paint colour development across the passenger car line up in partnership with Merkenich. The colour and materials team in Germany is around 12 strong now, and both teams liaise closely with each other, but also work globally with designers in the US, Turkey and China, plus the plant in Mexico.

"We do a lot of pre-program and early concept work in close collaboration with exterior and interior designers on many projects," says Francis. "As a colour and material designer you bring all your inspiration to your trend work, we research everything that inspires us in colour trends. Then we work with our suppliers, see what's feasible, what new pigments are coming through, what new effects are being developed in micas and flakes – we're constantly trying to push the boundaries."

In terms of changes in methods during her career, Francis says the following: "The process of working with designers is becoming more holistic, but there's still a long way to go. There's less separation now, more emphasis on teams working together. The outcome is a much more integrated product at the end of the process. Also, the importance of colour and material design in vehicles – the emotional appeal that it has for the customer – has grown over the last decade. Also in CVs, absolutely. The customers are demanding that much more in the products, they want that appeal and quality."

Ford's early metallic paints in the 1960s suffered from durability problems that would be unthinkable today. 'It typically takes about three years to develop a paint colour, from the start of the process to seeing them out on the road. One year is spent going from the trend input from the four global teams. We pull out what's relevant for that model year, what's relevant for those products and narrow it down. Then a couple of years going through all the feasibility, weathering tests and mastering before it actually hits the road. I'd love it to be much shorter but that's the reality.'

Around September each year, the colour and materials teams meet up to exchange ideas. "Everybody comes together to have a creative workshop. Not just paint, but all commodities, including leathers, interior finishes, grains etc.

"For CVs, we typically develop ten colours excluding special finishes," she continues. "A core palette of six colours then a couple of trend colours. With CVs we try not to change them too often, as fleets need consistency. We also look at new colours for Tourneo versions, some more spirited colours."

Testing has got tougher as time has gone on. 'CVs have a tougher specification than passenger vehicles, but, across the board, expectations are higher, so testing got harder. But new materials and finishes are able to meet that. In particular, the 1000 cycle Martindale test [for fabric balling and pilling] is hard for fabric suppliers to pass with something that is attractive, not simply functional.'

"There's lots more digital presentation nowadays, but in the end it's still important to have physical models in colour and materials to see real materials, to feel them and get a sense of depth of material. That cannot be replaced through digital work. Digital is a tool to get you to that end product, but finally it's a fully sensory experience that's required, not just a visual one."

Test paint panels

Reflecting on 50 years of change

From the initial £10.5 million cost, over £4.5 billion had subsequently been invested in Dunton by 2007. Today, that figure is something approaching £6 billion. And yet Dunton remains something of an unknown asset within the UK, with fairly low awareness of its significance within Ford's global product development activities and its importance as a major centre for engineering and design talent in the UK.

Whilst compiling this book, the author found many design staff who had fond memories of their time at Dunton, an atmosphere in which you were part of a highly competitive, yet quietly understated family. Fairly typical was the summary from Martin Burgess, who repeated the following reflection from the 1980s:

"There was a large degree of rivalry, particularly between the designers and the clay modellers and the designers and the design engineers ... And yet I suspect that those very tensions were in part responsible for the powerfully tight and effective design machine that was, Dunton Design."

That can be compared with Paul Wraith's summary of Dunton today, which still has a similar warmth behind it: "Today, there's an openness in the studios to look and learn. In the car industry there's a belief that the greatest things to work on are supercars, then high-performance luxury cars, followed by mainstream cars. Right down at bottom of the food chain is CVs. But what we are now doing on CVs has the ability to drive what we are doing on passenger cars. There are open reviews between the studios, peer reviews, sharing ideas and thoughts to keep the overall story growing. There's no hierarchy between the emotional importance of a flagship vehicle like Mondeo and a car for China. They all get the same level of scrutiny.

"We never stop, there's always a new challenge, a new objective and the studio should continue to shape and evolve, whether its interiors, exteriors, CVs, passenger cars, advanced or racing cars. There's a team here that can take it on board and deliver consistently good products.

The latest Fiesta range, launched in 2016, is a careful evolution of the outgoing model. Dunton had some involvement in early pre-program work, but the car was subsequently developed in Merkenich. The range comprises the Active, ST-Line, Vignale, and Style. Each version has unique bumpers, front foglight surrounds and grille treatments, to better differentiate it from the others. The Vignale is more luxurious, while the sportier ST-Line is slightly lowered, with a rear bib spoiler.

The Fiesta Active has a raised ride height to increase the SUV crossover quality, with a gloss black roof, black plastic lower body cladding, and roof bars.

Ford Design in the UK – 70 years of success

"Oddly, we do it in a way that is quite discreet too. There's something that has a resonance with Dunton and the UK, it's crazy. I was talking to an industry journalist at Goodwood last year from the *Daily Telegraph*, a guy very focused on industry and innovation in the UK. He hadn't even heard of Dunton. I explained – well, there's 6000 people there …"

As Ford's global product strategy continues to expand, the contribution of Dunton as one of the eleven Ford Design studios worldwide will continue to remain a vital force in Ford's continuing success.

The final word rests with Paul Wraith: "Dunton is a bit of a guerrilla setup, a secret. I don't know if that's a deliberate ploy but we don't go shouting about it. But there's an awful lot to shout about here."

The Dunton Design Center was recently refurbished, with a new exterior façade, and redesigned showroom area and studios. This was the first time the facility had seen a major revamp since the building opened in 1967.

Ford in the UK has used a number of different systems over the decades to denote model codes. The original coding lasted until the late 1930s:
- Model T 1908-'27
- Model A 1928-'32
- Model AA Fordson 30cwt truck 1931-'35
- Model AF 1927-'32
- Model B 1932-'35
- Model C 1934-'37
- Model Y 1932-'37
- Model 7Y Eight hp 1937-'39
- Model 7W Ten hp 1937-'39

Ford model code numbers

Just prior to the Second World War, Ford of Britain began using a series of 'E' codes, denoting 'England':
- E04A Anglia 1939-'48
- E93A Prefect 1938-'49
- E71A Pilot V8 1947-'51
- E493A Prefect 1949-'53
- E494A Anglia 1948-'53
- E83W Fordson 10cwt van 1938-'57
- EOTA Consul Mk I 1950-'56
- EOTTA Zephyr Mk I 1950-'56
- 100E Anglia & Prefect 1953-'59
- 103E 'sit-up-and-beg' Popular 1953-'59
- 100E Popular 1959-'62
- 105E Anglia 1959-'67
- 107E Prefect 1959-'61
- 109E/116E Consul Classic 315 1961-'63
- 113E Cortina Mk I 1962-'66
- 118E Cortina Mk I 1500 GT 1963-'66
- 120E Corsair 1963-'70
- 123E Anglia 1200 Super 1962-'67
- 204E Consul Mk II 1956-'62
- 206E Zephyr/Zodiac Mk II 1956-'62
- 211E Zephyr 4 Mk III 1962-'66
- 213E Zephyr 6/Zodiac Mk III 1962-'66
- 300E Thames 5cwt van 1954-'61
- 307E Thames 7cwt van 1961-'67
- 309E Thames 7cwt van 1200cc 1962-'67
- 400E Thames forward control van 1957-'65
- 508E Thames Trader truck 1957-'65
- 3008E Zephyr 6 Mk IV 1966-'71
- 3010E Zephyr 4 Mk IV 1966-'71
- 3012E Zodiac Mk IV 1966-'71
- 3022E Zodiac Executive Mk IV 1966-'71

Ford Design in the UK – 70 years of success

From the late 1950s, Ford of Britain began using codenames to supplement the numerical codes. During the 1970s with Ford of Europe, these morphed into a series of girls' names:

• 'Sunbird'	109E/116E Consul Capri 335 coupé 1961-'64
• 'Archbishop'	Cortina Mk I 1962-'66
• 'Buccaneer'	Corsair 1963-'70
• 'Redcap'	Transit Mk I 1965-'78
• 'Panda'	Zephyr/Zodiac Mk IV 1966-'72
• 'Colt' or 'GBX'	Capri Mk I 1969-'73
• 'New Anglia' or 'ECC'	Escort Mk I 1968-'75
• 'Diana'	Capri Mk II 1973-'78
• 'Carla'	Capri Mk III 1978-'86
• 'TC'	Cortina Mk III 1970-'76
• 'TC2'	Cortina Mk IV 1976-'80
• 'TC3' or 'Teresa'	'Cortina 80' Mk V 1980-'82
• 'MH'	Granada Mk I 1972-'77
• 'Eva'	Granada Mk II 1977-'82
• 'Gloria'	Granada Mk II F/L 1982-'85
• 'Bobcat'	Fiesta Mk I 1976-'83
• 'Brenda'	Escort Mk II 1975-'80
• 'Erika'	Escort Mk III 1980-'86
• 'Erika 86'	Escort Mk III F/L 1986-'90
• 'Toni'	Sierra 1982-'93
• 'Delta'	Cargo truck 1981-'86
• 'Apollo'	Orion 1983-'90

In 1982, Ford introduced a new worldwide system of numerical codes. 'E' for Europe, 'W' for world car, 'S' for sports, and 'V' for commercial vehicles, such as Transit. Under the Ford 2000 and later One Ford strategies, the regional part of the code was dropped, all programs becoming global.

• BE13	Fiesta Mk III 1989-96
• BE19	Fiesta Mk IV 1995-2002
• BE146	Ka Mk I 1996-2008
• B200	RS200 1986-'89
• B226	Fusion 2002-'12
• B256	Fiesta Mk VI 5 dr 2001-'08
• B257	Fiesta Mk VI 3 dr 2002-'08
• B299	Fiesta Mk VII 2008-'16
• B420	Ka Mk II 2008-'16
• CE14	Escort Mk IV 1990-'98
• ACE14	Escort Cosworth Mk IV 1992-'96
• CE99	Escort replacement (abandoned)
• C170	Focus Mk I 1998-'04
• C214	C-Max Mk I 2003-'10
• C307	Focus Mk II 2004-'10
• CDW27	Mondeo Mk I 1993-'96
• CD162	Mondeo Mk I F/L 1996-2000
• CD132	Mondeo Mk II 2000-2007
• CD340	S-Max, Galaxy Mk II 2006-'16
• CD345	Mondeo Mk III 2007-'12
• CD391	Mondeo Mk IV/Fusion 2012-
• DE1	Scorpio (Granada) 1985-'98
• SE161	Puma 1996-2001
• VE6	Transit Mk III 1986-'91 (initially 'Triton')
• VE64	Transit Mk IV 1991-'94
• VE83	Transit Mk V 'smiley face' 1994-2000
• V184/V185	'Transit 2000' Mk VI 2000-'06
• V227	Transit Connect Mk I 2002-'13
• V347/V348	Transit Mk VII 2006-'12
• V362	Transit Custom Mk VIII 2012-
• V363	Transit 2-tonne 2014-
• V408	Transit Connect Mk II 2013-
• VX62	Galaxy Mk I 1995-2006

Glossary of design terms

While not an exhaustive glossary of automotive design terms, the following are terms used by designers and engineers and are found throughout this book:

- 4WD Four-wheel drive.
- A-pillar, B-pillar, C-pillar, D-pillar The notation of the car's roof pillars, from front to rear. A 'six-light' design – such as the current Ford Focus – has an extra window behind the rear door and thus features a final D-pillar at the rear of the car. Whereas the A-pillar and C- or D-pillar are chiefly concerned with the style and flow of the greenhouse, the B-pillar is primarily functional, and thus often blacked-out to minimise its visual intrusion (see DLO).
- Alias The main CAD software used within design studios to create 3D digital models. The full title of the software is Autodesk Alias.
- Armature The frame or structure for a mock-up model or prototype. It is also used to mean the underlying substrate or structure for a component – for example, the instrument panel.
- Belt line The main dividing line between the lower body and the greenhouse. Typically the base of the side windows (UK colloquial term = waistline).
- Bench marking The process of evaluating and measuring the car project against key competitors in terms of dimensions, features, specification, best practice etc.
- BIW 'Body in White.' Originally, most steel bodies were painted in white primer at the initial paint stage. Nowadays, 'BIW' refers to the bodyshell of the car, either in a raw unpainted state or in its initial primer coat.
- Bulkhead The main structural firewall between the engine bay and the interior of the car.
- CAD Computer-Aided Design.
- Canson paper A type of coloured drawing paper, featuring a heavily textured surface. Popular in design studios in the '60s and '70s.
- Cant rail The structural section above the doors; the main box section at the edge of the roof.
- CAS Computer-Aided Styling. In some organisations it can also mean Creative Aesthetics and Styling – in other words, the team that uses CAS tools.
- Conté crayon A hard drawing pastel made from compressed powdered graphite or charcoal, mixed with a wax or clay base. They are square in cross-section.
- Dashboard See Instrument Panel.
- DI lamp Direction Indicator lamp. Shorthand for the orange turn signal lamps at the front and rear of the car.
- DLO 'Day Light Opening,' or the complete graphic shape of the side windows, including the B-pillar. Often outlined with a chrome finisher to emphasise the overall shape. This represents the main graphic element for the side view of the car.
- Door card Flat door inner trim panels, made of cardboard or hardboard until the 1970s. Now universally replaced by moulded items – more correctly termed door trim panels.

Ford Design in the UK – 70 years of success

- Di-Noc A highly stretchy 3M plastic film used to cover clay models to represent a painted finish. The film is typically painted in silver, although other colours can be used, such as dark grey for windows and headlamps. Di-Noc is also used as a quick tool to check highlights as the clay model is being developed.
- Escutcheon The surrounding to a handle or knob, such as a door armrest or interior door-release handle.
- Fender The front or rear panel surrounding the wheelarch, otherwise known as the wing. Due to the global nature of automotive design and the influence of Briggs (who always employed this term on drawings), the American word 'fender' is used in design studios.
- Foamcore A proprietary type of mounting board, typically used in graphic design studios. Available in varying thickness, it can be easily cut with a sharp knife or scalpel.
- FoE Ford of Europe abbreviation
- FWD Front-wheel drive.
- Greenhouse The glazed upper body of the car – in other words the entire cabin above the belt line, from the base of the windscreen to the base of the rear window.
- Graphics Any graphic shape or feature used on the surface of the car, such as the grille, the shut lines, the DLO, the windscreen or rear screen, the headlamps, or any louvres.
- GRP Glass-Reinforced Plastic, also called Fiberglass (US) or glassfibre (UK).
- H-point Hip point: this refers to the seating reference point, which is the hip joint of a standard seating mannequin. A number of regulations concerning packaging and vision angle are derived from this important interior datum point.
- Hard points Fixed engineering points on the car, determined often as a result of structural or legislative constraints, typical examples being the placing of the front bumper beam and the design of the crush structure.
- Header The structural section above the windscreen or rear screen, the main box section at the ends of the roof.
- Instrument panel The panel below the windscreen containing the instruments. The meaning has changed over time. Originally used to describe the (usually central) panel that contained only the instruments, it has now evolved to become the main term used to describe the entire dashboard assembly running across the whole width of the car. For consistency, we have used this term throughout the book, rather than 'dashboard.'
- IP Shorthand for instrument panel.
- Job One The first saleable car of the series produced on the production line
- Lightlines Paths of reflected light that run along a surface and make it possible to understand its sculptural form without reference to its outline shape.
- Lofting The drawing up and smoothing-out of body sections, full-size. Derives from shipbuilding parlance, where the ship's hull timbers would be drawn up in the roof area of the shipbuilder's workshop – the only area with enough clear floorspace to do this.
- LWB Long wheelbase – in other words, an extended-wheelbase version of the basic car.
- Mock-up The initial development model for any new car design. A non-functional representation of the exterior or interior of the car. A mock-up can be constructed from many different materials, including sheet metal, solid wood, clay, foam or glassfibre, depending on the eventual function and method of build available to the designer.
- Package The overall layout of the car, including the occupants, engine, wheelbase etc.
- Rear Deck The main horizontal surface of the trunk lid (or tailgate).
- RWD Rear-wheel drive.
- Scuttle Upper area of the bulkhead, directly below the windscreen. It contains the wipers, washer nozzles, bonnet hinges, air intakes for the heater, and so on – a complex functional area that requires careful design to integrate these features into a coherent whole. Also called 'cowl' (US).
- Shoulder line The intersection of the shoulder surface beneath the side windows and the vertical door surface. Not to be confused with 'belt line' – which (confusingly) lies above the shoulder.
- Shut line The gap between two panels. Also called 'shut gaps' (US).
- Six-light A six-light cabin has three windows on each side of the car – for example, the Focus. A car with just two windows is a four-light style – an example being the Ka+. The third window itself is also referred to as the 'six-light.'
- Stance The way in which a car sits on its wheels – a combination of proportions, wheel-to-body relationship and wheel size.
- Styling buck A mock-up model of an exterior or interior, typically using clay. Interior bucks may be part-models, eg just the front cabin and front seats.
- Tape drawing A 'drawing,' usually on Mylar transparent film, using photographic black tape of different widths. The tape drawing allows the designer to precisely refine and correct the lines of the car as it is translated into a 3D clay model. The slightly flexible nature of the tapes means that gentle curves can be created, the radius depending on the width of tape selected.
- Trunk Luggage compartment or boot. Due to the global nature of automotive design and the influence of Briggs (who always used this term on drawings), the American word 'trunk' is invariably employed these days in design studios.
- Tumblehome The slope of the side windows from vertical. Originally derived from naval architecture, where the sides of a galleon slope inwards above the water line.
- VP Vice President

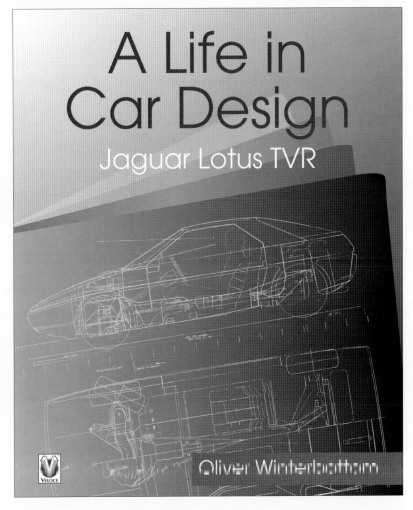

The Art Deco movement influenced design and marketing in many different industries in the 1930s, and the British motor industry was no exception.

This fascinating book is divided into two parts; the first explains and illustrates the Art Deco styling elements that link these streamlined car designs, describing their development, their commonality, and their unique aeronautical names, and is liberally illustrated with contemporary images. The book then goes on to portray British streamlined production cars made between 1933 and 1936, illustrated with colour photographs of surviving cars. This is a unique account of a radical era in automotive design.

ISBN: 978-1-845845-22-3
Paperback • 25x20.7cm • 144 pages
• 215 colour and b&w pictures

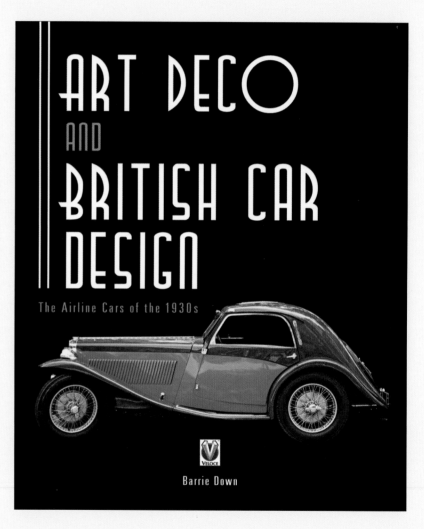

ART DECO
AND
BRITISH CAR DESIGN

The Airline Cars of the 1930s

VELOCE

Barrie Down

For more information and price details, visit our website at www.veloce.co.uk • email: info@veloce.co.uk • Tel: +44(0)1305 260068
* prices subject to change, p&p extra

New Edition! *How to illustrate and design Concept Cars* provides a clear, concise, step-by-step, easy to follow guide to drawing in the style of professional design studios. Includes 'trade tips' on rendering images, and showcase illustrations demonstrating techniques to produce great car art and design.
Covers all materials and methods.

ISBN: 978-1-787110-15-1
Paperback • 25x20.7cm • 128 pages
• 195 pictures

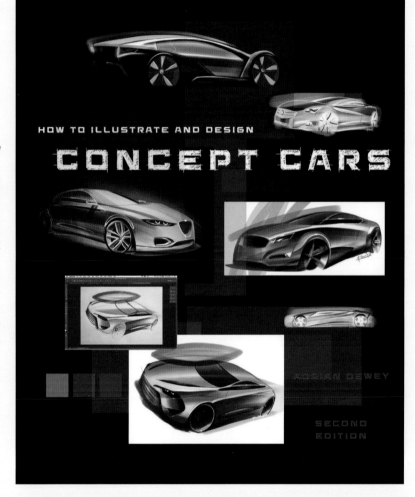

HOW TO ILLUSTRATE AND DESIGN

CONCEPT CARS

ADRIAN DEWEY

SECOND EDITION

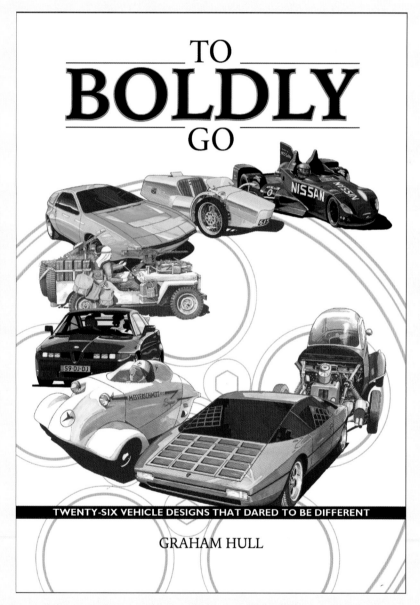

To Boldly Go, by Graham Hull, details 26 sometimes controversial vehicles, from 1911 to present, all solving different design challenges. From the Issigonis Mini that changed design and social mores, to racers so successful they were banned from competition, from cars produced in millions, to one-offs, all created by those marching to the beat of their own drum.

ISBN: 978-1-78711-002-1
Hardback • 22.5x15.2cm • 160 pages
• 79 colour and b&w pictures

For more information and price details, visit our website at www.veloce.co.uk • email: info@veloce.co.uk • Tel: +44(0)1305 260068
* prices subject to change, p&p extra

Index

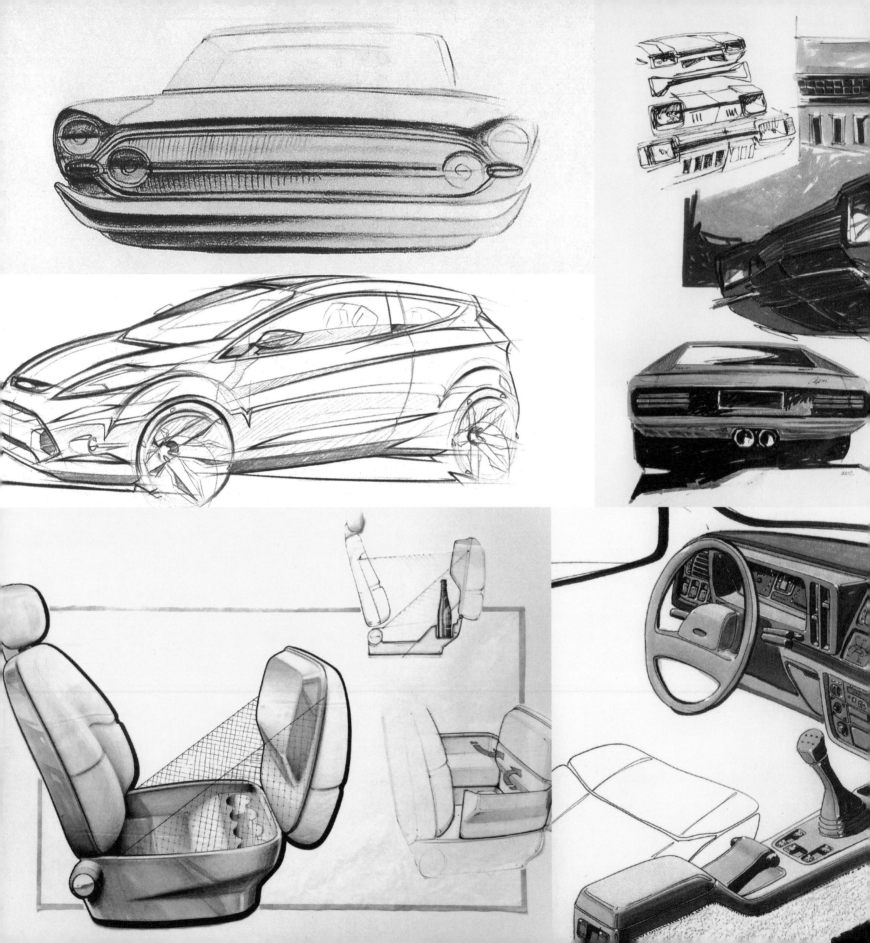